PADDLING
the
COLUMBIA

PADDLING
the
COLUMBIA

A Guide to All 1200 Miles of
Our Scenic & Historical River

JOHN ROSKELLEY

MOUNTAINEERS
BOOKS

Mountaineers Books is the publishing division of
The Mountaineers, an organization founded in 1906 and
dedicated to the exploration, preservation, and enjoyment of
outdoor and wilderness areas.

MOUNTAINEERS 1001 SW Klickitat Way, Suite 201, Seattle, WA 98134
BOOKS 800-553-4453, www.mountaineersbooks.org

Printed in the United States of America
Distributed in the United Kingdom by Cordee, www.cordee.co.uk
First edition, 2014

Copy editor: Jane Crosen
Design and layout: John Barnett / 4eyesdesign.com
Cartography: Ben Pease and Shizue Siegel, Pease Press
Shaded relief for maps 1–13 contains information licensed under the
    Open Government License—Canada.
Photos that show John Roskelley were taken by Joyce Roskelley.
All other photos were taken by John Roskelley unless noted otherwise.

Cover photographs: *Top*: Looking east over the Columbia River and Crown Point in
    Oregon to Bonneville Dam; *Bottom, left to right*: An unusually calm Lake Revelstoke
    a few miles south of Mica Dam, a map of a section of Kinbasket Lake, and the
    Interstate 5 bridge over the Columbia near Portland
Frontispiece and title page: *On Kinbasket Lake, British Columbia, in late fall*

Library of Congress Cataloging-in-Publication Data

Roskelley, John.
Paddling the Columbia : a guide to all 1200 miles of our scenic and historical river /
John Roskelley.
    pages cm
Includes index.
ISBN 978-1-59485-778-2 (pbk)—ISBN 978-1-59485-779-9 (ebook)
1. Canoes and canoeing—Columbia River—Guidebooks.
2. Columbia River—Guidebooks.
I. Title.
GV776.C66R67 2014
797.122097—dc23
                          2013045564

ISBN (paperback): 978-1-59485-778-2
ISBN (ebook): 978-1-59485-779-9

To John Osborn and Rachael Paschal Osborn,
the Pacific Northwest's John Muir and
Rachel Carson of the 21st century,
for their work to protect our environment

CONTENTS

OPPOSITE: Paddling in the strong current downriver from Bonneville Dam after launching from Hamilton Island

SEGMENT 2: MICA DAM TO THE US–CANADA BORDER

SEGMENT 3: US–CANADA BORDER TO CHIEF JOSEPH DAM

SEGMENT 4: CHIEF JOSEPH DAM TO McNARY DAM

SEGMENT 5: McNARY DAM TO CLATSOP SPIT

ACKNOWLEDGMENTS

Paddling the Columbia River was a long journey, both in miles and time, and I was always aware of how important others were to the adventure.

My wife, Joyce, was a willing companion who made our mornings and evenings when we were together the highlight of my day. Her days were just as long; her concerns just as great. We were a team, and that's how I managed to go the distance.

Bruce Hunt took me on my first kayak adventures on a number of lakes in Washington and Idaho. It was those adventures that led me to believe I would enjoy kayaking the Columbia. Bruce was my companion along Hanford Reach, and his knowledge and experience made this leg one of my favorites on the river.

My daughter, Jordan, joined me for the paddle from Fairmont to Radium Hot Springs. A four-year varsity pole-vaulter for the University of Oregon, she was fun to paddle with and showed me how powerful her shoulders were when a grizzly stood up on the bank of the wetland behind us. I didn't know a kayak could go that fast.

My parents, Fenton and Violet Roskelley, gave me my strength and tenacity to climb mountains and paddle rivers. They weren't able to see me finish, but I felt their spirit with every mile that brought me closer to the Pacific.

And finally, my admiration and respect go to editors Kate Rogers, Margaret Sullivan, Laura Shauger, and Jane Crosen; designer John Barnett; and cartographers Ben Pease and Shizue Siegel. Their skills and patience are why this book is in print.

PREFACE

My journey from the Columbia River's source, Columbia Lake, to its mouth at the Pacific began in 1993 when I decided that to know more about the Pacific Northwest, the place I call home, I needed to follow the path of exploration taken by David Thompson, Lewis and Clark, and other well-known explorers of a different age—down the river. I had driven roads and highways along the river since I was a little boy, crossed its width hundreds of times on bridges and ferries, and fished from its banks and on the numerous dam-created lakes. But I felt as though I still didn't know the Columbia—where it goes when it's out of sight; who benefits from its power and size; why we think we can pollute the carotid artery of this land; and what we have done to preserve the river's soul after two hundred years of use and abuse.

Originally, I planned to use a small jet boat and take my twelve-year-old son, Jess, and my seventy-year-old dad, Fenton Roskelley, down the river to fish and explore. We drove to Radium Hot Springs in April 1993 and decided to boat from Invermere to Golden as a trial run. We were a month too early. The river was virtually at flood stage, so rather than launch at Invermere, we put in below Radium at the Forsters Landing Road bridge in an eddy just out of the swift, milky-colored current. I had paddled this section from Invermere down to Radium Hot Springs once before in summer when the flow was smooth and quiet, like a lamb, but the river before us was wolf-like—powerful, filled with floating debris, and dangerous.

We set off upriver for Invermere, more as a test of the boat and water than as the beginning of our journey. The 90-horsepower jet engine worked hard against the current as we cruised along dodging logs and other debris being carried along in the torrent. Less than 2 miles (3.2 km) from the Athalmer Road bridge in Invermere our trip ended abruptly at the railroad bridge that crosses the Columbia. The floodwater roaring under the short bridge was so high we couldn't squeeze underneath. With the water getting even higher as the day progressed, we backed off and went back to Radium and pulled the boat out. Due to problems with the boat, and different workloads and lifestyles, we never returned together.

Six years later, I had an opportunity to paddle some lakes around Spokane with a friend who had two Necky Looksha IV sea kayaks. The quiet, surreal experience of gliding along the water so close to nature made me think once again of the Columbia. But it wasn't until I ended my work with the state of Washington in 2010 that I was able to focus on beginning the journey and, slowly through the years, accomplish my goal of kayaking the Columbia from source to mouth.

My plan was simple: begin the journey; paddle each leg consecutively; put in where I last took out; but do so as time and good weather allowed. I decided to paddle alone because I wanted to be on my own schedule, both on the river and when I chose to paddle, unless a family member wanted to join me or the leg had considerable risk. My wife, Joyce, always eager for the next adventure, would drive the support vehicle, dropping me at the put-in and picking me up at some point downriver. Her role of planning the food, looking for local activities and information, and monitoring my progress was instrumental in my final success. The plan worked, and in the end I paddled alone for all but 50 miles (80 km) of the journey.

I did not intend to write a guidebook. My purpose was the adventure—to learn about the river and myself as I paddled long stretches alone. But as I was paddling on a particularly beautiful though lonely stretch of Lake Roosevelt between Gifford Campground and Two Rivers, the idea of a guidebook took root. Not having seen a paddler on the river to that point, I realized that this amazing resource was completely underused by the very people who would protect it and be willing to challenge government and industry, when those entities' needs seemed to outweigh those of the public, tribes, and fish.

The challenge of paddling the Columbia is not physical or mental, but logistical—where to put in and take out, distances from point to point, underwater hazards, notable landmarks, places to camp, and things of interest along the route. In other words, knowledge is necessary to entice use. I didn't see another kayaker on the Columbia River from its source until Wenatchee, Washington, almost 700 miles (1126.5 km) into my journey, and then I didn't see another until Portland. These kayakers were simply paddling close by parks and recreating near shore, not paddling any distance along the length of the river. Rather than traveling alongside fellow paddlers, I was on the river with fishermen, tugs with barges, and oceangoing ships, but even they were few and far between. For the most part, except in highly urbanized areas, I was alone on the river and paddled most days without seeing another soul.

From the source to the mouth, the Columbia seemed to me overused by industries and power production and underused by paddlers, birders, and low-impact recreationists. Railroads, smelters, pulp mills, mining, recreation, shipping, commercial fishing, and power production all have taken a demanding toll on the river's environment, fish and wildlife, and shoreline. But despite all of these users and their history over the past two hundred years, the river somehow manages to clean itself enough so that some remnant of past salmon runs still return to their spawning grounds; bald eagles, blue herons, ducks, and other birds can be seen along its banks; and boaters, fishermen, and sunbathers enjoy its deceptively clear, cool water. The river today is a survivor on life-support that will not last forever unless we speak with our politicians, demand changes in how the river is used, and take major steps to right many of the past wrongs.

Paddling the entire Columbia River is not for everyone, no more than walking the Pacific Crest Trail end to end is for most hikers. What this guidebook does is open the river to everyone to paddle day-long legs or shorter distances, by providing knowledge of where to put in and take out based on physical ability or weather conditions. With knowledge comes confidence to accomplish small to large goals, and, yes, to paddle the entire river safely.

The Columbia River is a thread of life in the Pacific Northwest. A journey down any portion opens another world of nature's beauty, a history of man's dependence on the river, and an exploration of yourself. Do not hesitate—start the adventure.

COLUMBIA RIVER
SOURCE TO SEA

PREPARING FOR YOUR ADVENTURE

EQUIPMENT AND ESSENTIALS

When I launched my new sea kayak into the glacier-blue water of Columbia Lake, I wasn't quite your classic novice paddler—overdressed, undertrained, and unsure of even the basics—but just a stroke from it. Fortunately, I had watched and learned from an experienced paddler a limited number of times and knew enough to just keep me out of trouble.

An hour into the paddle, though, I knew I had made a critical error—I had purchased the wrong kayak. The boat's low-back-band seating system and small compartment made me feel as though I was in a medieval iron maiden. I couldn't sit for twenty minutes without writhing in pain and then pulling out. Rather than speak with a knowledgeable employee and expert paddler at a specialty store or attend one of the many kayak clinics available to new paddlers, I had purchased the boat sight-unseen based on a sale price. After two days of paddling on the Columbia River, I sold it online.

The first rule of thumb for a paddler is research. Never leave home without it! Before investing anywhere from a thousand dollars or more on a good polyethylene sea kayak to almost three thousand dollars for a high-end carbon-fiber or Kevlar kayak plus another thousand in accessories (such as a carbon-fiber paddle, personal flotation device, dry bags, pump, throw ropes, kayak cart, vehicle rack system, and other practical and safety necessities), do your homework. A good first step is to take a free paddlers' clinic held by certified experts and local store personnel at one of the nearby lakes or rivers. Jump into a dozen brands of kayaks and get a feel for the size of the cockpit; paddle the ones you feel comfortable in; use a variety of paddles; adjust and play with the rudder pedals; and test out the seating, even if you just sit on dry land.

The second rule is to buy equipment based on fit and function, not on fashion or price. If you want to stay on the water and paddle for longer distances, your comfort and safety are key. The old saying "You get what you pay for" is true for paddling. There may be a difference between what you can

Be prepared for a variety of weather and water conditions with equipment and clothing that you are familiar with and that is in good shape.

afford and what you'd like to buy, but there are great choices in equipment in just about every price range. Consider used as well. There are some great bargains on gently used equipment on Craigslist. This book is not intended to be a buyer's guide, but I would consider the following criteria before purchasing the basic paddler's kit.

Kayaks

Paddlers love to talk equipment, and your most important piece of equipment is your kayak. There is no kayak that is perfect for every situation. Buy one that fits your body size and intended purpose. Clearly, the first step is to speak with an experienced salesperson at a specialty store that sells a variety of brands and styles of kayaks. The second step is to take a clinic on the water and test-paddle a number of kayaks that fit your criteria. This is where you will learn not only about length, material, and design, but also specifics like cockpit size, foot and knee room, beam (width), flotation compartments or bags, waterline length, gear load, tracking, maneuverability, and even weathercocking.

I am not an expert, and this is not a gear buyer's book, but from my perspective, a good kayak for the Columbia River is a 14- to 17-foot (4.3 to 5.2 m) polyethylene sea kayak, your basic workhorse with watertight front and back compartments, a drop-down rudder, and an adjustable and comfortable seating system. As to the other criteria, you need to test-paddle a variety of boats and buy what is best for you. My recommendation for the Columbia is based on the length of the journey, big open water, and rough, rocky put-ins and take-outs. Fiberglass, Kevlar, and carbon-fiber kayaks are lighter, thus it takes less energy to paddle them—but they're more expensive and, given the rocky terrain along the shorelines and just beneath the surface on many of the legs, they could be subjected to some rough handling. If you don't mind the dings and damage, go with the lighter material.

I cannot emphasize enough how important comfort is to your selection of a kayak. Buy one with enough room to adjust your body position and with a seating system that feels like the bucket seat of a Porsche 911—well, almost. Low back-bands do not work for me, so I chose a kayak with an adjustable back for lean and height and a seat that could be raised or lowered. Be sure to sit in the kayak on dry land and adjust the thigh braces and pedals for your comfort and performance as well.

Whether you're paddling a kayak or canoe, it's important to remember to put everything in a compartment or connect the item to the boat securely, but without long tethers that can trap you under the boat. My kayak has bungee-cord rigging fore and aft of the cockpit within easy reach. This is where I secured my pump and other lightweight objects that I wanted close and handy. Inside the cockpit, I stored my drinking container in a tube attached underneath the forward deck, along with extra clothing; a cell phone in a waterproof container attached to my seat; extra food and drink behind the seat; and my camera in the built-in bottle holder in the front of my seat. The more miles I put in, the more organized I became. If you roll over, gear can disappear quickly if it's not well-attached.

Paddle

Paddles are almost as complicated in today's world as kayaks. They come in a variety of lengths for your kayak's beam size; in straight or bent shafts; different blade sizes and styles; and with or without adjustable feathering. The best policy is to buy the lightest and strongest you can afford. Your paddle is as important as your kayak and has to be comfortable and suited to your paddling stroke. I bought a carbon-fiber two-piece, bent-shaft paddle, not quite the lightest on the market, but one that was adjustable to my stroke and perhaps a bit stronger than the lighter, more expensive models. Carbon fiber and wood won't conduct cold, either. Your spare can be a bit cheaper, but also should be light and dependable.

PFD

A PFD, or personal flotation device, is the most important piece of safety equipment for the paddler. It is a federal requirement to have one available for each person on all boats. Although there is no law requiring an adult to wear the PFD while on the water, it is strongly recommended by the Coast Guard and experienced paddlers. Fit and function are priorities in choosing a PFD. Your vest should be Coast Guard–approved Type III or V, adjustable to your body style; should fit comfortably; and should be designed for paddlers with a back-pad length that is above your seatback.

The Columbia's water temperature is cold, especially in the spring, early summer, and winter. The river, which typically flows through a deep gorge, is a magnet for wind and storms. Hypothermia and shock from the low water temperatures are all too common and can lead to drowning. A wise paddler wears a PFD on any moving water and when crossing broad, open sections of reservoirs. Unless you have gills and your name is Chinook, wear your PFD on the Columbia. I went into the water once during my journey without a PFD, and by the time I managed to reach the shore, my extremities were numb, and hypothermia had set in.

Accessories

In addition to kayak and other basic equipment, you will need some accessories for safety, comfort, and convenience. I'll mention just a few essential ones here.

Your standard accessory list should include a bailer or bilge pump; throw rope; spray skirt; an extra paddle; dry bags for extra clothing, food, and electronics; a multitool; boater's whistle; a GPS device or cell phone or smartphone with GPS capabilities; and sealable plastic bags for human waste, toilet paper, and garbage. Some of these are in the Ten Essentials listed below. Sections along the Columbia are still without cell phone coverage, but in years to come that will certainly change.

My favorite accessory and one that I don't leave shore without is a thick gel-foam seat pad. Kayak seating is just now beginning to come out of the dark ages, so a bit of extra comfort is necessary to stay on the water.

Your Ten Essentials

Everyone has their own list of ten or more essentials that should be on the boat. Mine changes depending on where I'm paddling and the length of the trip. My background is in climbing mountains where every ounce has to be judged by its worth to the overall effort. I'm limited to what I can carry in my pack.

Paddlers are not as limited, but the principle is the same. Just because you have the space doesn't mean you have to fill it. Extra weight takes more energy and ruins more trips than windy weather. Think small and light. And remember: Leave no trace. You are passing through, and the next group of paddlers should never know you were there.

The Ten Essentials have changed throughout the years. Future technology will change the list even further. But, at this time, these are the items I believe are important to your comfort, safety, and responsibility to the environment:

1. Navigation (map and compass)
2. Emergency shelter
3. Sun protection (sunglasses, sun hat, sunscreen, and lip balm)
4. Insulation (wind gear, extra socks, athletic shoes, and a pile jacket)
5. Illumination (headlamp or flashlight)
6. First-aid kit (aspirin or ibuprofen, small bandages, and sting cream)
7. Fire (lighter or matches in a sealable container)
8. Repair kit (multitool with knife, and extra boat nuts and bolts)
9. Nutrition (extra food and high protein supplements)
10. Hydration (extra water)

FINDING YOUR WAY: MAPS, GPS, AND ROUTE ACCESS

The Columbia River is a path that ends at the Pacific—you may not know exactly where you are all the time, but you are not going to get lost. With the technology and information we have available today and in the future, paddlers can pinpoint their location within a few yards (2 m) anywhere on or near the river using a GPS device, smartphone, guidebook, or, if landmarks are visible, with an accurate topographic map and compass. When in doubt or in a deep fog, follow the shoreline.

My preference before paddling several of the more remote legs along the Columbia was to view Google Earth on my home computer or laptop while on the road, study the run of the river, and locate major landmarks such as mountains, bridges, dams, narrows, resorts, and creeks. It also enabled me to measure distances accurately, whether from put-in to take-out or between specific landmarks. In areas with smartphone coverage, I could also pull up Google Earth as a GPS source but in photo format, rather than lines and points on a screen. More than once, I printed screen shots from Google Earth or Google Maps at home to pinpoint put-ins, take-outs, and additional access points, and then handed them to my wife, Joyce, so she could find my final destination point.

Topographic maps, state atlases, government agency maps, state maps, and other resources have been the standby for generations of hikers and paddlers. This method of locating your whereabouts is still fairly accurate and the least expensive for use in the backcountry, and many are downloadable online. Paper maps also have one big advantage over the more accurate technology: no batteries. Simply put, maps are reliable and they also pinpoint roads and trails, boundaries, peaks and elevations. But in my opinion, maps and compasses are going the way of the sextant and will eventually be relegated to backup technology, rather than first choice.

No matter what you use—a map, GPS receiver, a guidebook, computer, or smartphone—practice using it and, if it is electronic, have a backup method and extra batteries, or know where you're going and how to get there.

SAFETY FIRST: WATER HAZARDS ON THE COLUMBIA RIVER

The Columbia River is a natural environment and, as such, has a number of hazards that can and should be avoided while paddling. Hazards can be divided into two categories: those inherent to the river, such as rapids; and those caused by human error, such as launching in bad weather. In more than 1200 miles (about 1900 km), the only time I felt in danger was when I didn't pay attention to my conscience, my gut feeling. Most hazards are like tiny waves—it takes a human to turn them into a tsunami.

There is a listing of kayak clubs and outfitters at the end of this book. Most of them provide paddling safety training and even a water rescue course for self-rescue and for rescuing other boaters. You can be miles from the nearest take-out on the Columbia. A lesson and practice in self-rescue with a certified instructor is a small price to pay for a safe journey.

I would love to proselytize about the danger of not wearing your PFD or paddling solo, but having broken both rules, I can't. I paddled all but a few miles of the Columbia alone for various reasons, and there were dead-calm, scorching days on the reservoirs behind the dams when I couldn't bring myself

Hazards include high-speed recreational boat traffic near fishing and recreational areas.

to wear a PFD. The PFD, though, was always within reach under a bungee cord on the kayak deck. There are lots of expert recommended dos and don'ts in every sport. But in the end, you're doing the paddling and making the choices. Do so using good judgment and common sense.

Here are some common hazards on the Columbia and tips for avoiding them:

Weather

The Columbia River flows between two major mountain chains in Canada; skirts between the desert plateau of eastern Washington and the snow-capped peaks of the Cascades; cuts through deep basalt canyons in Oregon and Washington;

twists and turns through the temperate forests near Portland; and ends in the cool coastal waters of the Pacific. In other words, the only weather you will not encounter along the route is an Atlantic hurricane—and yet, on windy days in the Columbia Gorge, you'll think that's exactly what you're in. Check the weather websites for forecasts in your exact location before and during your trip; never launch into a steady wind; and, if there are whitecaps on the river or you see a kite boarder smiling, be prepared to sit for a few days.

High Water

The Columbia runs high in the spring and early summer. High water carries trees, branches, and logging debris, and creates water features like whirlpools (more on these below). Some sections are best run at high water, such as Hanford Reach to the Pacific, but others, like from Lake Windermere to Kinbasket Lake, and Keenleyside Dam to China Bend, should be done when the water level is lower to avoid these problems. Current and historical flows can be found in the Resources section.

Rapids

There are several sections of Class II rapids along the Columbia River (see Legs 4 and 13). If possible, scout them out first by walking the shoreline or glassing them with binoculars from an observation point. Several can be portaged around in rough conditions, but if not, plan on paddling these sections in low water and wear your spray skirt.

Whirlpools and Eddies

There is nothing more intimidating than big, fast-moving water, and the Columbia River is known for its size and speed in some sections. Most of the historically well-known "holes" and monster rapids have been drowned in the backwaters of dams, but there are still some very dangerous whirlpools and eddies in the free-flowing water below Keenleyside Dam to Lake Roosevelt (Legs 13 and 14).

Whirlpools form mostly below islands and prominent landforms (headlands, points, and peninsulas) in moving water. The whirlpool that forms in high water behind Rock Island 2 miles (3.2 km) below the town of Trail is big enough to suck down the *Titanic*, and its eddy on the west shore will keep pulling you back in. This section (described in Leg 13) is best paddled in September/October early in the morning before the dam releases water. My advice also stands for the narrow canyon known as Little Dalles below Northport (see Leg 14). Paddle this section in low water or portage around, because there are known whirlpools at the head and tail of this 0.25-mile (0.4 km) feature.

Dams

There are excellent take-outs above the dams, sometimes just to the side of the spillway and at other times 1 to 2 miles (1.6 to 3.2 km) upriver. Make any crossings of the river far above a dam, and paddle close to shore prior to take-out. I never felt any strong current above the spillways until Bonneville Dam, but during spring flood stage there may be some strong flow at the pass-through dams.

Below the dams the water is fast and turbulent, at least for the first 0.25 to 0.5 mile (0.4 to 0.8 km). After a short distance, the water roils and boils and moves you along quickly, but there are no rapids you can't avoid. Stay in the smoothest area of the river and away from islands to avoid any whirlpools.

Recreational Boats and Jet Skis

Fishing boats, jet skis, wave boats, cabin cruisers—anything with horsepower and a throttle—are possibly the number-one manmade hazard for paddlers, the reason being that there is a human on the other end of that throttle. Keep in mind that boat pilots are distracted by pulling tubers, skiers, and surfers; spinning donuts; or looking for a fishing spot. We're not on their personal radar. Worse yet, we sit low in the water and can disappear between a few low waves.

Paddlers are generally safe near undeveloped shoreline, because the carbon-monoxide set fear submerged rocks, logging debris, and pilings. Near marinas, docks, sandy beaches, and open water, you are fair game. If they are coming in your direction, wave your paddle high above you; if you can see the whites of their eyes, catch their attention. The best way to avoid motor heads is to paddle early in the morning, and avoid urban areas and popular state park boat ramps past the witching hour of noon.

Tugs with Barges

Tugboats with barges work the Columbia from the mouth of the Snake to the Pacific in limited numbers. It's rare to see more than three or four in a full day of paddling. The tugs more often than not push two barges. The one directly in front of the tug is generally loaded and sitting low in the water. The second barge is usually unloaded and is breaking the surface tension for the deeper draft of the other. The combination of the tug and two barges creates three sets of bow waves followed by a tugboat prop wave. Away from shore, the large waves have a broad trough and are easily paddled, especially if you point your bow into the wave. Near shore is another story. Like all waves in shallow water, they grow in size and break over the crest, which can swamp or tip a paddler, so find a protected bay or stay in deeper water.

Tugboat pilots are professionals, have a commanding view of the river, and stay vigilant for all the crazies on the river, such as wind- and kite surfers, salmon fishermen, and, yes, the rare kayaker. But they can't see the first 100 yards (91 m) in front of the farthest barge. My advice is to stay out of the shipping channel—but if you can't, get out of the channel quickly, because tugs move deceptively fast.

Large oceangoing container ships are a frequent hazard on the lower Columbia.

Oceangoing Ships

The lower Columbia from the Pacific to Portland and Vancouver is an international shipping channel deep enough for ships carrying everything from Wyoming coal and eastern Washington wheat to Cascade logs and Japanese Subarus. If you paddle on the lower Columbia, at least one of these metal behemoths is going to pass you by. You won't hear them coming behind you, and the ones coming at you will be there in minutes. Again, stay out of the main channel west of Kelley Point (Leg 33), and when you see the bow and propeller waves coming, turn and point your bow into them, especially if you are near shore.

Wing Dams, Pilings, Piers, and Columns

The lower Columbia from Bonneville Dam to the Pacific has its own set of hazards, namely wing dams, pilings, and piers. Columns are under every bridge over the Columbia. For the most part, these are shoreline obstructions, although many are located hundreds of yards offshore close to, but not in, the main shipping channel.

Wing dams are closely spaced pilings connected by boards and placed in rows perpendicular to the current and tidal flow to focus erosion impacts up and down the river. By far, the majority of wing dams are rotten wooden structures that have been in the river for decades, if not centuries. In a strong current with maximum tidal flow, these obstructions act like sweeper trees in a flowing river. You can get pinned up against them and turned over. Paddle around them, never through them, because many of the pilings are broken off just beneath the surface.

Pilings are used to build structures over the water, hold docks and houseboats in place, and to secure boats, ships, and barges. They are usually placed close to or along the shoreline. Pilings have the same potential as a wing dam to trap or turn over a paddler. In a strong current and outgoing tide, make it a habit to pull in on the downriver side of pilings unless they are located in a protected bay or there is an eddy along the shore. The Astoria waterfront, for example, is lined with buildings built on tall pilings as thick as a forest. The deep shipping channel, thus the strongest current and tidal flow, is only several hundred yards offshore. Astoria, during an outgoing tide, is a good place to stay downriver of pilings when pulling into the shore along this waterfront.

Piers are shore-connected structures built on stilts or pilings that jut out into the channel. Like pilings, they can be strainers in a current or strong tide that may trap or flip a paddler. The safest approach to a pier in any flow is downriver.

Columns refer to vertical bridge structures in the water. Most bridges across the Columbia have at least two, and many have more, columns. There can be a strong flow past these columns in free-flowing river sections below a dam or from tidal flow. A good rule of thumb is to stay comfortably away from them to avoid small whirlpools and roiling water just behind the structure.

Tidewater

The legs below Bonneville Dam are susceptible to tides. The closer to the Pacific and the deeper the channel, the more pronounced the tidal effect on the river's flow. Check the tidal charts for the best times to paddle with the outgoing ebb tide, especially from Kelley Point west to Clatsop Spit's South Jetty at the mouth of the Columbia. Tides and tide changes are not a hazard, but the current they create through the manmade and natural obstacles in the river mentioned in this chapter can trap an unsuspecting paddler. Also, be aware that oceangoing vessels travel up and down the river with the tides.

A Note About Safety

Please use common sense. This book is not intended as a substitute for careful planning, professional training, or your own good judgment. It is incumbent upon any user of this guide to assess his or her own skills, experience, fitness, and equipment. Readers will recognize the inherent dangers in kayaking, canoeing, and stand up paddling, as well as in rivers and moving-water environments, and assume responsibility for their own actions and safety.

Changing or unfavorable conditions in weather, waterways, river flows, roads, trails, etc., cannot be anticipated by the author or publisher but should be considered by any outdoor participants, as routes may become dangerous or water unstable due to such altered conditions. Likewise, be aware of any changes in public jurisdiction, and do not access private property without permission.

This book contains only the personal opinions of the author. The publisher and author are expressly not responsible for any adverse consequences resulting directly or indirectly from information contained in this book.

—Mountaineers Books

HOW TO USE THIS GUIDE

Paddling the Columbia is a tool, like your paddle, to make your next trip on the river safer and more enjoyable, your decisions well informed, and your destination known. The information contained in this book is based on my first-hand experiences while paddling each leg of the river and my research before and after each adventure. Whether you intend to paddle the entire 1200 miles (1900 km) or try just a few day trips to experience the river, this guidebook is for you.

Like all guidebooks, though, it has its limitations, and it is important to adjust each day's paddle according to the variable conditions, specifically weather, time of year, flow of the river, and your mental and physical condition. The great thing about paddling on the Columbia is that everyone's adventure will be different, because the river environment changes daily and even hourly.

Common sense should be on every paddler's list of essentials and must never be left on the shelf at home or tucked away in a watertight compartment. The guidebook provides basic knowledge for things like routes, natural and manmade hazards, water movement, shipping, history, and environment, but it is how you use this information in combination with the weather and river conditions at the time you are about to paddle that will determine whether you enjoy your trip or find yourself in dire straits. To be prepared, take emotion off the table and consider the basics before you launch—time, wind speed and direction, flow rate, temperature, and distance. Then, if these basics make sense and you decide to paddle, put your focus and energy on the adventure and enjoy the challenge.

Preparation is the key to a successful adventure. Take the time to improve your paddling skills, or take a class from a qualified instructor. Read the safety advice in the previous section, and check other paddling resource books for safety and rescue techniques.

Paddling is a lot more enjoyable in a group, but if you intend to paddle alone, let someone know where you'll be and when you'll be back. Paddling with a partner also gives you the option of two vehicles for shuttling.

SEGMENTS AND LEGS

This guidebook divides the river into five distinct segments, bracketed by significant landmarks, further divided into thirty-five "legs" of various distances, most doable in a day by a physically fit paddler. Some legs will require two days, depending on flow rate, tide, and weather. Two of the segments are in Canada, two are in Washington, and the last is the dividing line between Oregon and Washington. If you do every leg, you will have paddled the entire Columbia.

Each leg is, for the most part, a day's journey (see Paddle Time below) between put-in and designated end take-out, with additional access points mentioned to allow for pulling out if conditions warrant or continuing even farther if desired. I encourage you to launch early in the morning, because typically the river is calm, the air temperature is cool, and an early start gives you some wiggle room to complete the leg in case the winds come up mid- to late afternoon.

As a solo paddler, but with a dedicated person to shuttle, I made good time by reducing my stops and paddling at a consistent speed. A larger group may take more time along the leg, just because everyone has different needs and expectations for rest stops, hydration, and food. Physically, I felt I could paddle farther than the distance of most legs but was limited by how long I could tolerate sitting in one position in my kayak. I shortened or lengthened some legs depending on whether they had flowing or dead water, but strong paddlers under good conditions should be capable of covering the longest legs and sometimes going even farther on sections with free-flowing river, tidal current, or both.

Information Blocks

The information blocks found in each leg provide details that can aid you during your paddle. Always keep in mind that wind, bad weather, season, flow, and tide will affect the paddle time, and plan accordingly. The Resources section has websites for land managers, government agencies, local clubs and outfitters, campgrounds, dams, history of the areas, weather and tide information, and other sites to help you along your journey.

Distance

The **distance** for each leg was measured along my own paddle route from designated put-ins to take-outs using Google Earth, and should be accurate to within 0.1 mile (160 m). Any time I could angle across the river to save time and distance during my journey, I did so, and this is reflected in the mileage. Your distance may vary by at most 1 mile (1.6 km) on any one leg depending on whether you follow the shoreline, choose to paddle the opposite side of the river, or, in good weather conditions, straighten your journey and paddle across the river or bays from point to point.

Paddle Time

The **paddle time** is an estimate of how long it should take for the average paddler to cover the entire leg under good conditions. I took the total distance of the leg and divided it by 3.5 mph and 4.5 mph (5.6 to 7.2 kmph) to cover a time range, and then took into consideration short breaks, flow, and shortcuts across bays and around points. Your physical condition, the type of boat and other equipment, wind, waves, tide, and current are just some of the variables that will increase or decrease the estimated time.

Possibly the most important criterion for completing a leg in a designated time is consistency in your pace. I can paddle fast and strong—for a short distance. But with sometimes 30 miles (50 km) or more to cover, I always set a pace I could paddle for hours and still feel strong at the take-out.

Each leg opens with a River View section that provides you with information about the day's paddle, like landmarks and access alternatives.

River View

The river view sections detail specific features, twists and turns, and points of interest you can expect to encounter over the day's paddle. Here you will find route descriptions, access alternatives, distances from point to point, and landmarks.

At the end of each section is a summary of generic and specific hazards the paddler may encounter on this leg. Generic hazards include low-temperature water, frequent wind, remote sections of the leg with limited access, confluence of incoming rivers, strong tides, and seasonal high flows. Specific hazards include known grizzly habitat, rapids, whirlpools, difficult shoreline access, frequent underwater objects, tugs with barges, ships, dam spills, wing dams, and recreational boaters.

Geographical place names and landmarks are called out in bold the first time they appear in a given leg's description.

Flow and Season

Flow is the movement of water downriver and will vary in power and speed throughout the year in those areas not pooled by dams. There is also a measurable flow in the reservoirs during the spring runoff downriver from the Snake–Columbia confluence, which can add 1 to 2 mph (1.6 to 3.2 kmph) in speed to your journey through the Columbia River Gorge, but don't count on it in the fall.

There are fourteen main-stem dams on the Columbia that are synchronized to control flow throughout the year for electricity, flood control, fish passage, and recreation. The dams normally hold back water at night and begin releasing water in the morning, but this may change during spring runoff. Check the websites of the United States Geological Survey (USGS) National Water Information System; Environment Canada Wateroffice; or the controlling public utility district (PUD) to find release times and flow rates at individual dams. Websites for these agencies can be found in the Resources section.

The Columbia has five natural free-flowing sections, in addition to the swift water within 5 miles (8 km) below the fourteen main-stem dams: (1) Columbia Lake to the Lake Windermere wetlands; (2) Lake Windermere to Kinbasket Lake; (3) Hugh Keenleyside Dam to Lake Roosevelt; (4) Priest Rapids Dam to Lake Wallula (Hanford Reach); and (5) Bonneville Dam to the Pacific Ocean.

Season is my broad recommendation for the best time to paddle a particular leg of the river and varies dramatically from the river's source to the mouth. For instance, the Columbia freezes over along the narrow, shallow sections from Columbia Lake to Kinbasket Lake, and it stays winter in the Kootenay Valley well into March. On the other hand, the lower Columbia from Bonneville to the Pacific may be paddled throughout the year, depending on the winter weather. During my journey, I paddled as early as the first week in March in the Columbia River Gorge below McNary Dam wearing just a light sleeveless shirt and shorts, and as late as mid-November north of Revelstoke fully clothed in insulated underwear, pile, and waterproof clothing. My rule of thumb is that the best time to paddle is anytime the wind is calm and the sun is shining.

Put-ins and Take-outs

Put-in and take-out locations, critical to a paddler, are detailed in the leg descriptions and shown on the maps, along with other river access points. For the most part, they can be accessed within a short distance from your vehicle, such as via a boat ramp facility or after a short drag or carry to the river from an unmaintained access point. The recommended put-in is listed first as primary, but on selected legs I include an alternative put-in for spring and flood-stage runoff, excessive turbulence, whirlpools, rapids, or even where lock access directly below a dam can make the primary put-in unsafe or difficult.

During my journey, I found the closest public access above and below the dams in order to paddle as much of the river as possible. Public access areas are generally located on land owned by government agencies—for example, the National Park Service and Army Corps of Engineers in the United States or BC Hydro and BC Parks in British Columbia, all of which are listed in the Resources section. The list of environmental, fish and wildlife, transportation, tribal, public utility, and regulatory agencies that have jurisdiction along the river is too lengthy to list here, but their extensive ownership ensures access to the river.

There are pockets of private ownership above the high-water mark scattered along the length of the Columbia, ranging from large farms to small lakefront lots. Private property is usually easy to distinguish, but if in doubt it is better to paddle farther to obvious public property than to trespass. The largest private landholdings belong to the railroads, which discourage public access because of liability. From McNary Dam to Bonneville Dam, where the tracks are on both sides of the river and along the shoreline, access to public launch areas and parks is near railroad crossings and bridges. There are areas close to the top and bottom of the main-stem dams, which are owned and operated by BC Hydro, county public utility districts, and the US Army Corps of Engineers, that have restricted or limited access. Pay attention to any signage and use caution launching anywhere near the dams.

The put-in and take-out distances from the dams vary. For instance, at Wells Dam you can put in a quarter mile (0.4 km) below the spillway, but above the dam, due to rough terrain and a railroad track, I found the most convenient take-out to be several miles (3.2 km) upriver at a Washington Department of Fish and Wildlife (WDFW) boat ramp facility. At other dams, like Grand Coulee, the situation was reversed. The take-out above the dam is just in front of the cable barrier, but the first good public access for put-in below the dam is several miles (3.2 km) downriver.

For the paddler, ease of access basically boils down to what agency or utility owns and operates the dam, when it was built, and if there was recreational mitigation required during relicensing, which usually resulted in a boat ramp facility nearby.

Services

Nearby **services** include motels, hotels, restaurants, gas stations, convenience stores, grocery stores, paddling stores, and other available resources. The quality and quantity of these services varies along the Columbia's course from source to mouth, ranging from completely self-contained camping to luxurious comforts in large urban centers.

There are good motels along most of the route, but be prepared to drive 25 miles (40.2 km) or more in some areas from your overnight lodging to the put-in, especially in Canada. During the tourist season and if you plan to paddle on a weekend, I strongly suggest booking a motel or hotel room in advance. On weekdays, facilities are more likely to be available on short notice. Of course, with smartphones (assuming you're in a good cell coverage area), locating a close motel and booking reservations are simple, but that doesn't mean there will be rooms available.

Paddling shops and outfitters are rare along the Columbia, so always have your full paddling kit, an extra paddle, specific bolts and nuts for your boat fittings and rudder, and a specialized tool kit in the car for repair.

Campgrounds along the Columbia offer a variety of amenities from a simple tent site to full-service park facilities.

Camping

Camping (and RV) facilities and access to public land for camping are fairly common along the river's route. Listed under this heading and located on the maps are most, if not all, of the government-built and -maintained camping facilities in British Columbia, Washington, and Oregon located within a 30-minute drive of the Columbia. Also listed are commercially operated campgrounds that are reasonably priced and near the paddle route. During midsummer and holidays campgrounds are generally booked, but before mid-June and after Labor Day you will have your choice of campsites in almost any campground that's open.

North of Revelstoke there are no motel/hotel services, so camping is a necessity. The river's shoreline is almost all Crown land (owned by the Canadian government) and available for public camping. Be sure to leave no trace and clean your site to original condition or better.

The Resources section includes a handful of regional sources of camping information.

Passage

Passage is based on my experience down this particular leg from put-in to take-out and paints a personal picture of what you may expect to see around the next bend, such as mountain vistas, wildlife and birds, adjacent terrain, near-shore hazards, landmarks, and geology. Your journey down any one of the thirty-five legs will most likely be different than mine in terms of weather and river conditions, but reading a personal account of the trip from put-in to take-out under the set of circumstances and conditions I experienced will give you another perspective of the river. Insight into my journey opens another door to understanding the Columbia: my first-hand knowledge will give you the keys to confidence and success in paddling the river.

MAPS

The **maps** included in this guide are as detailed as possible given size limitations. Included in each map are the principal put-ins and take-outs; additional river access points; state, provincial, and national parks; major highways and access roads; cities and towns; campgrounds and RV facilities; major mountain ranges; and incoming rivers and creeks.

It is important to familiarize yourself with the day's paddle route. The maps included in this guidebook are a good resource, but I encourage you to look at larger-format maps with greater detail, such as USGS topographic maps, Google Maps or Google Earth online, or on a GPS device. You have the technology literally at your fingertips to zoom in on any point of the river to determine where you will be and the terrain around you.

MAP LEGEND

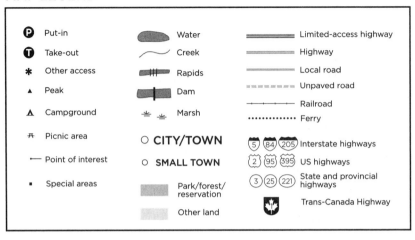

At the time of publication of this book, there are areas of the river, even in Washington, that do not have cell phone coverage, thus there are sometimes no mapping programs available via the Internet. This may change in the near future, but until then GPS satellite units are the only electronic map devices that will work along the entire length of the Columbia. I never felt the need during my journey to use a GPS device, but I finally did use the map feature on Joyce's smart phone once on the second-to-last leg (34) to find my way through the many low-lying sand islands in the Lewis and Clark National Wildlife Refuge to Astoria. It made me realize what I had been missing—knowledge—and that there was the need for this guidebook.

SIDEBARS

In addition to the information listed for each leg, I include detailed informational pieces about the river, the people who have influenced its development, and the environment through which it flows. The Columbia River basin has seen 10,000 years of human activity, including more than two hundred years of western settlement, and almost as many years of industrial use and abuse of the river basin's resources and environment.

Not much has changed since industrial fishing in the lower Columbia almost drove the salmon extinct in the late 1800s. We're still sending toxic chemicals and overflow sewage down the river, dredging the bottom, and removing more water to irrigate the desert, rather than send salmon fry downriver. Despite recent court rulings, hydroelectricity, industry, and agriculture still carry more weight than depleted and quickly vanishing runs of wild salmon. We've come a long way since David Thompson and Lewis and Clark explored and mapped the Columbia River, but we also have a long way to go to recover from our mistakes.

Paddling in the steady current alongside the Columbia Valley wetlands north of Spillimacheen

SEGMENT 1

COLUMBIA LAKE TO MICA DAM

Total Distance: 211.1 miles (339.7 km)

Segment 1 consists of six one-day journeys (legs) from the source of the Columbia, Columbia Lake, to the first dam on the river, Mica Dam, over 200 miles (321.9 km) north. The river flows through a glaciated, U-shaped valley between the Rocky Mountains to the east and the Selkirk Mountains to the west. The region is known as Kootenay country, which is where the Kutenai, a First Nations people, lived for thousands of years. The first 144 miles (231.8 km) pass through one of the largest wetlands in North America and on mostly free-flowing river. The final 67 miles (107.8 km) are on Mica Dam's gigantic reservoir, Kinbasket Lake, a remote and inaccessible body of water that creates its own weather. The paddle from the source to Mica Dam is one of the most spectacular river journeys anywhere in North America.

LEG 1: Canal Flats to Invermere

Distance: 29.9 miles (48.1 km)
Paddle Time: 6 to 9 hours

River View

The leg from **Canal Flats** to **Invermere** is a paddle across two major lakes, **Columbia Lake** and **Lake Windermere,** connected by a creek-like segment of the **Columbia River,** which slices through the Fairmont recreation area, Riverside Golf Course, and the **Lake Windermere Wetlands.**

Geographically, there seems to be no doubt where the Columbia River begins its journey—Columbia Lake. This spring-fed, light-blue pearl of water, headwaters of one of the world's great rivers, is nestled between the snow-capped **Rockies** to the east and the granite spires of the **Purcell Range** to the west. The lake's spectacular setting amid towering, snow-capped mountains,

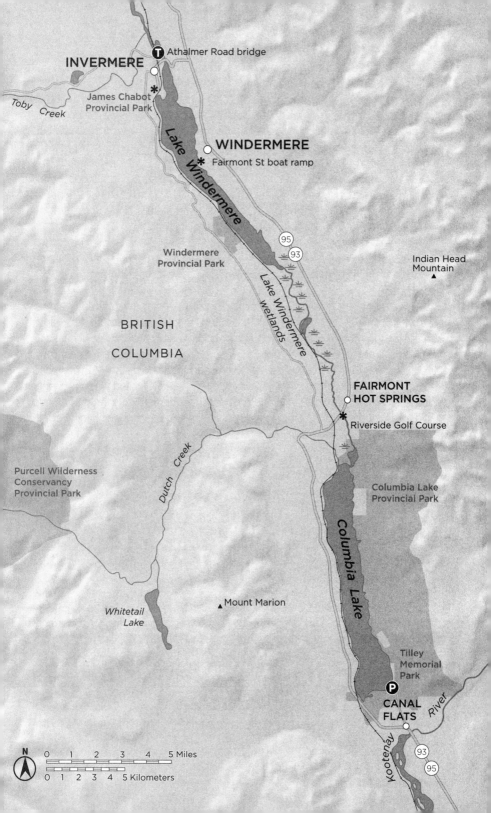

INVERMERE

T Athalmer Road bridge

*James Chabot
Provincial Park*

Toby Creek

Lake Windermere

WINDERMERE

Fairmont St boat ramp

95
93

Windermere
Provincial Park

Lake Windermere wetlands

BRITISH

COLUMBIA

Indian Head
Mountain ▲

FAIRMONT
HOT SPRINGS

Riverside Golf Course

Purcell Wilderness
Conservancy
Provincial Park

Dutch Creek

Columbia Lake
Provincial Park

Columbia Lake

▲ Mount Marion

Whitetail
Lake

Tilley
Memorial
Park

P

CANAL
FLATS

Kootenay River

93

95

N

| 0 | 1 | 2 | 3 | 4 | 5 Miles |
| 0 | 1 | 2 | 3 | 4 | 5 Kilometers |

evergreen forests, and relatively undeveloped shoreline sets the stage for hours, even days, of peaceful and enjoyable paddling.

Columbia Lake is fed by only one creek, **Dutch Creek,** which flows into the lake a stone's throw from where the Columbia River exits the lake and begins its journey north. Theoretically, Dutch Creek is the source of the mighty Columbia. It begins in the glacial ice beneath Saffron Peak, a 9665-foot (2946 m) peak in **Purcell Wilderness Conservancy Provincial Park** 40 miles (64.4 km) to the west, and meanders toward the Columbia River, gathering and building with stream after mountain stream. After 30 miles (48.3 km), the seasonally flooded, sometimes raging creek turns north as it passes Whitetail Lake and then drops 1000 feet (305 m) to Columbia Lake in 10 miles (16 km).

The gently flowing and meandering Columbia River between the two flatwater lakes is 13 miles (21 km) in length. The entire leg of 29.9 miles (48.1 km) can be done in one day, or at a more casual pace in two days by taking out on the south bank of the river at the British Columbia Highway 95 bridge. Both lakes have limited public access and boat ramps, but there are a few good spots on the banks of the moving creek or in the wetlands to take out. The boat dock ramp on the northwest end of Columbia Lake belongs to a private community association and is gated; do not use this facility as a take-out. There are homes along the river through the golf course and for a short distance farther downriver, so access for paddlers in this mostly privately owned area is limited to nonexistent.

Past the Fairmont Hot Springs community, the river meanders through islands of tall grass and mudflats before entering the Lake Windermere Wetlands. Paddle

Columbia Lake, the source of the river, sits beneath the rugged Rocky Mountains and the granite spires of the Purcell Range.

through the stiff reeds to the west shore near the railroad track and then north toward the lake. Your bow will slice through the hard reeds easily, but you'll have to fight them with your paddle. There is vehicle access and a boat ramp in Windermere 4.5 miles (7.5 km) from the wetlands, but if the water is calm and you're feeling strong, paddle the entire 8.5 miles (13.7 km) down the lake to the gravel beach on the northwest side of the **Athalmer Road bridge** in Invermere. The aboriginal Ktunaxa, who inhabited this area for thousands of years, called this place *Kwatagruk*, meaning "where the water leaves the lake."

Hazards include wind and waves on Columbia Lake and Lake Windermere; wayward golf balls along Riverside Golf Course; grizzly bears and mosquitoes in the wetlands; and uncontrolled, testosterone-driven jet ski and boat traffic on Lake Windermere.

FLOW AND SEASON: The flow rate depends on the season. April through June holds the potential for high, fast, and cold floodwaters from the snow-fed creeks off the peaks in the Purcell Range, whereas in July through October the water temperature climbs a few degrees and the paddling is much slower. In winter, Columbia Lake and Lake Windermere and most of the river freeze solid.

PUT-IN: Tilley Memorial Park, Grainer Rd exit off BC 95, then north to park and boat ramp.

TAKE-OUTS: South bank of Columbia River, 10.9 miles (17.5 km), south side of river at bridge off BC 95; Fairmont St boat ramp, 25.7 miles (41.4 km), Bench Rd off BC 95 to Fairmont St, Windermere; James Chabot Provincial Park, 29.5 miles (47.5 km), Laurier St and 3rd Ave in Invermere; Althalmer Rd bridge, 29.9 miles (48.1 km), northwest side of Althalmer Rd bridge on Laurier Rd, Invermere. All distances are from the Tilley Memorial Park put-in.

SERVICES: Canal Flats has limited services, including a restaurant, gas station, and guesthouse. Fairmont Resort, Windermere, and Invermere cater to tourists and vacationers and have a variety of good restaurants, grocery stores, parks, and motels.

CAMPING: There are many established camping areas and RV parks along BC 95, but book early if you visit during the summer season. Check with the Columbia Valley Chamber & Visitor Centre for details. If you are more adventurous, find an access road into Canadian government–owned (Crown) land where it is legal to camp.

DAVID THOMPSON

David Thompson, an early English-Canadian explorer and cartographer, has been described as the "greatest land geographer who ever lived" for his explorations and mapping of more than 2.4 million square miles (3.9 million km) of North America. After a brief period as a fur trader, Thompson was promoted to surveyor in 1794 by the Hudson's Bay Company. Frustrated with its policies, he left the company three years later and began work with the North West Company. In 1806, concerned about the Lewis and Clark Expedition, the North West Company directed him to explore the interior west of the Rockies.

Thompson and his French voyageurs established Rocky Mountain House on the East Saskatchewan River; Kootenae House near Invermere, British Columbia; Saleesh House near Thompson Falls, Montana; and Spokane House near Spokane, Washington, all at great risk to their lives from hostile Indian tribes and from running wild rivers. Thompson is best known for being the first European to navigate the entire length of the Columbia River. In 1810, he was directed by the North West Company to find a route to the Pacific. Armed with limited knowledge from the Lewis and Clark Expedition and other early explorers, Thompson reached the Columbia River just below Kettle Falls on June 19, 1811, about 500 miles (800 km) from the headwaters, after paddling down the Kootenay and Pend Oreille rivers, and then by horseback to Cusick, the Spokane House, and the Colville Valley. Thompson and his voyageurs then proceeded to paddle the rest of the Columbia River to Astoria in less than a month, reaching the port on July 15, 1811.

After a few days' rest, they began their return trip, reaching the mouth of the Snake River on August 5 and Spokane House on August 13. On September 2, 1811, the expedition put in at Kettle Falls to explore the only unknown and untraveled stretch of the Columbia—from Kettle Falls to the Big Bend where the Columbia turns from north to south (see Leg 6). They reached Boat Encampment, a site at the mouth of the Canoe River, just sixteen days later, completing the entire exploration of the Columbia River.

Thompson died in Montreal in relative obscurity on February 10, 1857, at the age of eighty-six.

Passage

As I slid my 17-foot touring kayak into the crystal-clear water at the south end of Columbia Lake to begin my journey to the Pacific, I could only imagine what David Thompson must have felt when he began his exploration of the Columbia River (see sidebar). In his world, the river was clear and clean, and flowed in its natural state more than 1200 miles (1900 km) to the sea; First Nations people hunted,

Getting comfortable at the Tilley Memorial Park boat ramp near Canal Flats for the first of many days on the river

CANAL FLATS

Canal Flats is located between the southern shore of Columbia Lake and the Kootenay River. Early entrepreneur William Adolph Baillie-Grohman built a canal from the Kootenay River to Columbia Lake to open up a north–south navigational system from Golden to Montana and to reclaim rich farmland he wanted from Kootenay Lake. The Canadian Pacific Railway and local farmers, fearing for their investments, put a stop to Baillie-Grohman's main plan of diverting the Kootenay, but he did complete the 45-foot-long (13.7 m) canal and lock system in 1889. Only two boats ever made the journey before the canal was closed in 1902.

fished, and built their villages along the banks throughout the river's basin, moving with the seasons; and salmon, exhausted by their instinctive journey from the Pacific, spawned and died by the hundreds of thousands in Columbia Lake. After two hundred years of western settlement, Thompson's world had disappeared.

I had no illusions that I would find undeveloped land along the length of the Columbia River, as the river has been a source of transport and industry for most of those two hundred years, but I hoped that by paddling alone with the limited information I could find for paddlers, I would enhance and contribute to my daily adventures. At times, this provided for more excitement than I cared to experience, but in the end I felt more like the explorer and geographer David Thompson, and less like the more technologically dependent traveler that I usually am.

Columbia Lake, 8.4 miles (13.5 km) long, 1.2 miles (2 km) wide, and averaging only 15 feet (4.6 m) deep, is sparsely populated. Other than a few fishermen seeking kokanee, whitefish, and a variety of trout species, there is very little motorized boat traffic. I put in at Tilley Memorial Park in Canal Flats Provincial Park, a well-maintained facility a little less than a mile (1.6 km) from Canal Flats with a concrete boat ramp and newer dock. Setting off in a slight headwind, I paddled along the east shoreline just far enough offshore to avoid the reeds and shallows.

The paddle was quiet, peaceful, and relatively inaccessible; the Canadian Pacific Railway runs the length of the west side, and the east side is roadless park and wildlife habitat. I set off early because severe winds often form in midafternoon from the north, and thunderstorms are common in the heat of summer; the weather can change in a paddle stroke.

The Columbia River begins at the northeast end of the lake within the Eastside Columbia Lake Wildlife Management Area and adjacent to **Columbia Lake Provincial Park,** a user-maintained park with rustic boat access and no facilities. I picked my way around some reedy, shallow areas and entered the flow. It felt good to be on the river as it picked up speed and passed over a short section of shallow rapids near the BC 95 bridge.

I pulled over to a rocky access on the south side of the river just before the BC 95 bridge on the Columbia where my daughter, Jordan, was waiting to join me for the paddle through the wetlands. She put in, and we followed the easy, smooth flow through the **Fairmont Resort and Riverside Golf Course** in a series of horseshoe bends until we reached the backwaters and wetlands of Lake Windermere.

Once it reaches the wetlands, the river cuts a channel about 3 to 6 feet (0.9 to 1.8 m) deep through high, mud-banked grass, brush, and marshlands. I noticed that where the mud bank drops to the river, larger animals had trampled the grass to get to the water. Jordan and I heard the rustling of a big animal running in the grass behind us, and when we turned our heads, there was a grizzly on his hind legs staring at us from 50 yards (45.7 m) away. After a brief look at us, he dropped and disappeared in the 5-foot-tall (1.5 m) grass. Needless to say, we covered the marsh area at a brisk pace.

At times, I found it difficult to determine which channel led to more open water, but even when we made mistakes, we could either back up or charge right through the tall reeds. There was not a clear and obvious channel to Lake Windermere from the marsh in the late season, so we paddled west adjacent to the railroad track and then north through the aquatic reed grass to the lake. As we broke through the tall reeds, the rain of interesting critters and spiders dropping into our boats prompted us to stop and put on our spray skirts. Even though we couldn't see the lake at first, we could hear the drone and whine of boats pulling water tubes and toys filled with kids, and jet skis mindlessly turning donuts in the lake.

As we found out that afternoon, the lake provides its own challenges, not just rough water due to boat traffic, but an afternoon mountain storm as well. We paddled the length of the lake to the Athalmer Road bridge in choppy water after a brief stop at the Fairmont Street boat ramp in Windermere. The sandy beach take-out next to the bridge was easy to access with the vehicle and a perfect spot to end the day.

LEG 2: Invermere to Spillimacheen

Distance: 36.3 miles (58.4 km)
Paddle Time: 7 to 10 hours

River View

The leg from **Invermere** to **Spillimacheen** begins in the slow-moving river shallows and wetlands north of **Lake Windermere,** but the flow quickly escalates

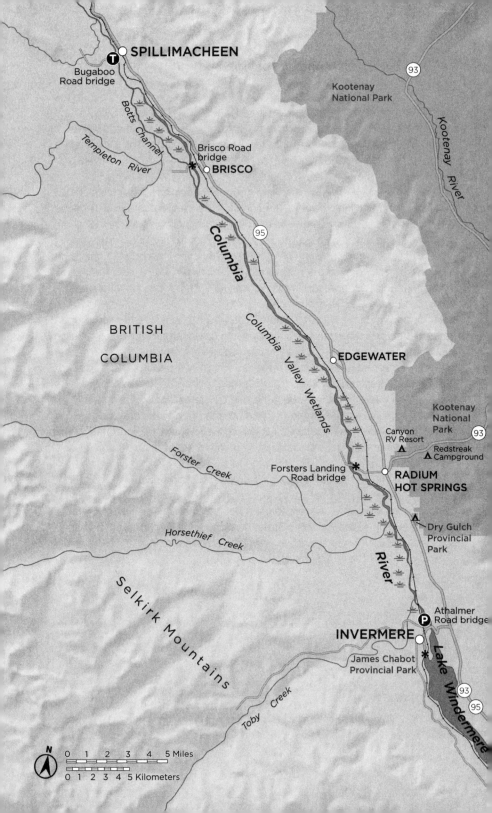

HISTORY OF THE KTUNAXA

Ktunaxa First Nations people lived in the lands known as the Kootenay region of southeastern British Columbia for more than 10,000 years. Their traditional territory included areas of Alberta, Montana, Washington, and Idaho, and they migrated with the hunting and vegetation cycles. Upon the establishment of Indian reservations in the late 1800s, the present-day Indian bands were created: Columbia Lake, Saint Mary's, Tobacco Plains, Lower Kootenay, Shuswap, Kootenai Tribe of Idaho, and Ksanka bands. The Ktunaxa language is unique and is not linked to any other in the world.

into a strong current at the confluence of **Toby Creek** 1.4 miles (2.2 km) from the bridge. Toby Creek dramatically changes the character of the Columbia from its casual, almost nonexistent flow to that of a more powerful body of water. As defined as a line in the sand, the clear, clean wetland-filtered water from Lake Windermere suddenly disappears into the churning, milky-colored glacial water plunging steeply from the icy lakes high in the Purcell Range.

The first 10-mile (16 km) section from Invermere to **Radium Hot Springs** is floated and paddled by hundreds of locals and tourists during the summer season. It usually takes less than 2 hours and is perhaps the most popular section for nonmotorized boating on the entire length of the Columbia.

After the entry of the narrower but more powerful Toby Creek, the Columbia widens and slows a few miles downstream and begins its steady, meandering flow to Kinbasket Lake over 100 miles (160 km) to the north. The main channel flows at a good pace between the **Columbia Valley Wetlands,** the longest continuous wetlands in North America, on the west and the exposed mud and glacial till cliffs, wetlands, and forested slopes on the east where the Canadian Pacific Railway tracks limit access to the river. **Horsethief Creek** is the only major creek that enters the Columbia prior to Radium Hot Springs, but it has little impact on the flow at this point. The best take-out on this leg is at Radium Hot Springs, 10.3 miles (16.6 km) downstream, but to make it a full day, continue your journey to Spillimacheen. There are multiple channels to choose from as the river runs its course, most of which eventually braid back to the main channel. During low water, though, it is possible to run into a logjam in a side channel, so observing the flow and looking for the stronger current will keep you in the main channel.

This leg is rich in birdlife, from song sparrows to the common loon. At every bend in the river, an osprey or bald eagle would be sitting atop another snag watching me as I paddled by, and great blue herons did that leap of faith they do from the reeds as I entered their private wetland dining room. Kokanee (landlocked sockeye salmon, see sidebar in Leg 10) were rising, and their small fry could be seen along the banks and in the wetland. Few fishermen or paddlers venture north of Radium Hot Springs, but this makes for a quiet and peaceful sojourn through one of the world's most productive wetlands.

Hazards include turbulent water at the entrance of Toby Creek; milky-colored water that hides underwater snags, piles of branches, and logging debris known as strainers; and swarms of mosquitoes.

FLOW AND SEASON: The flow is a steady 2 to 3 mph (3.2 to 4.8 kmph) on average during the summer and fall. Spring, on the other hand, turns Toby Creek into a raging torrent, which makes this time of year dangerous because of large floating debris and submerged snags. This leg is best paddled in summer after the spring melt, but can be done through October.

PUT-IN: Athalmer Rd bridge, northwest side, Athalmer Rd off BC 95, Invermere.

TAKE-OUTS: Forsters Landing Rd bridge, 10.3 miles (16.6 km), Forsters Landing Rd off BC 95, Radium Hot Springs; Brisco Rd bridge, 29 miles (46.7 km), Brisco Rd off BC 95, Brisco; Bugaboo Rd bridge (Bugaboo turn-off), 36.3 miles (58.4 km), Westside Rd off BC 95, Spillimacheen. All distances are from the Athalmer Rd bridge put-in.

SERVICES: Invermere is a full-service community, and its restaurants are excellent. Radium Hot Springs has a few restaurants, a grocery store, and many mini-mart/gas stations, plus an internationally known hot springs. Both communities have numerous motels. Brisco and Spillimacheen have very limited services.

CAMPING: There are several provincial park and commercial campgrounds along BC 95 and BC 93, but again, book early if you visit during the peak tourist season. The closest campgrounds are: Dry Gulch Provincial Park, 2.8 miles (4.5 km) south of Radium Hot Springs on BC 95; Kootenay National Park, Redstreak Campground, 1.6 miles (2.5 km) from Radium Hot Springs on BC 93; Canyon RV Resort, Sinclair Creek, Radium Hot Springs on BC 93. Or drive any logging or former skid road on the west side of the valley and find a meadow or flat area to pitch a tent. Be prepared, though, to be ravaged by mosquitoes.

Passage

I've paddled the first portion of this leg to Radium several times and, as with all rivers, the season and snowmelt can turn an easy paddle into a fight for

COLUMBIA VALLEY WETLANDS

The Columbia Valley Wetlands, 112 miles long (180 km), comprise the longest continuous wetlands remaining in North America and cover an area of 64,000 acres (24,000 hectares). As a designated wildlife management area since 1996, the wetlands are protected by stringent environmental regulations. Beginning in 2009, all motorized vessels are banned from the wetlands and engine size for boats on the river channel is restricted to 20 horsepower. More than 260 resident and migratory bird species, 11 species of large mammals, and numerous reptiles, including painted turtles, live in or migrate through the wetlands. Species of concern include the northern leopard frog and the white sturgeon. Listed species include the prairie falcon and the short-eared owl.

The Columbia River is wild and free flowing from Invermere to Kinbasket Lake.

Rocky Mountain bighorn sheep frequent the cliffs above the Columbia River near Radium Hot Springs.

survival. In fact, one spring with exceptionally high floodwater, I was unable to go underneath the Canadian Pacific Railway bridge which crosses the river less than 2 miles (3.2 km) from Invermere because the floodwaters were almost hitting the bottom of the bridge. As you will observe during your paddle, there are many huge slash and woody debris piles along the banks and blocking smaller channels, evidence that the Columbia can be immensely powerful and destructive during flood events.

I put in on the northwest side of the Athalmer Road bridge. The beach is a public area easily accessed from the Invermere side of the river and not fancy (unless you think a fiberglass porta-potty is a paddler's throne), but it's the best access facility I found for the next 100 miles (160 km). I paddled in moderate flow following a channel, for the most part, and then the river slowed as it entered a wide wetland area near the confluence of Toby Creek. Here I pulled the straps tight on my PFD and set off down the Columbia, which abruptly changed character from a mild-mannered, slow-moving freshwater creek to a surging, milky- to dun-colored river, which grabbed my boat and quickly sent me northward. The river is completely opaque at times from the glacial wash out of Toby Creek, so I stayed alert for telltale signs of underwater snags in the channel and sweepers at the horseshoe bends. I paddled down the center, while the river hugged the east side of the valley up against the steep, glacier-deposited till which forms the hillside above.

Within an hour, I was at the first possible take-out on the northeast side of the Forsters Landing Road bridge below Radium Hot Springs, and ready for a break. It has good vehicle access and a mud and silt bank. I stayed river left of the big island just before the bridge, but under certain conditions either channel around the island will allow you to enter the eddy at the access north of the bridge.

As on almost every leg on the Columbia, I was the only self-propelled boater on the river, and the next 26 miles (42 km) were no exception, possibly because public access is difficult, resulting in a long paddle. I paddled easily with the flow, which snaked its way down the center of the wetland another 6.5 miles (10.5 km) to **Edgewater,** a possible emergency exit, then continued along the east side of the valley. About 27 miles (45 km) into this leg and a mile (1.6 km) from Brisco, the river forked into two main channels. I chose the right-hand channel to Brisco, which is primarily a large lumbermill on river right, and then paddled another 0.5 mile (0.8 km) to the Brisco Road bridge. On the west end of the bridge, I pulled the kayak alongside a narrow opening in the tall grass and bushes and stepped out to stretch my legs, and immediately regretted wearing swim trunks. The voracious mosquitoes hadn't bothered me while I was paddling on the open river, but at the stop they were on me in swarms in seconds.

The final 8 miles (13 km) to the **Bugaboo Road bridge,** I paddled in the main channel near the railway on the east side of the valley. Less than a mile

(1.6 km) from the bridge, the left channel, which had forked just before Brisco, entered the river on my left but had little effect on the flow. I knew from scouting this leg the afternoon before that the only reasonable access and take-out was about 100 yards (91 m) inside a side channel southwest of the bridge. I paddled to the narrow shoreline below the road, pulled the boat onto the bank, and then dragged it up steep gravel to a wide spot in the road. It was a rough take-out, but the best along the river for many miles.

LEG 3: Spillimacheen to Golden

Distance: 44.2 miles (71.1 km)
Paddle Time: 9 to 12 hours

River View

The leg from **Spillimacheen** to **Golden** has difficult and limited access because of the wetlands and railroad along the eastern side. This seems to limit entry by boats with motors and anything larger than kayaks or canoes. The river volume varies greatly from season to season, but after the spring thaw, the river has a strong, steady flow supplemented by the many side creeks entering the wetland from the **Selkirk Mountains** that rise to the west and the **Rocky Mountains** to the east. The valley, a classic glaciated half-pipe, is so flat along this section that the Columbia frequently braids into smaller channels.

From Spillimacheen, take Westside Road off British Columbia Highway 95 and drive 0.25 mile (0.4 km) to the bridge. Both east and west sides have access, but there's a side road across the river to the west side where you can park off the main road, unload your boat, and launch from a small inlet into the main flow of the river. Within 1 mile (1.6 km) the lighter blue-colored southern braid of the **Spillimacheen River** enters from the west and 1.5 miles (2.4 km) farther its northern braid comes in. Neither have an impact on the flow.

The main channel is obvious for the first 5.7 miles (9.2 km). At this point, there is a smaller channel that I call the Harrogate cutoff with good flow that breaks off river right and follows the east bank past Harrogate and sometimes comes close to the railroad line. After 6 miles (10 km), it joins the main flow again. The stronger and main flow continues for 0.3 mile (0.5 km) past the Harrogate cutoff to a short but abrupt turn to the west and necks down to a smaller river because of the few large braids that separate and flow into wetlands and smaller channels. At the turn there are log and brush piles pushing you to go straight into a smaller channel, but there are several good passages through them. Missing this turn is not critical, but will send you into a smaller channel that in low-water conditions may end in vegetation. All but the smallest braids typically join the main flow again about 5.7 miles (9.2 km) downriver.

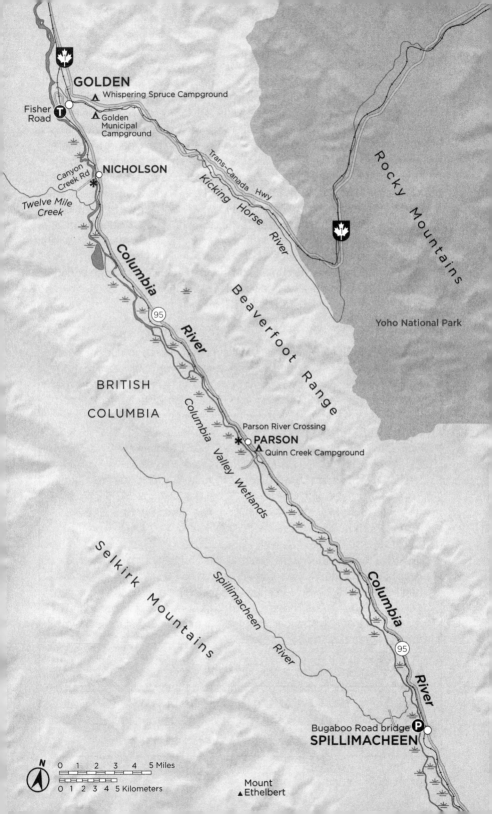

For the next 6.8 miles (10.9 km), the now obvious main stem of the Columbia gathers side channels, braids from the wetlands, and small side creeks, mostly from the Rocky Mountain front, and reaches the **Parson River Crossing Road,** the first good access point to take out, if needed. Six miles (10 km) from **Parson,** the river separates into two equal-sized stems. Go river left; the stem to the right, although not a complete dead end, enters a large, vegetated, nonflowing wetland before exiting into the main stem again. The two stems join again in 4 miles (6.4 km), and the main flow is generally obvious for the next 10.2 miles to **Nicholson** and the **Canyon Creek Road bridge,** another access point. The only major creek entering the Columbia through this area is Twelve Mile Creek, just 1.2 miles (1.9 km) from the bridge. From Nicholson to the **Golden Airport/Fisher Road** take-out, a distance of 5.5 miles (8.9 km), the Columbia leaves the wetlands and numerous braiding and once again becomes a river within a channel.

Hazards include a strong current; low-temperature water; hidden underwater snags, branches, and fallen tree strainers along the banks; inaccessible and remote locations; and dead-end channels.

FLOW AND SEASON: The flow in the main channel continues at 2 to 3 mph (3.2 to 4.8 kmph). Spring has snowmelt and high water, so watch for large floating debris and submerged snags. The best time to paddle this leg is in summer after the spring runoff, but also consider September and October, as the fall colors are spectacular through the wetlands.

PUT-IN: Bugaboo Rd bridge, off BC 95, Spillimacheen.

TAKE-OUTS: Parson River Crossing (Crestbrook Rd), 18.4 (29.6 km), BC 95, Parson; Canyon Creek Rd, 38.7 miles (62.3 km), BC 95, Nicholson; Fisher Rd, 44.2 miles (71.1 km), 5th Ave S and 9th St S off BC 95, Golden Airport. All distances are from the put-in.

SERVICES: Spillimacheen, Parson, and Nicholson have limited services, such as gas and convenience stores. Golden is located on Trans-Canada Highway 1 and is one of the major cities in the Kootenay Valley. It has numerous bed-and-breakfasts, lodges and motels, numerous restaurants and fast food businesses, multiple gas stations, canoe and kayak rentals, and several grocery stores.

CAMPING: Golden has several campgrounds for tent and RV camping, including the Golden Municipal Campground and Whispering Spruce Campground. Quinn Creek Campground is nearby on BC 95, Parson; and the Kinbasket Lake Resort is 30 miles (50 km) north of Golden off T-C 1. Contact Tourism Golden for more information.

OPENING UP THE ROCKIES:
THE CANADIAN PACIFIC RAILWAY

There was seldom a day while paddling between Columbia Lake and Golden that I wasn't aware of the proximity of the Canadian Pacific Railway (CPR), which has a track south from Golden to the United States along the river—so close, in fact, that the rock ballast on which the track is built is often the "bank" of the river. The CPR opened up the Rockies and British Columbia. Rail not only connected Canada from east to west, but brought hundreds of thousands of immigrants, miners, farmers, loggers, and visitors west. The main transcontinental line reached Golden in 1884 from Kicking Horse Pass, and the city's tourism department believes, "Golden would simply not exist without the Canadian Pacific Railway."

Taking a short break near one of the few access points between Radium Hot Springs and Golden

Passage

I put in below a siding road in a side channel just across the Westside Road bridge. It felt good to enter the flow of the main stem from quiet water, catch the current, and relax with the easy flow. The river for the first 5.7 miles (9.2 km) stays in one channel, but then braids into multiple channels, all having about the same flow. One channel river right was tempting, but had a narrower entry, so I paddled farther to another Y. I started down the direct channel, but it seemed narrow, so I paddled back to the other stem, floated over some ripples in front of a large drift pile on a gravel bar, and then followed this tree-lined channel through, the numerous lakes and ponds on either side. There were a lot of smaller braids exiting and entering my channel, but I found it easy to follow the flow.

The braiding was less after 11.7 miles (18.8 km), and the river followed one channel to Parson, where I pulled out on the northeast side of the Parson River Crossing Road bridge for a short break—and it was short. The mosquitoes were on me in minutes, and I was quickly enveloped in my own cloud of the buzzing critters. I hopped back in the kayak and they disappeared as I made my way downriver.

Six miles (9.7 km) from Parson, I found myself at another Y, but it seemed as though the stem flowing straight (river right) lost current ahead, and I could see vegetated wetland as the channel spread out. Thinking this might be a dead end, I turned and followed river left and was glad I did. The channel flowed to the east

Old hunting and fishing cabins can still be seen along the banks in the more remote sections of the Columbia River wetland.

side of the valley and followed the timbered slopes above me, while avoiding the lakelike river to the west. Within 4 miles (6.4 km), the river consolidated all its braids, and I found the next 10 miles (16 km) easy to navigate and the current strong and steady. I didn't stop at Nicholson, as the mosquitoes in Parson had taught me that my paddling shirt was a draw for the little buggers for miles around. The Columbia was locked into its channel from Nicholson to Golden for the next 5.5 miles (8.9 km) and, despite paddling near two urbanized areas, Nicholson and Golden, I felt the river was remote and wild.

As I approached my planned take-out below Fisher Road, which runs alongside the airport landing strip, I edged over to the 10-foot-high (3 m) east bank and caught the shoreline eddy into a low-lying muddy landing. Joyce, who was watching for me, dropped down to the water's edge and pulled me into the gravel and mudflat to end the leg.

LEG 4: Golden to Kinbasket Lake Resort

Distance: 34.3 miles (55.2 km)
Paddle Time: 6 to 9 hours

River View

The leg from **Golden** to **Kinbasket Lake Resort (Beaver River)** has the only significant section of rapids on the Columbia for almost 200 miles (321.9 km). River access is limited and, once you are past the **Trans-Canada Highway 1 bridge,** plan on paddling down the gorge to the resort.

There is a wide choice of rough put-ins along **Fisher Road,** which parallels the airport runway on the west, from the confluence of the **Kicking Horse River** and **Columbia River** to an opening along the bank 1 mile (1.6 km) from the confluence and near the south end of the runway. The launch is in swift water. Find the center of the river and move away from the confluence of the Kicking Horse River, and then continue along the easternmost channel downriver from the Kicking Horse Drive bridge. The river braids around gravel bar islands 1.7 miles (2.7 km) from the bridge. I took the east channel, which put me alongside the T-C 1, but it was shallow in places. There are several more gravel-bar islands to go around in the next 6.3 miles (10.1 km), plus numerous, smaller channels that weave in and out of the wide valley, but then the river consolidates and takes one channel.

The **Blaeberry River** enters the Columbia 11 miles (17.7 km) from the Kicking Horse Drive bridge. If it's roaring in the spring, keep river left. The Columbia takes a right-hand bend after the Blaeberry River delta and flows near T-C 1 for another 7.5 miles (12.1 km), meandering around the occasional big gravel bar, and then goes under T-C 1 near **Donald.**

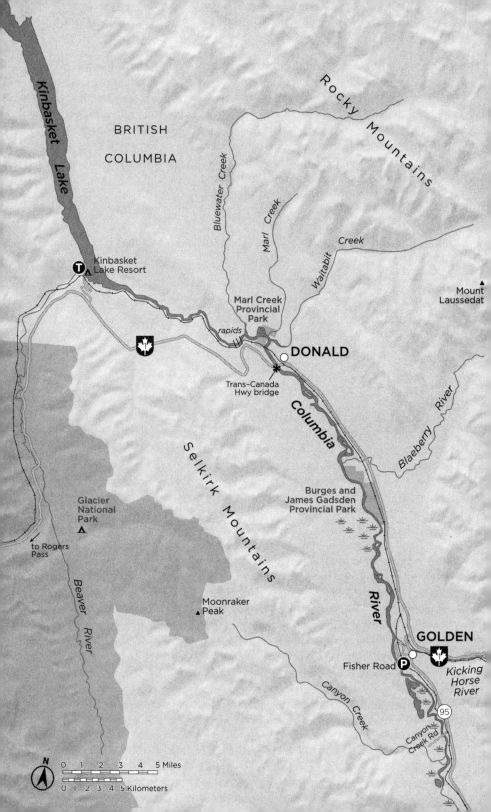

THE ROCKY MOUNTAINS

The Rocky Mountains stretch more than 3000 miles (4800 km) from northern British Columbia to New Mexico and form the Continental Divide where rivers east of the divide flow to Hudson Bay, the Atlantic Ocean, and the Gulf of Mexico and where rivers west flow to the Pacific. Mount Robson, 12,972 feet (3954 m) in British Columbia, is the highest peak in the Canadian Rockies. The mountain range was formed between 80 and 55 million years ago by the folding of layers of ancient seafloor beds, which created a high plateau of sedimentary and metamorphic rock. The Rockies we see today are the result of intense erosion over those millions of years. The Columbia River flows north from Columbia Lake through the Rocky Mountain Trench, an immense valley running north–south, and formed between the Rockies and the Columbia Mountains (Purcell, Selkirk, Monashee, and Cariboo mountains).

Just 1.1 miles (1.8 km) from the T-C 1 bridge, the river passes beneath a Canadian Pacific Railway bridge, and then 0.5 mile (0.8 km) farther makes a sweeping U-shaped bend and ends up flowing west. There are shallow riffles in this area on the inside of the bend, but no rapids. Almost 4 miles (6.4 km) from the T-C 1 bridge is a smaller U-turn to the left. Just after the turn you will hear rapids. The river makes a short sweep right, narrows, and enters a rock-walled gorge.

The only rapid in this section of the river is shortly before a protruding rock buttress that the Columbia hits, bounces off, and flows around. To avoid the main rapid, keep right. There's a lot of surface turbulence for a few hundred yards along the vertical cliffs downstream, but nothing so severe that it will overturn your boat.

Once you are past the rapid and narrows, paddle river left or center away from the vertical limestone walls. The river slows and continues through the steep-walled gorge another 8 miles (12.9 km) where flow stops from the back-waters of **Kinbasket Lake.** At the mouth of the river there may be rafts of windblown logging debris clogging the entrance to the south end of the lake. Once you are clear of the logs, branches, and floating bark, it is another 2.2 miles (3.5 km) across the lake to Kinbasket Lake Resort and the take-out on the west shore. If the wind is blowing and the lake looks rough, paddle directly to the west shoreline and follow it closely to the lodge.

Hazards include rapids, dead snags, log and brush piles, fast-flowing and low-temperature water, inaccessible and remote locations, and logging debris in the lake. There are also numerous grizzly bears in this area, so watch for bear activity if you pull out along the leg.

FLOW AND SEASON: The Kicking Horse River will add volume to the flow, especially in spring or early summer, which increases turbulence at the river's mouth. The Columbia picks up speed as it enters a gorge north of T-C 1, but soon slows as the backwater of Mica Dam turns the Columbia into Kinbasket Lake. The best time to paddle this leg is August through October.

PUT-IN: Fisher Rd west of Golden Airport runway, south end (primary); or confluence of the Kicking Horse and Columbia rivers off Fisher Rd (secondary). Fisher Rd is reached from 5th Ave S and 9th St S off BC 95.

TAKE-OUTS: T-C 1 bridge, 20.1 miles (32.3 km), near Donald, southwest side of bridge; Kinbasket Lake Resort, 34.3 miles (55.2 km), Columbia West Forest Service Rd off T-C 1. Distances are from the Fisher Rd put-in on the south end of the airport runway.

SERVICES: Golden is a full-service community with excellent motels, lodges, bed-and-breakfasts, grocery stores, gas stations, restaurants, and paddler facilities. Kinbasket Lake Resort provides nice cabins overlooking the lake and is a perfect spot for an early-morning getaway for a paddle of the two legs to Mica Dam 66.4 miles (106.9 km) north. The lodge also has a small store with resort food.

CAMPING: The Golden area has several campgrounds for tent and RV camping, including the Golden Municipal Campground and Whispering Spruce Campground, Golden; Quinn Creek Campground, off BC 95, Parson; the Kinbasket Lake Resort, 30 miles (48.3 km) north of Golden off T-C 1; Illecillewait Campground, west side of Rogers Pass; and Glacier National Park, off T-C 1. For the adventurous, there are numerous old logging and skid roads on public land along the west side of Kinbasket Lake, but be prepared—this is grizzly country.

Passage

This leg with its short section of whitewater is one of the most enjoyable day trips on the Columbia, and chances are you will not encounter any other parties on the river. In Golden, my put-in was a small sand-and-mud beach directly below the road that runs along the west side of the airport runway and about 0.5 mile (0.8 km) above the confluence of the Kicking Horse River and the Columbia. The airport has few flights coming and going, so Joyce and I camped in the grass alongside the river.

The Columbia River grows in size from Invermere to Golden as it is fed by multiple creeks and streams from glaciers in the Rocky Mountains and Selkirk Mountains.

I paddled this leg in mid-September, and the water was fairly low and the air temperature cool. The Kicking Horse River had minimal impact on the flow and speed of the Columbia at this time of year, but I suspect it can be a handful for a paddler during spring or summer runoff. I found only a few access points once I passed under the Kicking Horse Drive bridge in Golden. The river channel held together for just a few miles before entering a floodplain where it broke into multiple braids. I tried to follow the strongest flow, but twice was caught in a shallow side channel where the gravel bottom of the river reached up and grabbed me, then let me go after a good scraping.

After the delta of the Blaeberry River, I followed a channel that came close to the T-C 1 a number of times for over 6 miles (9.7 km) to the T-C 1 bridge near Donald. The first good take-out from Golden was at the bridge, and I stopped for a short break and to speak with Joyce who had been motioning for me to pull over. "Did you know there are rapids farther downriver?" she asked. "Well, not really," I admitted. She proceeded to tell me about her conversation with a knowledgeable lady in Golden whose husband knew the river well. "Are you sure you want to keep going?" A little bit of knowledge is a scary thing. I had been paddling along with not a care in the world, and now I was faced with uncertainty. I quickly responded "Hell, yes," although as usual, talking is a lot easier than doing. I was 20.1 miles (30.9 km) out from my put-in with 15 miles

(24.1 km) farther to go and no access. My concern, of course, was overturning in the rapids.

The river flowed past Donald and then turned west. After a long S-bend, I paddled through a short U-turn until I was headed south and the river narrowed. I was 3.8 miles (6.1 km) from the T-C 1 bridge and could hear the rapids as I took the corner, so I pulled out onto a gravel bar just upriver to scout the entrance, flow, and exit of the rapid. I plotted my paddle route, got back in the kayak, and launched into the flow. The river made a sweeping right turn to avoid a vertical rock buttress, so I paddled as close to the inside corner as possible to avoid being shoved by the powerful flow into the limestone cliff that juts out on river left. I was through the rapid and into the canyon a lot more quickly than the time it took to worry about it.

Once I had passed the rapids, I was swept along with the river as it rushed through the high cliffs for another 2 miles (3.2 km), and then was able to relax as the river slowed before entering the backwaters of Kinbasket Lake, about 8 miles (12.9 km) from the rapids. Reaching the slack water of the lake, I found the bay clogged with wind-deposited logging debris, including old log booms connected by cable to hold log rafts near both shorelines. I found a clear path through the debris on river left. Once clear of the logging debris, I angled the 2 miles (3.2 km) to Kinbasket Lake Resort over calm open water.

LEG 5: Kinbasket Lake Resort to Central Columbia River Reach

Distance: 32.5 miles (52.3 km)
Paddle Time: 7 to 10 hours

River View

The leg from **Kinbasket Lake Resort** to **central Columbia River Reach** passes beneath a region of the **Selkirk Mountains** in British Columbia few people will ever get to see. **Kinbasket Lake** is the immense reservoir created by the backwater of Mica Dam and has two long, narrow reaches of similar length: the Columbia River Reach, which runs southeast from the dam and the route we paddle; and the Canoe River Reach, which runs northwest to Valemount, British Columbia. The Columbia River Reach leg is 66.4 miles (106.9 km) between Kinbasket Lake Resort and the take-out above Mica Dam. The journey from the south end of Kinbasket Lake through the Big Bend country to the dam is one of the most remote and inaccessible areas of British Columbia, and I suggest the paddle be done in at least two stages (this leg and Leg 6) in approximately 30-mile (48.2 km) sections.

There are a limited number of decent take-outs along this leg and no public vehicle access, although there is one logging road far above the lake. **Bear**

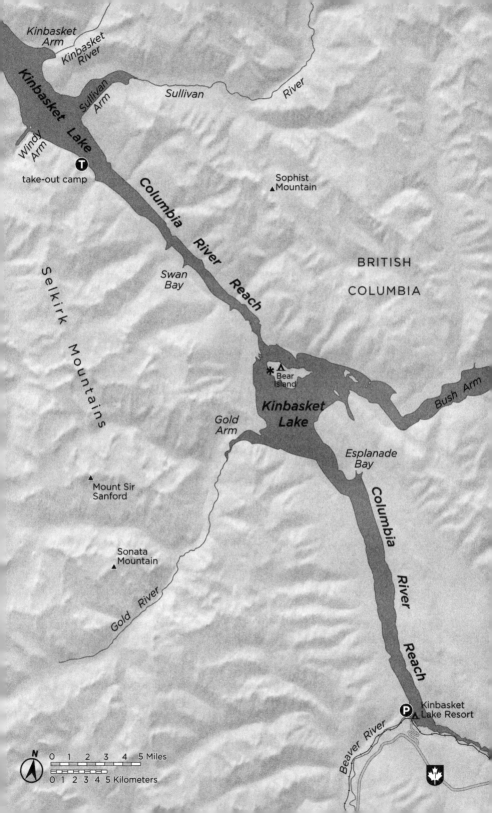

KINBASKET LAKE

Kinbasket Lake is the 170-square-mile (430 sq km) reservoir created by the 1973 construction of Mica Dam on the Columbia River. The original lake at the Big Bend where the dam was later built was named Kinbasket Lake in 1866 by Walter Moberly, after a chief of the Secwepemc Tribe who guided his survey team. The reservoir consists of two long, narrow reaches, the Canoe River Reach and the Columbia River Reach, approximately 120 miles (193 km) long. Its widest point is a little more than 20 miles (32 km).

Island, 19.3 miles (31 km) from Kinbasket Lake Resort, has excellent places to camp, although the locals insist it is named Bear Island for a reason. North of Bear Island the shoreline has eroded from the raising and lowering of the reservoir into steep glacial till undercut banks, with some vertical rock walls. The shoreline is lined by stacked wind-deposited logs, downed trees, and logging debris.

From the boat dock at Kinbasket Lake Resort located at the mouth of **Beaver River,** paddle close to the west shoreline past a solitary cabin located behind a prominent point 6 miles (10 km) from the lodge. Continue hugging the west shoreline for another 6 miles (10 km) where the lake starts to widen and turns a few more degrees to the northwest. Across the lake from here is **Esplanade Bay.** From a prominent point, it's 2.8 miles (4.5 km) to where the lake abruptly opens up into a large bay with several deep arms—**Gold Arm** to the west and the deep, long **Bush Arm** to the east. There are also a number of islands, of which Bear Island is the largest and most obvious.

In calm conditions, cross the 4.5 miles (7.2 km) from where the large bay opens to Bear Island, keeping in mind this will take close to an hour in big, open water. If there is any wind, the safe alternative is to follow the northwest shoreline, cross Gold Arm, and paddle the shoreline to the narrows beyond Bear Island. The wind and waves can come up quickly in this bay, so it's important to take this into consideration before embarking from the shoreline.

From a logical take-out near the center of Bear Island, paddle 1.6 miles (2.6 km) around the island to a 0.3-mile-wide (0.5 km) narrows or entrance to the continuation of the Columbia River Reach. Stay along the west shoreline in the reach for the rest of the journey to Mica Dam. Approximately 6.3 miles from the narrows and 27.2 miles (43.8 km) from Kinbasket Lake Resort is **Swan Bay,** a small but noticeable opening in the reach. Begin looking for a reasonable take-out and campsite as you paddle the next 5 to 6 miles (8 to 9.7 km) and the end of Leg 5. The shoreline along the reach is steep glacial till in places, sometimes vertical and rocky. Decent campsites are few and far between.

Hazards include sudden storms, high winds and large waves, underwater snags and rocks near the shoreline, large floating logging debris, cold water temperatures, and grizzly bears.

FLOW AND SEASON: This is a dam-created reservoir, and there is no perceptible flow. The best time to paddle this leg is April through October, although there's a chance of snow and below-freezing temperatures later in October.

PUT-IN: Kinbasket Lake Resort boat ramp, Columbia West Forest Service Rd off T-C 1.

TAKE-OUTS: Bear Island, 19.3 miles (31 km); my camp, 32.5 miles (52.3 km), old skid road landing on the west shoreline (GPS coordinates: N 51°52'25.70", W 117°54'01.50").

SERVICES: There are no services once you leave Kinbasket Lake Resort. Be prepared and pack everything you think you will need, including a tent, sleeping bag, stove, raingear, dry clothes, and food. In September, I spotted one boat in two full days of paddling to Mica Dam. Be self-sufficient or paddle with two or more people.

CAMPING: Almost all land in this area is Crown land and open to camping. You can camp along the lake or find a clearing off a secluded logging or slash road just about anywhere off the main highway. Start looking for a campsite along this leg an hour before you intend to camp. Take-outs are limited, except on Bear Island. There are a few low-angled slopes above the undercut banks, and even fewer shoreline areas free of debris that provide possible campsites. The owner of Kinbasket Lake Resort and several locals warned me that there is a healthy grizzly bear population throughout this area, so consider carrying pepper spray if you plan to spend time on shore.

Passage

I can't say for sure how many fishermen boat on Kinbasket Lake, but when I paddled this leg in mid-September, the lake was deserted. Due to the size and extent of woody debris floating in the lake, ranging from small pieces of bark to 100-foot logs left from past logging operations, recreational boating is hazardous. It seems as though even fishermen are reluctant to use the lake. This makes for a quiet and enjoyable paddle for those of us in kayaks or canoes.

GRIZZLY COUNTRY

Fact: While paddling in British Columbia, you are no longer at the top of the food chain. That honor belongs to the grizzly, an omnivore that can weigh up to 800 pounds (363 kg), reach a height of 8 feet (2.44 m), and sprint 30 miles per hour (45 km per hour). The grizzly is easily recognized by its wide, concave face; high, hump-backed shoulders; short, round ears; and grizzled light brown to nearly black coat.

If you are lucky enough to see a grizzly in the wild—at a distance—it is the experience of a lifetime. But if your encounter is close or you surprise one on the trail, stand your ground, face the animal, talk, and slowly edge away at a walk while facing it. Running may elicit a chase response from such a large predator. The best defense from interrupting a bear over a fresh kill or getting between a sow and its cubs is to make lots of noise while in their territory. Normally, bears want nothing to do with you. You smell, you make funny noise, and you taste like . . . well, you know what.

When I pulled out on the rocky shore of Bear Island, I kept an eye out for the island's namesake.

Entering the narrows on Kinbasket Lake just northwest of Bear Island

I packed the two watertight compartments in my kayak with camping gear and food, and then launched from the dock below the lodge at 6 AM, staying close to the west shoreline. There was one cabin just a few miles out, but from that point on I was on my own. Joyce would drive west over Rogers Pass to Revelstoke, and then north on British Columbia Highway 23 to Mica Dam. We planned to meet somewhere near the dam on the evening of my second day.

The rugged peaks of the Selkirk Mountains, with some of the most spectacular glaciated peaks in British Columbia, rise steeply from the lake, the slopes covered in a patchwork of second-growth timber and clear-cuts. It's sometimes hard to believe timber could be harvested from the almost vertical slopes. At about 15 miles (24.1 km) from the lodge, the 1-mile-wide (1.6 km) Columbia River Reach widened into a bay as much as 6 miles (9.7 km) wide east to west and 5 miles (8 km) over open water to Bear Island, the first land I would reach across the bay. There was no wind, so rather than take the long route around, hugging the west shoreline, I set off directly across the open water, knowing that just a breeze on a lake this big would result in huge swells and whitecaps.

Paddling far out from shore on open water always makes me feel as though I'm not even moving, so I measured my speed and distance by spotting one of the many logs floating in the lake and timing how long it took to reach it. After paddling for an hour across the open expanse, I landed briefly on Bear Island. The shoreline was alternately gravelly, swampy, or rocky, but easy to pull out on.

After a snack, I continued around the west side of the island, avoiding the weedy shallows close to shore and then entered another narrow section of the Columbia River Reach, averaging less than 0.5 mile (0.8 km) wide over the next 15 miles (24.1 km). The banks of the channel were undercut from the raising and lowering of the reservoir water, with some short vertical cliffs. Along with old harvested logs floating along the shoreline, I saw trees with root balls still attached that had recently eroded out from along the banks, fallen into the lake, and drifted to shore. I watched carefully for submerged branches and stumps, which are plentiful and a hazard near any shoreline on Kinbasket Lake.

An afternoon storm blew in from the south about an hour into the narrow section of the reach. With waves crashing over my stern, wind at my back, and a hard rain dampening my spirits, I stepped out of my kayak after 9 hours onto a large log, and then dragged and lifted my boat to the top of several garbage can–sized boulders. I unpacked and made camp on the remnants of an overgrown skid trail, which had evidently been used many years ago to dump logs into the lake for transport. As night fell, I threw another piece of driftwood on the fire, found a dry spot under the tarp, and fell asleep to the rhythmic patter of raindrops.

LEG 6: Central Columbia River Reach to Mica Dam

Distance: 33.9 miles (54.6 km)
Paddle Time: 7 to 10 hours

River View

The leg from your take-out near the center of the **Columbia River Reach** to **Mica Dam** will vary in length depending on where you camped the night before. I split the distance and my take-out was approximately 33.9 miles (54.6 km) from the dam. This leg has many more opportunities to pull out to rest or camp because of the lower-angled slopes off the **Selkirk Mountains** to the southwest. You will also notice an increase in small motorized boats as you approach the 25–30-square-mile (64.8–77.7 sq km) bay behind the dam

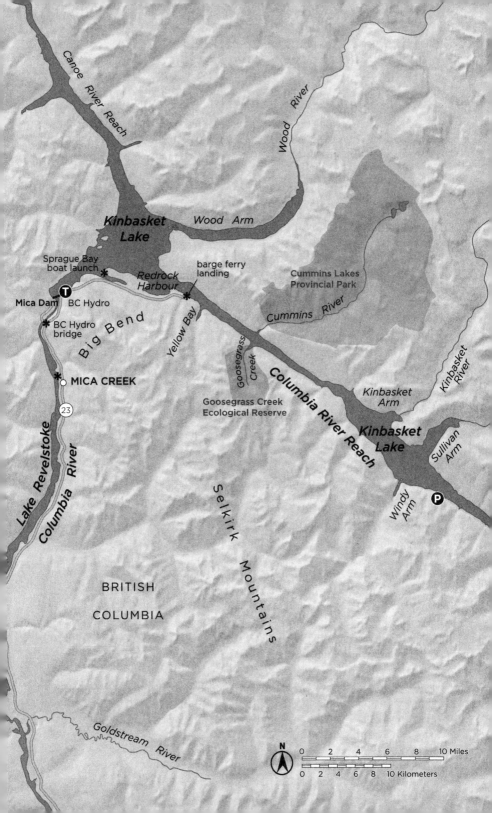

DAMS ALONG THE COLUMBIA

The Columbia River has 14 hydroelectric dams on its 1200-mile (1930 km) main stem. They exist for flood control, navigation, stream flow regulation, storage and delivery of stored water, reclamation of lands, recreation, and generation of hydroelectric power. In the list below, USACE stands for US Army Corps of Engineers, and PUD stands for public utility district.

DAM	YEAR COMPLETED	OPERATOR	POWER (in megawatts)	HEIGHT
Rock Island Dam	1933	Chelan Co PUD	624	38 ft (12 m)
Bonneville Dam	1937	USACE	1189	197 ft (60 m)
Grand Coulee Dam	1942	USACE	6809	550 ft (168 m)
McNary Dam	1954	USACE	980	183 ft (56 m)
Chief Joseph Dam	1955	USACE	2620	236 ft (72 m)
The Dalles Dam	1960	USACE	1780	260 ft (79 m)
Priest Rapids Dam	1961	Grant Co PUD	956	178 ft (54 m)
Rocky Reach Dam	1961	Chelan Co PUD	1300	93 ft (28 m)
Wanapum Dam	1963	Grant Co PUD	1038	185 ft (56 m)
Wells Dam	1967	Douglas Co PUD	840	160 ft (49 m)
Keenleyside Dam	1968	BC Hydro	185	171 ft (52 m)
John Day Dam	1971	USACE	2485	183 ft (56 m)
Mica Dam	1973	BC Hydro	2805	800 ft (244 m)
Revelstoke Dam	1984	BC Hydro	2480	574 ft (175 m)

that separates the **Canoe River Reach** to the north and the Columbia River Reach to the south.

This leg is very similar to the paddle from Bear Island. From your camp along the west shoreline, the 0.5-mile-wide (0.8 km) channel expands to 2.5 miles (4 km) wide just a few miles from your campsite in the reach. About 5 miles (8 km) from my take-out and river left is **Windy Arm,** a 1.2-mile-long (1.9 km) narrow bay with a small island at its mouth. This is the termination of Windy Creek, which drains the Adamant Peaks deep in the Selkirk Mountains. On the northeast side across the reach is **Sullivan Arm,** an immense bay 4.5 miles (7.2 km) long that drains the Sullivan River. Just north of Sullivan Arm is **Kinbasket Arm**, a much smaller bay that drains the **Kinbasket River.** Under calm weather and water conditions, paddle the open water to the other side of Windy Arm, but if it is windy, hug the west shoreline, which will add only a short distance to your paddle.

Approximately 13 miles (20.9 km) from the old skid road landing where I camped, the reach narrows again to less than 0.5 mile (0.8 km). There are several small bays along river left, none of which are good landmarks until the half-mile-long, V-shaped bay at **Goosegrass Creek** 18.4 miles (29.6 km) along the reach. For the most part, if you need to pull out, you will still have to find a way through drift logs piled like toothpicks sloshing along the shoreline or use the more stable logs to stand and exit your boat.

The next recognizable landmark is **Yellow Bay,** a mile-deep (1.6 km) cleft into the shoreline, 4.7 miles (7.6 km) past Goosegrass Creek and 22.9 miles out from my campsite. No need to stop on the gravel beach on the northeast side of the bay, because just 2.2 miles (3.5 km) farther is a logging truck barge ferry landing with a good take-out and access to the road to Mica Dam, if weather or water conditions force you off the lake.

Within 0.7 mile (1.1 km) of the ferry landing is **Redrock Harbour.** Cross the 1.4-mile (2.3 km) mouth and within 3 miles (4.8 km) round the point to **Sprague Bay** with a boat launch facility across the bay. Continue paddling 2.3 miles

Looking southeast from Yellow Bay across the Columbia Reach

(3.7 km) to the take-out above the dam, weather and water conditions permitting. This short section can be a hard paddle into a fierce headwind drawn up the Columbia River from the Revelstoke side and over the dam.

Hazards include weather-related high winds and waves, underwater snags and rocks near the shoreline, large floating logging debris, cold water temperatures, and possibly grizzly bears.

FLOW AND SEASON: There is no perceptible flow in Kinbasket Lake. The best time to paddle this leg is between April and October.

PUT-IN: Same as your take-out for Leg 5, or a variation. My take-out for Leg 5 was at an old skid road/log landing 32.5 miles (52.3 km) from the Kinbasket Lake Resort (GPS coordinates: N 51°52'25.70", W 117°54'01.50").

TAKE-OUTS: Logging truck barge ferry landing, 9.7 miles (15.6 km), BC 23; Sprague Bay boat launch, 3.5 miles (5.6 km), BC 23; BC Hydro boat launch, 0.5 mile (0.8 km), BC 23. All distances are upstream from Mica Dam.

SERVICES: There are no services at Mica Dam or along BC 23 from Revelstoke.

CAMPING: Almost all land in this area is Crown land (owned by the Canadian government) and open to camping. You can camp along the lake or find a clearing off a secluded logging or slash road just about anywhere off BC 23. There are no accommodations in this area. Be self-sufficient.

Passage

Several miles (3.2 km) beyond my campsite along the rough shoreline, the lake widened to over 2 miles (3.2 km), but since it was still early morning with no wind or waves, I cut across from point to point almost 4 miles (6.4 km) in front of Windy Arm rather than take the longer shoreline. I didn't have to make many decisions as to the route. There are a few bays that break the shoreline, but otherwise the lake was straight as a paddle. I knew to stay close to the southwest shoreline, so I would be on the correct side of the lake to make the turn west to Mica Dam.

Past Windy Arm, the reach narrowed and I kept close to the undercut bank of the shoreline. As I crossed the small bay at the head of Trident Creek, I could see several 9000–10,000-foot (2743 to 3048 m) glaciated peaks, including

Trident Mountain and Dolphin Peak. This was one of the few places along the paddle where I had a clear view up a canyon to see the peaks in the Selkirks. My paddle route directly below the forested slopes close to the shoreline and the deep, twisting canyons limited good views of the many spectacular peaks I knew were above me.

This was still big water with a long, straight channel for wind and waves to develop. I was also aware that I had not seen any recreational boaters since the day before, so at midday when I started to feel the wind at my back, I stopped and put on my spray skirt. I was glad I did. As I paddled past the bay at Goosegrass Creek, a little more than halfway to the dam, the waves came up, and I was paddling in whitecaps within just a few minutes.

Even though I knew British Columbia's economy was based on timber, I was surprised at the extent of the logged area above Kinbasket Lake, the size of the clear-cuts, and their close proximity to the shoreline. I wondered if the government had sufficient regulations controlling the timber industry to protect

The barge ferry used to transport logging trucks and other vehicles across the Columbia River Reach

the creeks, streams, and rivers from sediment and increasing water temperature. Throughout my journey, I found evidence of past indefensible logging practices the length of the Columbia River. It is difficult for me to see change in the industry, but it is coming as better machinery and modern scientific methods replace outdated and abusive practices, and as a society we evolve to be better stewards of the environment. Even so, industry representatives and many government agency personnel defend the clear-cut, as if a forest is like a corn patch rather than an ecosystem.

Once I was past Goosegrass Creek, which is also the name of the ecological reserve in the drainage, I paddled 6 miles (9.7 km) with waves breaking over my stern past Yellow Bay to a barge ferry landing used to transport logging trucks and other machinery from the logging operations taking place on the northeast side of the reach. There were numerous log landings and skid roads along the shore to pull out on before the ferry landing, but the landing was more convenient and, with the wind and waves I was fighting, I was considering taking out before the dam.

I knew I didn't have far to go to the take-out above the dam, so I launched from the landing and paddled 0.5 mile (0.8 km) around a small rounded peninsula, and then crossed the 1.5-mile-wide (2.4 km) Redrock Harbour before finding protection from the wind and waves again along the shoreline for a few brief moments. As I turned the corner and faced west toward the dam, the wind was directly into my bow. I crossed Sprague Bay and found relief at one of several unmaintained boat launches along the shoreline, but this was temporary, as I again paddled around a small peninsula protecting the boat launch area and faced the full strength of the wind coming over the dam. There were a few more small bays I managed to hide behind as I covered the last couple of miles (3.2 km) to the take-out, but anytime I left the protection of the small bays and entered the open water, I struggled to make headway.

Joyce met me at a boat launch a short distance from the dam at dusk as the wind picked up another notch near the narrow opening above the dam and the rain became a soaker, so typical of the interior ranges of British Columbia. I had finally reached the northernmost extent of the Columbia River.

OPPOSITE: Fog and wind greeted me as I approached Mica Dam.

SEGMENT 2

MICA DAM TO THE US–CANADA BORDER

Total Distance: 247.1 miles (397.7 km)

Segment 2 details seven one-day journeys on the Columbia from Mica Dam to the US–Canada border, beginning with the pristine waters of Lake Revelstoke, paddling through the remote stretches of the Arrow Lakes, and finishing along the free-flowing wild water below Keenleyside Dam to the border. Mica Dam is at the northern end of the Big Bend, where the Columbia takes an abrupt U-turn from its northern flow to the south and cuts a deep valley between the Selkirk Mountains, now to the east, and the Monashees to the west. The river has two more dams, Revelstoke and Keenleyside dams; passes by the larger towns of Revelstoke, Castlegar, and Trail; and adds the Kootenay and Pend Oreille rivers to its flow.

LEG 7: Mica Dam to Downie Creek Arm

Distance: 46.7 miles (75.2 km)
Paddle Time: 10 to 13 hours

River View

The leg from **Mica Dam** to **Downie Creek Arm** is a stretch of the river lined with thick stands of cedar and hemlock that carpet the steep slopes below the towering and spectacular **Selkirk Mountains** to the east and the **Monashee Mountains** to the west. As if the Columbia suddenly realizes that flowing north is the wrong direction, the river turns abruptly at Mica Dam and flows directly south for the border.

BC Hydro, which operates all three main-stem dams on the upper Columbia, discourages paddlers from putting in directly below the face of Mica Dam. Therefore, the best access is an easily reached concrete pad from a former building site on the west shore 2.3 miles (3.7 km) downstream from the dam

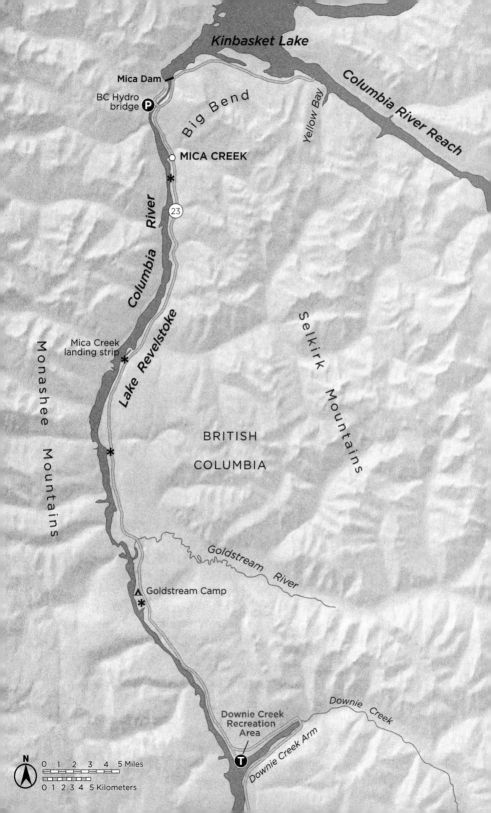

THE COLUMBIA RIVER TREATY

The Columbia River Treaty, a 1964 agreement between Canada and the United States, ensures cooperative development and operation of four dams for power and flood control in the upper Columbia River basin, two of which are on the main stem of the Columbia: Mica Dam and Keenley-side Dam. The trans-boundary treaty provides Canada with half of down-stream US power in exchange for flood control, and other benefits. Per the agreement, the two Canadian dams are set to release water to meet demand, rather than rely on seasonal flow. The treaty's flood-control plan is set to expire in 2024 and be replaced by on-demand flood-control needs, unless a new agreement is reached.

As of October 2013, the US Army Corps of Engineers began the public hearing process to take comments on the draft recommendations to the Department of State regarding what a modernized treaty will look like. Environmental groups and tribes along the river want to add ecosystem function and restoration, fish passage at Chief Joseph and Grand Coulee dams, and modernized flood-control systems to power production and flood control as the main goals to any renegotiated treaty.

and 300 yards (274 m) below the blue steel girder–built bridge crossing the Columbia and leading to the Nagle Creek drainage.

The east shoreline has numerous unmaintained take-outs, primarily where short sections of the old Mica Highway disappear into Lake Revelstoke, and at the many temporary logging truck ferry crossings. Before paddling off, locate the most easily accessed take-out from British Columbia Highway 23, known as the Big Bend Highway. BC Hydro maintains a boat launch and picnic area on the north shore of **Downie Creek Arm,** the only maintained facility for 46.7 miles (75.2 km). Avoid taking out at **Downie Creek,** a small private community. The west shoreline also has unlimited places to take out for a rest or to relax during your journey, but no vehicle access.

The Columbia is still a small river below Mica Dam that widens and narrows to the changing topography, but within just a few miles, any flow from the dam disappears into 80-mile-long (128.7 km) **Lake Revelstoke,** the backwaters of Revelstoke Dam. From the put-in, the Columbia flows straight south for 10 miles (16 km), begins another easy 10-mile sweep slightly southwest, and then takes an equally easy sweep the final 25 miles (40.2 km) to the southeast before opening like the jaws of a grizzly bear at Downie Creek Arm. The water temperature is cold enough to give you an "ice cream" headache if you go in, but the river's channel is always 0.75 mile (1.2 km) or less, so it would be a short swim to shore. A lightweight wetsuit in early spring is warranted.

Hazards include swift flowing water below the dam, underwater snags near the shoreline, hypothermia (if you go in), and grizzly bears.

FLOW AND SEASON: Flow rate will depend on the season and release from Mica Dam, but in general, the Columbia quickly loses any power as it enters Lake Revelstoke within 2 to 5 miles (3.2 to 8 km) downstream from the put-in. The best months to paddle are June through October, although I thoroughly enjoyed the serenity as I paddled several of the legs below Mica Dam in mid-November.

PUT-IN: A former mill site on the west shore 2.3 miles (3.7 km) below the face of Mica Dam and 300 yards (274 m) downstream from the blue girder bridge.

TAKE-OUTS: Mica Creek landing strip river access, 16 miles (25.8 km), BC 23; Goldstream Camp, 33.2 miles (53.4 km), BC 23; Downie Creek Recreation Area, 46.7 miles (75.2 km), BC 23. All distances are from the put-in. There are many additional unmaintained access points along the east side of the river.

SERVICES: There are no services north of Revelstoke (see Leg 8), a full-service community with motels, grocery stores, bakeries, and paddler specialty stores.

CAMPING: Camping is allowed free of charge on Crown land, which includes both shorelines of the Columbia River from Revelstoke to Mica Dam.

Passage

I paddled most of this leg in mid-November, despite the chilly temperatures and snow on the ground. The weather report called for more snow, but no wind, and the release from Mica Dam was minimal. The best put-in was on the west shore 300 yards (274 m) downstream from a steel girder bridge used by BC Hydro to access the dam, and by logging trucks removing timber from the Monashee Mountains.

I was alone on this trip, so I locked my mountain bike to a tree downstream near the Mica Creek landing strip, drove back to the put-in, and launched into a 3–4 mph (4.8–6.4 kmph) current and crystal-clear water. The river swept me downstream for several miles (3.2 km), past the Canadian Mountain Holidays Lodge built just above the shoreline of the river, and then 1 mile (1.6 km)

BALD EAGLES ALONG THE COLUMBIA

British Columbia is second only to Alaska in the number of bald eagles, even though their range includes almost all of North America. Bald eagles develop their white head plumage after reaching reproductive maturity at four to five years old, and live an average of twenty years in the wild. They are the second-largest bird of prey in North America, averaging 7 to 14 pounds (3.2 to 6.4 kg), with a wingspan of almost 7 feet (2.1 m), which allows them to reach flight speeds of 43 mph (69.2 kmph) and dive speeds of up to 99 mph (159.3 kmph). Females are typically 25 percent larger than males.

For a variety of reasons, including the pesticide DDT, which thinned the bird's eggshells, the bald eagle was placed on the US Endangered Species list in 1967. With regulations in place and DDT banned, the bald eagle is recovering and was delisted in 2007.

farther to **Mica Creek,** BC Hydro's living quarters for dam personnel. From Mica Creek I was alone on the river for the next 4 hours.

The river is as clear as glass along the route, and on windless days this clarity gives the paddler the impression of being suspended in midair. It also provides a fish buffet second to none for the numerous eagles that perch on dead snags lining the banks and great blue herons stalking the shallows at every bend of the river. Just past Mica Creek, I entered the backwaters of Revelstoke Dam, where the river runs due south, widening and narrowing as the topography changes. I paddled point to point, crossing the river several times in a straight line before a slight wind, and the resulting waves had me hugging the east shoreline to my campsite on the river at the southeast end of the Mica Creek gravel landing strip 16 miles (25.8 km) downriver.

Early the next morning, after brushing the fresh layer of snow off my boat, I put in again and paddled for the logging truck ferry landing at **Goldstream Camp,** another 17.2 miles (27.7 km) downriver. Again, the river varied in width throughout the paddle, but in one idyllic spot below 9000-foot (2743 m) peaks to the west it narrowed to less than 200 yards (183 m) wide. I found that about every 6 miles (9.7 km), there was a seldom-used or abandoned logging truck ferry landing, which made for good spots to pull out to stretch, rehydrate, and eat. Occasionally an old motorized barge or ferry was still at the landing attached to a cable, which was strung under the river to the other side.

The Columbia is still a small river in the Big Bend country, and it heads due south with very few curves. When it wasn't too windy, I simply paddled in line of sight from protruding peninsula to peninsula. Around 29 miles (46.7 km) downriver from my put-in below Mica Dam, I paddled through a 400-yard-wide (366 m) narrows where **Goldstream River** on the east and a minor creek on the west emptied into the Columbia.

I pulled out several times to wait out an intermittent pesky wind, as the early-winter weather changed hourly. After 5 hours of paddling, I reached the log truck ferry landing at Goldstream Camp, 4 miles (6.4 km) downstream from Goldstream River. The site has good vehicle access and a nice place to camp. That afternoon, I hopped on my bike and rode back upriver along BC 23 to retrieve my vehicle, stopping only once to let a cow moose and her calf mosey across the deserted highway.

From Goldstream Camp, the Columbia flows so directly southeast for 12.7 miles (20.4 km), it's as if the channel was cut using a straightedge. The next morning, I paddled downriver touching each side of the channel multiple times as I tried to take the most direct line to Downie Creek Arm. Just before the arm, I stopped briefly on the beach at the residential area of Downie Creek, then turned east into Downie Creek Arm, a huge bay compared to the narrow river, and finished my journey to the Downie Creek Recreation Area boat ramp.

Looking down on Mica Dam with its spillway on the left

LEG 8: Downie Creek Arm to Revelstoke Dam

Distance: 32.7 miles (51.6 km)
Paddle Time: 7 to 10 hours

River View

The leg from **Downie Creek Arm** to **Revelstoke Dam** is a paddle on a much broader **Lake Revelstoke** than below Mica Dam. The width of the lake averages around 0.75 mile (1.2 km) but can be well over a mile (1.6 km). From the **Downie Creek Recreation Area boat ramp** on the north shore of Downie Creek Arm, cross the 1 mile (1.6 km) of open water to the river's east shoreline and paddle this shoreline for the next 32 miles (51.5 km). The Columbia takes a long curve to the southeast before turning due south, and following the east shoreline prevents you from having to cross big, open water.

British Columbia Highway 23 parallels the river, climbing and dropping in elevation as the steep, rough terrain dictates. Where the road comes close to the Columbia, there are a number of opportunities to take out along the paddle route if the wind creates difficult and dangerous conditions. Most are unmaintained remnants of the old highway above the portions that were covered by Lake Revelstoke.

The first good access from Downie Creek Arm is 10.2 miles (16.4 km) out and only 0.7 mile (1.1 km) before the BC 23 bridge over **Mars Creek** and the prominent peninsula jutting out into the river. It's an old road remnant slightly hidden behind a bump in the shoreline. There are several more road remnants prior to reaching the good take-out between Holdich Creek and Kelly Creek with its long, narrow bay 15.2 miles (24.5 km) from the put-in. Again, there are additional spots to stop and relax, but the next good take-out is south of **La Forme Creek,** 21.9 miles (35.2 km) out and recognizable by the third major highway bridge along the paddle route. From La Forme Creek it's less than 5 miles (8 km) to the south end of **Martha Creek Provincial Park,** which has excellent public facilities and a boat ramp. The main take-out, though, is another 5.1 miles (8.2 km) downriver at a **BC Hydro boat ramp** and less than 2 miles (3.2 km) from the top of the dam.

This paddle has spectacular views of the **Monashees** to the west, immense slopes of forested terrain, steep cliffs, beautiful bays, and an occasional waterfall into the lake. You won't be without the constant vigilance of wary eagles taking fish out of the river like it was a barrel.

Hazards include big, open water; wind and waves; and some fishing boat traffic in Downie Creek Arm.

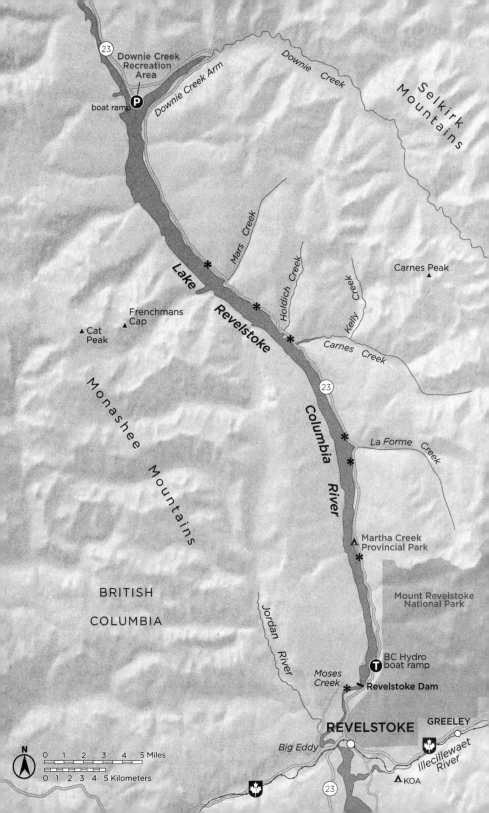

DALLES DES MORTS (DEATH RAPIDS)

Prior to the building of the three Canadian dams, there were more than twenty rapids, narrows, known whirlpools, and other dangerous features on the Columbia River between Columbia Lake and the US border. Dalles des Morts, 3.7 miles (6 km) north of Downie Creek Arm, a particularly violent stretch of the river, deserved its moniker as Death Rapids. A number of fatal accidents occurred here, including the death of twelve travelers in the autumn of 1838.

The rapid was known for its 12–15-foot-high (3.7–4.6 m) rollers and a flow as fast as a racehorse. According to Lewis Ransome Freeman, who rowed the Columbia with expert boatmen in 1920, as recounted in his book *Down the Columbia* (see the Resources section): "For a quarter of a mile below where the rolling waves ceased to comb there was a green-white chaos of whirlpools and the great geyser-like up-boils where the sucked down under water was ejected again to the surface."

The small lakeside community of Downie Creek sits on the shore of Lake Revelstoke at the mouth of the Downie Creek Arm.

FLOW AND SEASON: Flow is imperceptible on Lake Revelstoke. I paddled this leg in midsummer, and it was relatively free of other boaters. The best time is between May and October.

PUT-IN: Downie Creek Recreation Area and boat ramp, BC 23.

TAKE-OUTS: Unmaintained old highway remnant, 8.7 miles (14 km), BC 23; Mars Creek, 10.2 miles (16.4 km), unmaintained old highway remnant, BC 23; unmaintained old highway remnant, 13 miles (20.9 km), BC 23; Holdich Creek, 15.2 miles (24.5 km), BC 23; La Forme Creek, 21.9 miles (35.2 km), unmaintained old highway remnant; Martha Creek Provincial Park, 26.8 miles (43.1 km), BC 23; and BC Hydro–maintained boat ramp, 31.8 miles (51.2 km), BC 23. All distances are from the Downie Creek Recreation Area boat launch off BC 23.

SERVICES: All services are available in Revelstoke, including excellent restaurants, good motels, grocery stores, and paddler supplies. There are no restaurants, grocery stores, or motels north of Revelstoke.

CAMPING: Camping along the river is allowed free of charge on Crown land, which includes most of both shorelines from Revelstoke to Mica Dam. Typically, campers use the access roads to the old highway remnants and the shoreline for camping. There are also forty-six maintained campsites at Martha Creek Provincial Park, the only provincial park on this reservoir.

Passage

I launched from the Downie Creek Recreation Area boat ramp just after sunrise on a calm June morning. I was alone, except for a few fishing boats in the distance. The beauty of Downie Creek Arm is the 4 miles (6.4 km) of unobstructed view east toward the glaciated 9600-foot (2926.1 m) Argentine Mountain and other peaks in the **Selkirk Mountains.** Once across the arm, I hugged the east shoreline, not only the shortest distance along the curve but also adjacent to possible take-outs in case of wind, which frequent this big lake. Directly off my bow to the south and across the river was **Frenchmans Cap,** a rugged 9400-foot (2865.1 m) mountain in the Monashees surrounded by other glaciated 9000-foot peaks (2743.2 m).

For spectacular beauty, the Columbia along this section is hard to beat. With the Big Bend Highway terminating at Mica Dam, there is very little traffic on the road, especially in mid- to late September. Additionally, there is no

The steep shoreline along Lake Revelstoke has thick, rainforest-like undergrowth below a forest of towering red cedar and Douglas fir.

railroad, making this stretch peaceful and relatively quiet, a pleasant improvement over the paddle from Invermere to Golden.

Approximately 15 miles (24.1 km) from the launch is a deep, narrow bay and a bridge where the highway spans **Carnes Creek.** The mountains along this section to the dam seem to spring from the river's edge. I could hear cars on the highway, but there were few motorboats to interrupt a perfect day.

After 26 miles (41.8 km), I reached Martha Creek Provincial Park, which has a white sandy beach and is a popular camping spot and boat launch area. Despite storm clouds building over the mountains, the tubers, ski boats, and jet skis were active, giving the small bay a noisy, carnival-like atmosphere. But considering the calm day, exquisite scenery, and occasional common loon and bald eagle, I expected a much bigger crowd. I stopped for a late lunch at the park and then continued paddling toward the dam, arriving at the BC Hydro boat ramp 1.9 miles (3.1 km) short of the dam in the early afternoon.

LEG 9: Revelstoke Dam to Shelter Bay (Upper Arrow Lake)

Distance: 30 miles (48.3 km)
Paddle Time: 6.5 to 10 hours

River View

The leg from **Revelstoke Dam** to **Shelter Bay** is rich in birdlife and framed by spectacular mountain scenery. The steep mountainous terrain that characterized the river valley from Mica Dam is set back from the Arrow Lakes and replaced by hundreds of square miles of forested slopes leading to snow-capped peaks. The mountains are still spectacular, but visible at a distance rather than perched directly above the river. The **Upper Arrow Lake** valley is wider, and the shallow marshland attracts geese, ducks, and a variety of shore birds.

Public access to the river is limited just below the dam, although there is a good put-in off the Westside Road at the **Moses Creek** spawning channel 1.1 mile (1.8 km) from the spillway. Be aware of **Big Eddy,** a well-known 90-degree trap-like bend just north of Trans-Canada Highway 1 that creates a giant whirlpool in high water in a bowl-like feature at the turn 3 miles (4.8 km) from this put-in at Moses Creek. In low water, like in October, it's an easy and pleasant 4-mile (6.4 km) paddle past Big Eddy to the T-C 1 bridge. Stay river left at the bowl and glide with the current over the gravel bed just under the surface, letting the river catch and sweep you along the left shoreline. You can scout this section from the Westside Road as you drive up to the put-in.

The best put-in in high water is off a gravel-and-mud beach on the southwest side of the highway 5 miles (8 km) from the dam spillway. Flow can vary

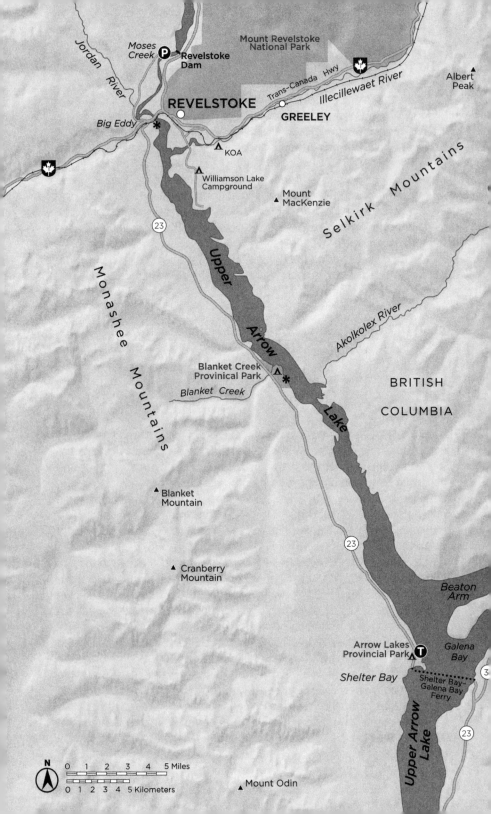

THE SINIXT

The Sinixt, known as the Arrow Lakes Indians or Lakes Indians, are the First Nations people of the West Kootenay region of British Columbia and northeast Washington. Sinixt translates as "Place of the Bull Trout." Archaeological material uncovered at Deer Park north of Castlegar (British Columbia) suggests that people came north from the Interior Plateau nearly 10,000 years ago.

Once the explorers, miners, and land grabbers began to arrive in the early nineteenth century, it didn't take long for the Sinixt to dwindle in numbers and lose their tribal lands. Once the salmon failed to return upriver after the construction of the Grand Coulee Dam in 1942, and much of the bottom land around the original Arrow Lakes was flooded in 1968 by the construction of Keenleyside Dam, the Sinixt, like so many tribes, lost their traditional way of life and never fully recovered. As spoken by a Sinixt elder, "Buried beneath the waters are the graves of our First People and their history."

In 1956, the Canadian government declared the Arrow Lakes band of the Sinixt extinct even though many Sinixt tribal members live on the Colville Indian Reservation, in the Slocan Valley, and are scattered throughout southern British Columbia.

from the dam depending on the season, but in general there is a powerful, smooth current under the highway that continues for several miles (3.2 km) before it disappears in Upper Arrow Lake. There are two bridges within 250 yards (229 m) of this launch area. Stay centered between the bridge pilings to avoid their turbulence, and continue to follow the west shoreline around the first bend, paddling with the flow to the southeast. Two miles (3.2 km) below the bridge put-in and at the southern end of the town of **Revelstoke,** the **Illecillewaet River** enters from the east, but it has no impact on paddlers.

During midsummer, Upper Arrow Lake, the reservoir for Keenleyside Dam above Castlegar, reaches to within several miles (3.2 km) of Revelstoke and eliminates any flow. Again, depending on the season, there are large marsh areas and sandy shallows in the bays on either side of the river, as well as several remote beach areas.

The river can be over a mile (1.6 km) wide below Revelstoke, but narrows to less than 400 yards (366 m) in some places. Upper Arrow Lake widens to 1.7 miles (2.7 km) abruptly at **Beaton Arm,** 24.5 miles (39.4 km) from the put-in. In calm weather, it's an easy paddle south across the bay to the campground take-out at **Arrow Lakes Provincial Park;** if there is wind, though, paddle along the west shoreline, which is somewhat protected by the point off Shelter Bay. To the northeast is 10-mile-long (16 km) Beaton Arm.

Hazards include turbulence and hydraulics at Big Eddy below the Westside Road put-in, underwater obstructions below the bridge put-in, afternoon storms, wind and waves, sand bars and shallows.

FLOW AND SEASON: Flow below the dam is turbulent and fast, but slows 5 miles (8 km) downriver at the unmaintained public launch area below the T-C 1. A flow of 2 to 4 mph (3.2 to 6.4 kmph) for several more miles (3.2 km) can be expected. The paddle is mostly on Upper Arrow Lake. The best time to paddle is from April to October.

PUT-INS: Moses Creek off Westside Rd, 1.1 miles (1.8 km) from Revelstoke Dam (low water); southwest corner of T-C 1 (high water).

TAKE-OUTS: Blanket Creek Provincial Park, 17.5 miles (28.2 km), BC 23; Arrow Lakes Provincial Park, 33.5 miles (53.9 km), BC 23 at Shelter Bay. All distances are from the Westside Road put-in.

SERVICES: All services are available in Revelstoke, including excellent restaurants, good motels, grocery stores, and paddler supplies.

CAMPING: Vehicle-accessible camping is available at Blanket Creek Provincial Park (see Take-outs); Arrow Lakes Provincial Park (see Take-outs); Martha Creek Provincial Park, above Revelstoke Dam off BC 23 (see Leg 8); Williamson Lake Campground, south Revelstoke, near airport; and KOA Campground Revelstoke, Oak Dr off T-C 1.

Passage

I was excited to begin my journey from Revelstoke to Upper and Lower Arrow lakes. Paddling these two long, wide bodies of water would prepare me for Lake Roosevelt and other large reservoirs farther downstream.

I searched for a put-in close to Revelstoke Dam and found two potential launch sites, but in mid-July the dam was releasing a high volume of winter runoff. The turbulence and hydraulics, especially at Big Eddy, a toilet trap–like bowl and bend in the river 4 miles (6.4 km) from the dam where the river backs up on itself, seemed too dangerous for my sea kayak, so I put in at an unmaintained gravel bar on the southwest side of the Trans-Canada Highway. Big Eddy was so well known to early explorers that the town of Big Eddy just south of the feature was named after it, and Revelstoke was first known as "The Eddy" because of this whirlpool feature. (I returned later in October when the flow was much smaller, put in at Moses Creek, and found Big Eddy to be easily passed by paddling river left.)

Revelstoke Dam's 574-foot-high (175 m) concrete face holds back Lake Revelstoke, an 81-mile-long (130 km) reservoir.

There were a few fishermen in motorboats anchored in the bays near Revelstoke, but for most of the paddle I had the river to myself, except for a number of great blue herons in the reedy shallows, rafts of ducks, and of course, bald eagles. To benefit from the steady flow and avoid shoreline hydraulics, I moved away from the shallows and marshes, but stayed river right for the entire journey to Arrow Lakes Provincial Park. I hardly noticed the Illecillewaet River, which enters the Columbia at Revelstoke, even though it too was running high.

Within 4 miles (6.4 km), the west shoreline changed from marsh and rural residences to deep forest and steep bluffs. The river is framed by Revelstoke's ski area on **Mount MacKenzie** to the east and the snow-capped **Monashees** to the west. I barely heard a sound of human activity on this section of the river, although British Columbia Highway 23 is squeezed down to the river by the rising peaks above where the Columbia narrows to less than half a mile (0.8 km) about 12 miles (19.3 km) from my put-in.

I reached Blanket Creek Provincial Park 3 hours into my journey. British Columbia provincial parks are excellent facilities, and this one was no exception. After Joyce picked me up at Shelter Bay later in the day, she and I returned to Blanket Creek to camp, and we felt it was one of the nicest parks along the Columbia.

Four miles (6.4 km) from Blanket Creek, the river bottlenecks and turns due south. This area was very shallow along river right, and in low water you can hit sand or weeds, but in mid-July I enjoyed a clean run through deep water. Three hours after leaving Blanket Creek, Upper Arrow Lake widened abruptly where the 10-mile-long (16 km) Beaton Arm of Upper Arrow Lake entered the bay from the east. I would have hugged the west shoreline if there had been anything but a breeze, but this was one of the finest days I had on the river, so I made the long, open-water paddle to Arrow Lakes Provincial Park and pulled out next to the park's recreational boat launch just before Shelter Bay.

LEG 10: Shelter Bay to Nakusp

Distance: 29.3 miles (47.2 km)
Paddle Time: 7 to 10 hours

River View

The leg from **Shelter Bay** to **Nakusp** begins with a 2.8-mile (4.5 km) open-water crossing of **Upper Arrow Lake,** and then follows the rocky and jagged east shoreline due south to Nakusp.

Begin this leg in windless conditions. The prevailing wind is from the south and southwest, and you don't want to be on this leg if the wind is kicking up waves all the way from Nakusp. From the beach or boat ramp at **Arrow Lakes Provincial Park,** paddle around the rocky point off Shelter Bay, and then set off across the bay for the east shore after one of the Galena Bay–Shelter Bay ferries passes by. The two ferries move in opposite directions and travel quickly, so timing is everything to avoid some bow and prop turbulence and to get out of their path.

The passage to the east shore is across one of the largest open-water areas on the upper Columbia. Upper Arrow Lake is as straight as the shaft of an arrow here, and you can see over 21 miles (33.8 km) downriver, so be prepared for big rollers or rogue waves even if the weather is calm at Shelter Bay. The east shore is rocky, steep, and vehicle access is very limited. Access to shore to rest or walk can be difficult because of the terrain, but there are numerous small rock coves and a few small sandy beaches protected from wave action for easier take-outs. The lake drops in elevation in the fall, and access to the shore can be even more difficult in some places. In calm conditions, you can paddle from rocky point to rocky point to avoid at least five wide bays, rather than follow the undulating shoreline.

The west shore is similar, but it is more susceptible to a southwest wind. You will also have to make the 2-mile (3.2 km) crossing at some point in your

▲ Cranberry
Mountain

23

Arrow Lakes
Provincial Park ⛺ Ⓟ

Shelter Bay

*Galena
Bay*

Shelter Bay–
Galena Bay
Ferry

31

23

BRITISH

COLUMBIA

▲ Mount Odin

**HALCYON
HOT SPRINGS**
◦

Halfway   River

Halfway
River ✳

Upper

Arrow

Lake

Monashee Mountains

23

✳

Kuskanax Creek

NAKUSP
◦

Ⓣ ▲ Nakusp
Recreation Park

6

6

Upper
Saddle Mountain
▲

0 1 2 3 4 5 Miles
0 1 2 3 4 5 Kilometers

journey, and the chance of wind and waves later in the afternoon in this mountainous terrain over cold, open water is almost a sure bet.

If you need to pull out early, there are take-outs with vehicle access at **Halfway River,** 13.6 miles (21.9 km) from the put-in, and just above Nakusp where British Columbia Highway 23 approaches the shoreline about 25 miles (40.2 km) from Shelter Bay. Nakusp has a south-facing bay just beyond **Kuskanax Creek's** obvious wide, sandy delta. The designated take-out is next to the swimming beach at the **Nakusp Recreation Park.**

Hazards include the two ferries crossing between Shelter Bay and Galena Bay; recreational boaters; big, open water; high winds and waves; and submerged rocks and stumps near shore.

FLOW AND SEASON: There is no perceptible flow in Upper Arrow Lake. The best time to paddle this leg is between April and October.

PUT-IN: Arrow Lakes Provincial Park boat ramp, 350 yards (320 m) from the Shelter Bay ferry dock, BC 23.

TAKE-OUTS: Halfway River logging site, 13.6 miles (21.9 km), BC 23; Nakusp Recreation Park, 29.3 miles (47.2 km), west end of Broadway St W off BC 6, Nakusp. All distances are from the Arrow Lakes Provincial Park boat ramp.

SERVICES: Revelstoke, 30 miles (48.3 km) north from Shelter Bay, is a full-service community with nice motels, good restaurants, grocery stores, gas stations, and paddling supplies; Nakusp is a small town, but with nice motels, good restaurants, a grocery store, bakery, and gas stations.

CAMPING: Vehicle-accessible camping is available at Blanket Creek Provincial Park, 16 miles (25.8 km) north of Shelter Bay (see Leg 9); Arrow Lakes Provincial Park (put-in); Nakusp Recreation Park, Nakusp; and McDonald Creek Provincial Park, 7 miles (11.3 km) south of Nakusp.

Passage

I picked a perfect mid-July day to paddle this leg. The put-in is protected from wind and wave by the granite promontory that creates Shelter Bay, so as I rounded the protruding cliff, I was surprised to find chop and mild rollers. One of the two early-morning ferries had just landed at Shelter Bay and was taking on vehicles. Rather than take the chance of getting caught in the ferry route, I hung back along the rock and, as soon as it passed on its way to Galena Bay, set out for a point on the east shore. I had the river to myself again, except for

BC FERRIES ON THE COLUMBIA RIVER

Three ferries cross the Columbia River in British Columbia, all on the Arrow Lakes south of Revelstoke. BC ferries are considered part of the highway system and are free. They are Upper Arrow Lake Ferry, which crosses 30.4 miles (49 km) south of Revelstoke on BC 23, between Shelter Bay (west side) and Galena Bay (east side); Arrow Park Ferry, across the junction of Upper and Lower Arrow lakes at Arrow Park, 13.7 miles (22 km) south of Nakusp on BC 6; and Needles–Cable Ferry (Needles–Fauquier Ferry), across Lower Arrow Lake, about 36.7 miles (59 km) south of Nakusp on BC 6, between Fauquier (east side) and Needles (west side).

One of two ferries making the 2.8-mile (4.5 km) crossing from Galena Bay on the east side of Upper Arrow Lake to Shelter Bay on the west side

the ferries, and the crossing seemed to go on forever. Even though there was no wind, rollers from wind action more than 20 miles (32.2 km) south broke over my bow until I was sheltered by the east shoreline. I measured my progress and speed by selecting one of many large branches or logs floating on the surface and watching it go by.

KOKANEE

Kokanee are landlocked sockeye salmon that frequent cold, clear lakes and reservoirs found in the upper reaches of the Columbia River, such as the Arrow Lakes. An adult kokanee averages 3 to 5 pounds (1.4 to 2.3 kg) depending on the availability of zooplankton, its main food source. The smooth-skinned fish reach sexual maturity in their fourth year and begin the spawning cycle by turning from bright silver to red, with hooked jaws and teeth on the males. Kokanee migrate in September and October from the lakes into side streams and creeks to spawn, but will also spawn along lake gravel shores as well, laying their eggs in reeds or nests they build with their tails in the gravel. The adults die after spawning, and the eggs hatch in 110 days.

Keenleyside, Revelstoke, and Mica dams reduced kokanee spawning habitat, restricted migration, and removed nutrients needed for growth. Efforts are under way to solve these problems and reverse the kokanee's decline in the Arrow Lakes and other reservoirs.

Once near the east shore, I paddled close, skirting solid rock outcrops that rose from the water or advanced from the steep cliffs above the shoreline. The water was so clear, it was as if I was looking through a glass-bottomed boat. I could see the bottom of the river and into the depths as I passed over underwater cliffs and old drowned stumps. Occasionally, I would surprise a kokanee or rainbow trout and, with one flick of its tail, it would disappear, its green-colored back blending into the pristine water.

Protected from the rollers and waves by the shoreline, I cut across a wide bay, passing the resort at **Halcyon Hot Springs,** situated on a forested bluff almost 100 feet (30.5 m) above the lake and just over 8 miles (12.9 km) out. I selected a prominent point along the shore with a small sandy beach to pull out for a break. Be patient on selecting a place to take out to rest. The shoreline is mostly rough granite that can damage your boat, but small sandy beaches turn up at the most opportune times.

Even though I was out among the rollers again at about the 12-mile (19.3 km) mark, I paddled across the big bay at Halfway River and then stayed along the shoreline to a prominent rocky point 20 miles (32.2 km) out. Here the lake turned to the southeast for the final 10 miles (16 km) to Nakusp.

On the outskirts of Nakusp, I passed the rusted hulk of the no-longer-used **CRSS beehive burner,** a relic of past logging practices, which sits on the fan-like Kuskanax Creek delta 1.5 miles (2.4 km) from the Nakusp Recreation-Park. It was a quick paddle around the delta to the beach at the park where I pulled out.

LEG 11: Nakusp to Fauquier

Distance: 32.3 miles (52 km)
Paddle Time: 7 to 10 hours

River View

The leg from **Nakusp** to **Fauquier** is a spectacular paddle from the wide, southern end of **Upper Arrow Lake,** through a section between the two Arrow Lakes known as the **Narrows,** and down the first 11 miles (17.7 km) of **Lower Arrow Lake.** The lake averages 2 miles (3.2 km) wide for almost 7 miles (11.3 km) from the Nakusp Recreation Park beach.

The best route from Nakusp is angling across the lake to **Bahamas Beach** spit, a prominent point 6.8 miles (10.9 km) to the south. It is one of the longest open-water paddles on the entire journey, but on a windless morning, one of the classic experiences on the Columbia. But only make this crossing in good weather. If there's any wind, follow the east shoreline south from Nakusp.

Once to the prominent sandy point along the west shore, turn the corner and continue along the shoreline for another 3 miles (4.8 km), cutting across the bays or stopping to relax on one of the many recreational beaches. Angle across the lake again and follow the south shoreline to the **Arrow Park Ferry,** 11.6 miles (18.7 km) from Nakusp and just before the lake makes a wide sweeping turn to the south. The turn will have sandy-bottomed shallows, so stay offshore a short distance.

Either side of Upper Arrow Lake is great paddling for the next 9 miles (14.5 km) with easy pull-outs to relax, but if you want to reach the **Burton Historical Park and beach,** stay along the east shore. One mile (1.6 km) past the park, the lake bottlenecks to less than 0.5 mile (0.8 km) and begins to take another broad turn to the south toward Fauquier. As you leave the Narrows and Upper Arrow Lake, the cliffs, ribs (inset in the rock face), and gullies to the north rise 5200 feet (1585 m) directly above the river in less than 4 miles (6.4 km), an impressive jump of almost a mile (1.6 km) from the bottom of the canyon.

From the Narrows, angle across the lake to **Caribou Point,** an obvious rock buttress on the south shore. British Columbia Highway 6 is inset along the cliffs 100 feet (30.5 m) above the water, but due to cliffs and boulders along the shore, is inaccessible as a take-out. From Caribou Point, paddle along the southeast shoreline across the small bays. This can be another windy stretch, especially in the afternoon. The **Detta Beach** boat ramp in Fauquier is 6 miles (9.7 km) from Caribou Point.

There are many beaches on this leg to take out on for rests, but only a small number with vehicle access.

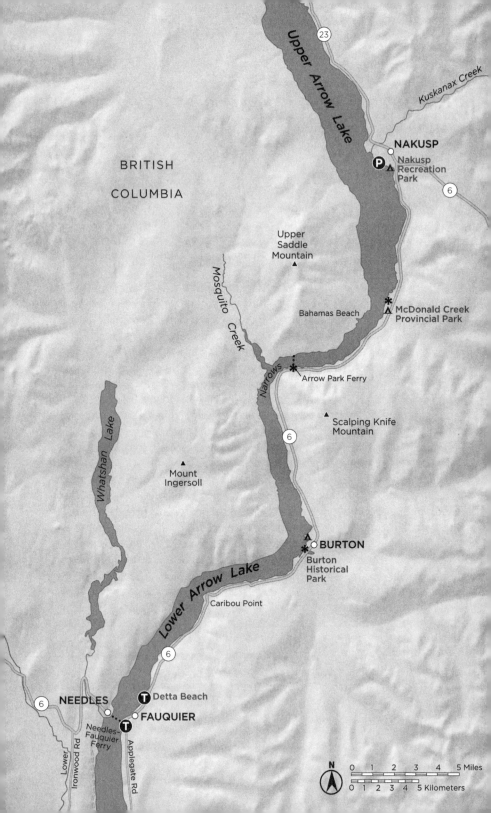

Lake Revelstoke's crystalline-clear water comes from the glacier-fed streams running off the slopes of the Rockies, Selkirks, and Monashees.

With more than 630 miles (1014 km) of shoreline, Lake Roosevelt has some of the finest paddling along the Columbia.

Highway 101 passes above old building pilings along Astoria's historic waterfront.

At nearly every bend in the river, expect to see a great blue heron jump from the shallows or wetlands, oftentimes chastising paddlers with its harsh croaking. *(Photo by Heather Roskelley)*

Grizzly bears roam the shoreline and thick forests found along the river as it flows through British Columbia. *(Photo by Chris Hudson)*

Water is released over the Grand Coulee Dam spillway during a high-water event in July.

Basalt flows throughout the Columbia Basin cooled at different rates, resulting in unusual columnar patterns in the walls and pillars along the river.

A gulp of double-crested cormorants in their roosting tree on a sand island along the west shore of Lake Wallula

Bald eagles frequent the river from source to mouth due to the shoreline habitat and the numerous species of fish it supports. *(Photo by Heather Roskelley)*

One of the tourist stern-wheelers that dock at Stevenson, Washington, on their way up and down the navigable reaches of the Columbia

Paddlers will enjoy the sand-and-gravel beach take-outs, deep bays, and magnificent views of the Monashee Mountains on their journey down Lake Revelstoke.

Herds of Rocky Mountain elk live in the forests throughout the Kootenay Valley and along the Columbia River in British Columbia.

The two basalt columns in Wallula Gap known as the Twin Sisters

Storm clouds part over the river below Bonneville Dam.

Paddling below Revelstoke Dam immediately upriver from the big water trap known as "Big Eddy"

Hazards include big, open water; wind and waves; motorboats and jet skis in the afternoons near Nakusp; and the Arrow Park Ferry.

FLOW AND SEASON: There is no perceptible flow in the Arrow Lakes. The best time to paddle this leg is between April and October.

PUT-INS: Nakusp Recreation Park beach, west end of Broadway St W of BC 6, Nakusp; Nakusp wharf, Nelson Ave SW off Broadway St E in Nakusp.

TAKE-OUTS: McDonald Creek Provincial Park, 7 miles (11.3 km), BC 6; Arrow Park Ferry dock, 11.7 miles (18.8 km), BC 6; Burton Historical Park beach, 20.5 miles (33 km), Burton, BC 6; Detta Beach and boat launch, 32.3 miles (52 km), Fauquier, BC 6; Needles–Fauquier Ferry landing dock beach, 33 miles (53.1 km), Fauquier, BC 6. All distances are from the Nakusp Recreation Park beach.

SERVICES: Nakusp is the go-to village in this part of the Kootenay because of its restaurants, quaint hotel, motels, grocery stores, convenience stores, and bars. Fauquier has limited services, such as a motel/restaurant, grocery store, and gas station.

CAMPING: Nakusp Recreation Park, Nakusp; McDonald Creek Provincial Park, 7 miles (11.3 km) S of Nakusp on BC 6; Burton Historical Park campground, Lake View Park Rd, Burton, BC 6; unmarked side roads on Crown land off BC 6.

Passage

Upper Arrow Lake was like a sheet of glass when I launched from the community beach in Nakusp at 8 AM in early July. With almost 2 hours of open-water paddling to reach the sandy Bahamas Beach spit, which I could see protruding from the west shoreline 6.8 miles (10.9 km) downriver, calm conditions were a priority to me for an extra degree of safety while paddling alone. If there had been any wind or waves, I would have followed the east shoreline with its small bays and protruding peninsulas. This is a spectacular paddle with thick forests rising steeply from the Columbia to the summits of **Saddle Mountain** to the west and the monolithic **Valhallas** to the east. More than once, I stopped paddling and just sat and gazed at the beauty around me, enjoying the quiet of wilderness.

Once I reached Bahamas Beach in McDonald Creek Provincial Park and at the beginning of the Narrows, I followed the west shoreline as the lake

NAKUSP

The Nakusp area on the Columbia River had two village sites used by three aboriginal Indian tribes, the Shuswap, Sinixt, and Ktunaxa, between 3000 and 5000 years ago.

European settlers arrived in the area in 1890, driven by the Big Bend Gold Rush of 1865. There were no roads or railways between the Kootenay mining areas and Vancouver, so men and mining equipment were transported by stern-wheeler up the Columbia from Washington to the port of Nakusp and then Revelstoke. The completion of Hugh Keenleyside Dam in 1968 raised the level of the Arrow Lakes by 80 feet (24 m), drowning a number of important First Nations archaeological and burial sites; forcing thousands of people to relocate, and submerging entire towns. Nakusp survived the rising water and lost only two streets and some industrial land.

One of the numerous waterfalls that cascade into the Arrow Lakes from the heavily forested eastern slopes of the Selkirks

narrowed to 0.5 mile (0.8 km) and made its first snakelike turn to the west. Blue herons, fishing the reed and weed beds in the bays between fine sandy beaches nearby, squawked noisily soon after taking flight as I interfered with their lunch plans. Two miles (3.2 km) into the turn of the river, I rounded another prominent point and spotted the Arrow Park Ferry another couple of miles (3.2 km) downriver as it made its journey across the Columbia. Knowing the river made another bend to the south just after the ferry landing, I angled across the river aiming for the ferry landing and, once there, took a short break. From the ferry landing, I paddled river left around the big bend where the Columbia skirts **Scalping Knife Mountain** on the east and across from the fern-shaped fjord of **Mosquito Creek** on the west, and followed the shoreline 9 miles (14.5 km) to the old town site of **Burton**. The sandy, beach-like shoreline and many shallow bays make this leg a paradise for shorebirds, ducks, geese, and bald eagles.

Burton is at the south end of the Narrows and at another bend in the river, so I paddled across to the west shore once more and entered Lower Arrow Lake. The north shoreline is accessible to pull out on if necessary, but above the shore the terrain changes to steep rocky ribs and deep canyons that lead to the summit of 6622-foot (2018 m) **Mount Ingersoll.** I could see another southern bend in the river, so I angled 2.5 miles (4 km) across the river to Caribou Point, where solid base rock is exposed in vertical cliffs and massive boulders that plunge into the Columbia.

I wasn't done with the long, open paddles. Just past Caribou Point, I aimed for another small peninsula 3.5 miles (5.6 km) downriver and avoided the longer shoreline along river left. Almost every snag along this stretch of river had an eagle or two. The fish were rising all around me, and I'm sure I interrupted more than one eagle's meal. Past the final protruding point, it was only 2 miles (3.2 km) to Detta Beach and a little farther to the Needles–Fauquier Ferry boat launch.

LEG 12: Fauquier to Keenleyside Dam

Distance: 45.5 miles (73.2 km)
Paddle Time: 9 to 12 hours to Deer Park; 11.5 to 16 hours to Keenleyside Dam

River View

The leg from **Fauquier** to **Keenleyside Dam** is in one of the Columbia's most inaccessible and remote areas, and best done in two days: a 34.4-mile (55.4 km) paddle from Fauquier to **Deer Park,** the first take-out with vehicle access from Fauquier; and a short 11.1-mile (17.9 km) finish to the dam the next day.

From **Detta Beach,** it's a short paddle of less than 0.75 mile (1.2 km) to the **Needles–Fauquier Ferry landing** in Fauquier. The cable ferry begins daily

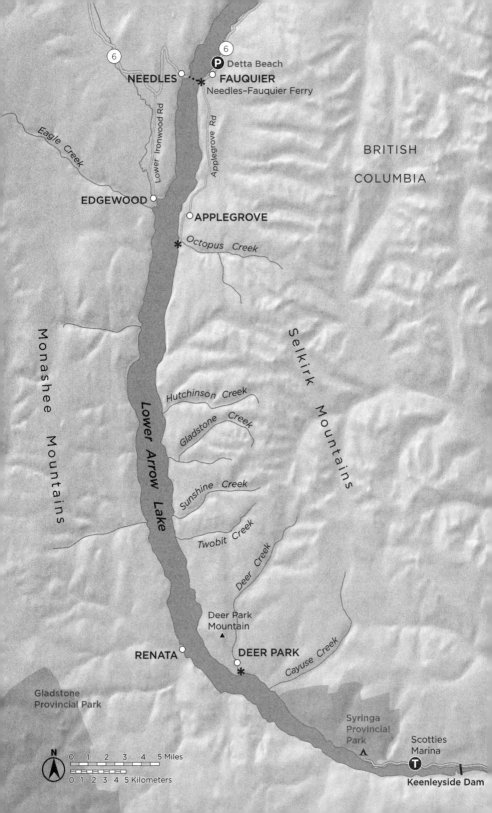

A rough take-out along the rocky shoreline of Upper Arrow Lake

operation at 5 AM and ends at 10 PM, takes 5 minutes to cross, and makes the crossing on the half hour. Stay well off from the landing as you go by, because the ferry operates by a cable in the river.

The route is simple—follow the east shoreline for the entire journey. You may hear an occasional logging truck using its air brakes high above the river or see a fishing boat somewhere along the route, but for the most part, you will enjoy one of the Columbia's true wilderness areas.

It takes the Columbia over 40 miles (64.4 km) to gently curve from the southeast to the southwest and then to Keenleyside Dam. The shoreline is typically bordered by rocky outcrops and cliffs; thick, Douglas fir forests; steep mountainous terrain above the river; and scattered small, sandy or pebbly beaches on the prominent points or amid the outcrops, great for stopping to rest and stretch. There are some homes near the shoreline close to Fauquier, but except for a log landing on the **Octopus Creek delta** 9.6 miles (15.5 km) from the launch, which has access to Applegrove Road, there is no vehicle access.

Hazards include remote, inaccessible areas; big, open water; sudden storms leading to wind and waves; submerged obstacles, including rock, stumps, and logging debris.

FLOW AND SEASON: There is no perceptible flow in the Arrow Lakes. The best time to paddle this leg is between April and October.

PUT-INS: Detta Beach boat ramp and beach, Fauquier; Needles–Fauquier Ferry landing beach.

TAKE-OUTS: Octopus Creek, 9.6 miles (15.5 km); Deer Park public boat ramp, 34.4 miles (55.4 km), off Broadwater Rd from Castlegar, Deer Park; Scotties Marina, 45.5 miles (73.2 km), 2.8 miles (4.5 km) on Broadwater Rd from Keenleyside Dam. All distances are from Detta Beach, Fauquier.

SERVICES: Fauquier has several motels, gas stations, and a small grocery store. Nakusp, the only big village along this section of river, has a better selection of restaurants and other facilities. Deer Park is strictly residential and has no commercial services, but it is on the road from Castlegar, a full-service community (see Leg 13).

CAMPING: *Near Fauquier.* McDonald Creek Provincial Park, 7 miles (11.3 km) S of Nakusp; Burton Historical Park campground, Burton; unmarked side roads on Crown land off BC 6. *Near Deer Park.* Syringa Provincial Park, Broadwater Rd, Lower Arrow Lake.

Passage

There are not many paddle legs on the Columbia River where there isn't a road somewhere nearby. Kinbasket Lake is one such leg; **Lower Arrow Lake** south of Fauquier is another.

I packed my kayak with a few extras, such as warm clothes, running shoes, and additional food and drink, before launching from Detta Beach in Fauquier at 6:30 AM. Joyce would take the long way around, 144 miles (233 km) through Nakusp, New Denver, Slocan, Castlegar, and then to Deer Park.

The Needles–Fauquier Ferry had just departed, so I paddled past the landing dock and began my journey south. There were a few small farms along the eastside lakeshore and a small number of homes far above in the trees overlooking the lake, but for the most part any sign of habitation disappeared within a few miles. I paddled close to the shore with the curve of the river, cutting across the many narrow bays from tiny peninsula to rocky point, avoiding the larger pieces of logging debris that are common on this leg. Seldom was I more than 0.25 mile (0.4 km) from land. The rock cliffs, crystal-clear water, jagged shoreline, and thick, green forest made this one of my favorite paddles on the Columbia. I didn't see another soul for over 20 miles (32.2 km).

It was a long way to Deer Park, but the exceptional beauty of this area, with numerous eagles in almost every bay, made the hours seem like minutes as I glided along under cloudless skies. Almost 10 miles (16 km) from Fauquier, I passed the only possible take-out for the next 21 miles (33.8 km) at Octopus Creek. Applegrove Road, a logging road running south from Fauquier, drops to the shoreline to cross the creek. On the delta of the creek is a log landing with vehicle access.

The next slight bend in the river's direction is over 7 miles (11.3 km) from Octopus Creek, where the river turns due south, and I could see 15 miles (24.1 km) of open water before me. There still wasn't a breeze on the water, but if a storm had brewed from the south, I wouldn't have made Deer Park. This pipe-straight, 1–1.5-mile-wide (1.6–2.4 km) section could be a nightmare for a paddler under bad conditions.

Nine miles (14.5 km) from the bend and past four large creeks, **Hutchinson Creek, Gladstone Creek, Sunshine Creek,** and **Twobit Creek,** I turned the last prominent point around **Deer Park Mountain**. Two miles (3.2 km) from

Hugh Keenleyside Dam is the first dam on the upper Columbia with a navigational lock. The earthen and concrete dam is 171 feet (52 m) high and holds back Upper and Lower Arrow lakes.

Deer Park the wind suddenly picked up, and I had to use small bays to hide in to make any headway. At 5:30 PM, I paddled into the small, sheltered bay at Deer Park, a lakeside community with no services. Joyce was nearby on a dock having a glass of wine with one of the many wonderful Canadians we met along the journey.

The next morning, after we camped in waist-high grass in a meadow on Deer Park Mountain, I launched from Deer Park and paddled along the northeast shoreline and Syringa Provincial Park, known for its Douglas fir forests, vertical cliffs, and numerous wildlife species, including Rocky Mountain sheep. I passed the privately owned marina 9 miles (14.5 km) from Deer Park and paddled several more miles (3.2 km) to the public boat launch and Scotties Marina in under 3 hours. Paddlers can also take out 2.2 miles (3.5 km) farther downriver at an unmaintained boat ramp on the southwest shore accessed off Arrow Lakes Drive just above the dam.

LEG 13: Keenleyside Dam to the US–Canada Border

Distance: 22.5 miles (36.2 km), Giro Park;
　　　　　　31.5 miles (50.7 km), international border
Paddle Time: 3 to 6 hours

River View

The leg from **Keenleyside Dam** to the **US–Canada border** is one of the most challenging sections of water on the Columbia for a paddler. Below the dam, the river is wild and free-flowing and the flow rate can exceed 200,000 cfs during the snowmelt months between May and August. If you are a well-seasoned paddler and comfortable in fast water coupled with turbulence, strong eddies, and large whirlpools, then this is the paddle for you. If not, do this section in low water or pull out at **Giro Park** in **Trail**.

There are two USGS monitoring stations along this leg; the first is at **Birchbank,** British Columbia, just upriver from Trail, and the second is at the international boundary. The international boundary station has hourly flow readings, but can be misleading for this leg because of the confluence of the Columbia and **Pend Oreille rivers** just before the monitoring station. Before putting in below Keenleyside Dam, check the daily flow data at both monitoring stations on the USGS website (see Resources section for websites). Historically, April has the lowest flow rate and the dam holds back water overnight, so an early-morning launch also ensures less flow, but late September and October are also a low-flow period. Keenleyside Dam begins to release more water around 9 AM, and within hours the river can increase flow as much as 25,000 cfs.

POISONING A RIVER: TECK-COMINCO'S LEGACY OF POLLUTION

The zinc and lead smelter and refinery complex in Trail, British Columbia, has been in operation since 1896. The corporate name changes frequently, but is presently Teck Resources Limited. What matters is the legacy of pollution this one corporate facility has left on the Columbia River, adjacent lands, and the hundreds of thousands of people of the Pacific Northwest. The EPA estimated that the smelter sent 400 tons of slag into the Columbia every day, at least 23 million tons between 1896 and 1995, when the company finally agreed to install an interim slag collection system. The slag sent down the smelter's No. 12 sewer pipe into the river created the upper Columbia River's toxic black sand beaches and poisoned fish.

The slag contained twenty-five different heavy metals and chemical compounds, including lead, arsenic, mercury, chromium, sulfuric acid, nitrate solutions, and ammonium sulfate—chemicals that would melt a lab rat inside out or have been known to cause ulcerative colitis, Crohn's disease, and cancers in humans.

In 2010, Teck paid $2 million to remove and clean Black Sand Beach in Northport, Washington, of 5000 cubic yards of contaminated sand. Floodwaters in 2011 turned the cleaned beach into black sand again. Since then, the company has lost its battles with the Confederated Tribes of the Colville Reservation and the state of Washington in the highest courts in its effort to deny responsibility for cleanup. Two million is just a start to what Teck is going to have to pay to clean up its "legacy."

The Columbia below Keenleyside Dam flows due south and snakes through the Castlegar–Trail valley in a shallow gorge through eroded glacial till and stream deposits down to bedrock. Even though the paddle is through a relatively urban area, the river is far enough below the urbanized benches above the gorge, that at times you'll think you're paddling in a remote area of British Columbia.

There are three bridges within 4 miles (6.4 km) of the dam. Stay centered between the pilings. Five miles (8 km) downstream is the confluence of the Columbia and the **Kootenay River**. There can be some rapids and strong turbulence before and after this section. Your paddle line should be river right and center. Be aware of whirlpools along the east shoreline just after the confluence. It's a good rule of thumb to stay clear of any protruding land formation, like a rock buttress, where the water is moving this fast and paddle the natural V of the river where eddy lines converge. An example of this is **Waterloo Eddy** at

The Teck-Cominco smelter discharged toxic slag into the river, leaving behind heavy metals and chemical compounds that can be found on the beaches and in the fish of Lake Roosevelt.

the mouth of **Cai Creek** 8.7 miles (14 km) out. Keep river right as you approach and pass the obvious gravel peninsula and eddy it creates. There is a small rock island 10 miles (16 km) from the launch and several large gravel islands 14 miles (22.5 km) out. Past the gravel islands, the river cuts through a deep canyon with no easy access or take-outs.

There are rapids from a large rock island and a few smaller ones 19.4 miles (31.2 km) from the put-in. You may see whitewater kayakers play-boating here. Paddle river left to avoid the main rapids around the island. Several miles farther downstream on the east shore is Giro Park, a well-maintained park in Trail with a boat ramp and beach area. Stay in the center of the river past the rock outcrops on the east until past the small bay swimming area, and then paddle hard to catch the eddy into the boat ramp. For many paddlers, this is as far as you'll want to go, depending on the flow rate.

It's another 9.4 miles (15.1 km) to a vehicle-accessible take-out 1.4 miles (2.3 km) upriver from the mouth of the Pend Oreille River and 2 miles (3.2 km) from the international border. From Giro Park, the Columbia passes through downtown Trail, running east for several miles (3.2 km) before turning due south again through a short section with large rock islands in the center of the river known as **Rock Islands.** This area is treacherous in high water because of the

PULP MILLS ON THE COLUMBIA

The Pacific Northwest is known for timber, logging, and wood product manufacturing. Pulp mills are the manufacturing facilities that use the wood and convert wood chips and other plant fiber into a thick fiberboard that can be shipped to a paper mill for further processing. The mills were typically located on rivers to take advantage of a way to transport logs and ship the final product, along with a plentiful supply of fresh water and dam-created energy.

Pulp mills create jobs, bring tax revenue to the communities, and produce paper products. But mills are detrimental to water quality, discharging into the river chemicals used in the manufacturing process. Seven large pulp mills still operate along the Columbia discharging various amounts of effluent, which typically contains arsenic, cadmium, chromium, copper, lead, mercury, and zinc. Prior to the US Environmental Protection Agency and the Canadian Department of Environmental Quality updating their discharge regulations in the early 1990s, pulp mills dumped cancer-causing 2,3,7,8-TCDC, dioxins and furans, as well as other chemicals into the river, which are still found in elevated amounts in fish.

whirlpools and eddies created by the big island and a satellite island just downstream. In low water, river right between the big rock island and the west shore is the best route through this area. There's turbulence between the whirlpool off the island and the shore eddy, but the flow here is strong and will pull you through. It's a dangerous route in high water due to extreme hydraulics off the large center island, which creates a giant whirlpool (it's a boat-eater!) that captures a large section of the river, and a very large and strong shore eddy coming back upriver. Portage is a difficult, but safe alternative.

Six miles (9.7 km) below Giro Park, the Columbia pinches to less than 0.1 mile (0.16 km), but flows nicely in the center and beyond the reach of the eddies. Just beyond the pinch is **Beaver Creek Provincial Park,** which has a maintained boat launch/take-out on the east shore. The main take-out, though, is downriver another 3.5 miles (5.6 km). Stay river left where the Columbia jogs to the east 2.5 miles (4 km) south of the Beaver Creek boat launch to avoid rapids and squirrely water near a rocky bluff. This area of the river has protruding rocks, hydraulics, and rough water river right and center. The take-out is on the east shore in a small bay protected by a gravel bar. There is an eddy line off the gravel bar, so paddle hard and cross it at a 45-degree angle to access the take-out.

If you float past the mouth of the Pend Oreille River, wear a bulletproof vest, as you will have reached the border and raised the ire of the US Office of Homeland Security, and they do not take paddling across the border lightly.

Hazards include fast-moving turbulent water; large hydraulics, such as whirlpools and eddies; bridge pilings; rapids; large rock islands; American Homeland Security.

FLOW AND SEASON: Flow is variable from 35,000 cfs in October/ November to over 200,000 cfs in July. The best time to paddle is in low water, typically in March/April and September/October.

PUT-INS: Unmaintained rough access, 0.4 mile (0.6 km) from spillway, north shore, Broadwater Rd; unmaintained vehicle access, 1.7 miles (2.7 km), Broadwater Rd (primary); Robson public boat ramp, 3.3 miles (5.3 km), Broadwater Rd, Robson.

TAKE-OUTS: 1st Avenue Park, 8 miles (12.9 km), Kinnaird; Giro Park boat ramp, 22.3 miles (35.9 km), BC 3B to 1st Ave, Trail; Beaver Creek Provincial Park boat ramp, 28.9 miles (46.5 km), Beaver Creek Park Rd off Waneta Hwy; unmaintained gravel bar boat access, 31.4 miles (50.5 km), 1.4 miles (2.3 km) upriver of Pend Oreille River–Columbia River confluence, off Waneta Hwy. All distances are from the put-in off Broadwater Rd primary put-in, unless noted otherwise.

SERVICES: All public services are available in Trail, Castlegar, and surrounding small towns, including chain motels, grocery stores, restaurants and fast food, gas stations, and convenience stores.

CAMPING: Syringa Provincial Park (above Keenleyside Dam); Beaver Creek Provincial Park (see Take-outs).

Passage

After days of paddling calm water on the Arrow Lakes, I looked forward to being swept along in a current and picking up a few "easy" miles. The day before my intended launch, Joyce and I drove British Columbia Highway 22 between Castlegar and Trail, BC 3B from Trail east, and the Waneta Highway south to the international border multiple times to scout the river, which is difficult to see for the most part. But what was visible from the road was fast and turbulent from the early-summer runoff.

The Columbia snakes its way through the Castlegar–Trail valley in a deep trough, so access is difficult, if not impossible, along some stretches of the river. My best information came from four whitewater kayakers putting kayaks on their vehicles alongside BC 22 between Castlegar and Trail. They had been play-boating in a hole and rapids behind some large rocks in the river just above Trail. They gave me some good information about avoiding those rapids, and when I told them I was paddling a sea kayak to the border, they all agreed I should not go through the Rock Islands below Trail. Too dangerous with the river this high, they said. After glassing (through binoculars) the Rock Islands area that afternoon, I had to agree with them. The center island was creating a whirlpool and eddy system behind it spanning two-thirds of the river that looked as though it could swallow the *Titanic*.

I launched from a gravel beach 1.7 miles (2.7 km) from the face of the dam at 9:30 AM because the lower launch site was less turbulent. The huge Celgar Pulp Mill was directly across the river, and production was noisy and smelly. The Celgar mill was the first of seven pulp mills I would pass on my way to the ocean.

The river was running high and more water was being released as I paddled into the main flow and sped downriver 2.8 miles (4.5 km) to a public boat dock in **Robson,** 650 yards (594 m) upriver from the Castlegar–Robson Bridge and the point of no return. I vacillated, sitting at the dock talking with Joyce. The river seemed to me overpowering and too risky, and I had not even reached the mouth of the Kootenay River coming in 2 miles (3.2 km) downriver. As I was about to take out and come back when the river had less water, a jet skier, who

Checking gear at the Giro Park put-in across from the Teck-Cominco smelter complex

had just buzzed upriver from near the border, landed at the boat launch and said the river was high, but "smooth." You won't have any trouble, he said. That was easy for him to say, I thought, with 90 horses under his butt, but I liked his "go for it" attitude, so I thanked him, made the decision to give it a try, and pushed off.

I paddled river right under the bridges, giving the pilings plenty of breathing space, as the Columbia made a sweeping turn to the south. I was concerned about the hydraulics and turbulence at the confluence with the Kootenay River, but the Columbia absorbed this extra flow as if it were drinking a cup of water. The river was flowing at 122,000 cfs and growing, and I could feel its power and size. I stayed close to the center of the river from the confluence for 9 miles (14.5 km) to the gravel islands to avoid the shoreline turbulence and at least one big whirlpool that formed downstream off a protruding cliff area on the east shore. The whirlpool was big enough to drag me close to its vortex, but I paddled hard and pulled out of it and was swept downriver.

The river widened and became shallow at the gravel islands. A side channel skirted the small gravel island on river left and then doglegged to river right around the larger island. I didn't like the turbulence and waves in the side channel, so I went river right following the overflow around the smaller island and caught the main channel as it circled the larger island downriver. Once I was past the gravel islands, I stayed in the center again for 4 miles (6.4 km) to avoid the numerous whirlpools and hydraulics near the shorelines. Despite being in a populated valley, this section of the river is inaccessible and remote, and I felt vulnerable.

I heard the rapids where the kayakers were play-boating before I could see them. The entire width of the river had rough water and rapids, but having scouted this from the bank of the river the day before, I knew to stay river left and center to avoid the rocks in the river. I paddled through like it was smooth water. From the rocks and rapids, it was a quick 3 miles (4.8 km) to Giro Park. This was a tricky area, as the protruding rocks on the east shore create strong hydraulics just before the park's boat ramp in a small bay. Given the size and power of the river, I started angling over to the hidden boat launch area right after passing the rocks. The flow in this section was powerful and fast, so I had to paddle hard and hit the eddy line at a 45-degree angle to catch the eddy and pull into the boat launch bay. I took the whitewater kayakers' advice and ended my day's paddle at the park after just 3 hours of paddling, deciding to paddle through the Rock Islands area in much lower water.

I returned to Giro Park to finish off the leg to **Waneta** above the border in late September. The river was flowing at a reasonable 41,000 cfs, a third of the volume of water I paddled from the dam to Giro Park. This time I was paddling with Chris Ryman, an expert paddling instructor who, with his wife Andrea, owns and operates Endless Adventures located in Crescent Valley, BC. Joyce pulled the "I will never drive for you again, if you paddle this section alone" card, so Chris joined me for this short section.

We put in at Giro Park and drifted and paddled in the mild current for the next 3 miles (4.8 km) in the Columbia's deep trough below residential homes and industrial buildings perched along the bank. As we entered the area of Rock Islands, Chris was telling me about the garbage he and other kayakers remove from the river during the year. I liked his motives and enthusiasm to clean up the river. The river needs more like him.

There were still a lot of eddy lines off the shores and fast water hitting the center island, but nothing like it was at 122,000 cfs. We paddled into a V shape of water between the whirlpool on river left and the eddy line on the river right and kept paddling until the hydraulics let us go and we were swept farther downstream. Past the big center rock island and the smaller satellite island below it, the rest of the paddle seemed like a calm day on the Arrow Lakes.

We passed the Beaver Creek boat ramp 5.8 miles (9.3 km) out, and then 2.5 miles (4 km) farther, lined up in the center of the river as it turned abruptly 90 degrees to the east where some small rock islands and shallows created the last of the rapids before our take-out. The river picked up speed close to the Waneta take-out, but I spotted Joyce along the gravel bar, and Chris and I angled through the eddy line and caught the smooth water near shore to where she was waiting with Clifford, our big brown Labrador, to end a great morning with Chris on the river.

In low-water conditions, kayakers should paddle river right in the Rock Islands area below Trail, following the natural V between the whirlpool on river left and the eddy on river right.

Paddling instructor Chris Ryman and Haunch from Giro Park across from the Teck-Cominco smelter for our paddle to the Waneta take-out.

SEGMENT 3

US–CANADA BORDER TO CHIEF JOSEPH DAM

Total Distance: 183.2 miles (294.9 km)

Segment 3 covers five one-day journeys from the US–Canada border to Chief Joseph Dam, through some of the most scenic, wild, and remote country in Washington. This segment has everything from fast and turbulent, free-flowing water below the border to one of the longest reservoirs along the Columbia, 130-mile-long (209 km) Lake Roosevelt. The river leaves the deep valley and mountainous terrain of British Columbia and winds its way south through the forested foothills of the Kettle River Range; along hidden coves and sandy beaches near the confluence of the Spokane River; and into the basalt and granite-walled canyon that leads to Grand Coulee Dam, down Rufus Woods Lake, and ends at Chief Joseph Dam.

Despite its popularity as a summer destination, the shoreline along Lake Roosevelt is sparsely populated. The surrounding country has large wheat farms east and south of the river, while to the north are the pine forests and shrub-steppe land of the Confederated Tribes of the Colville Indian Reservation. On this segment you will find the most remote and inaccessible section of the river in the United States, Rufus Woods Lake.

LEG 14: US–Canada Border to Evans Campground

Distance: 30.8 miles (49.6 km)
Paddle Time: 7 to 9 hours

River View

The leg from the **US–Canada border** to **Evans Campground** has everything a confident, experienced paddler would want and then some. But for us mortals, the free-flowing Columbia along this leg can be exciting, wild,

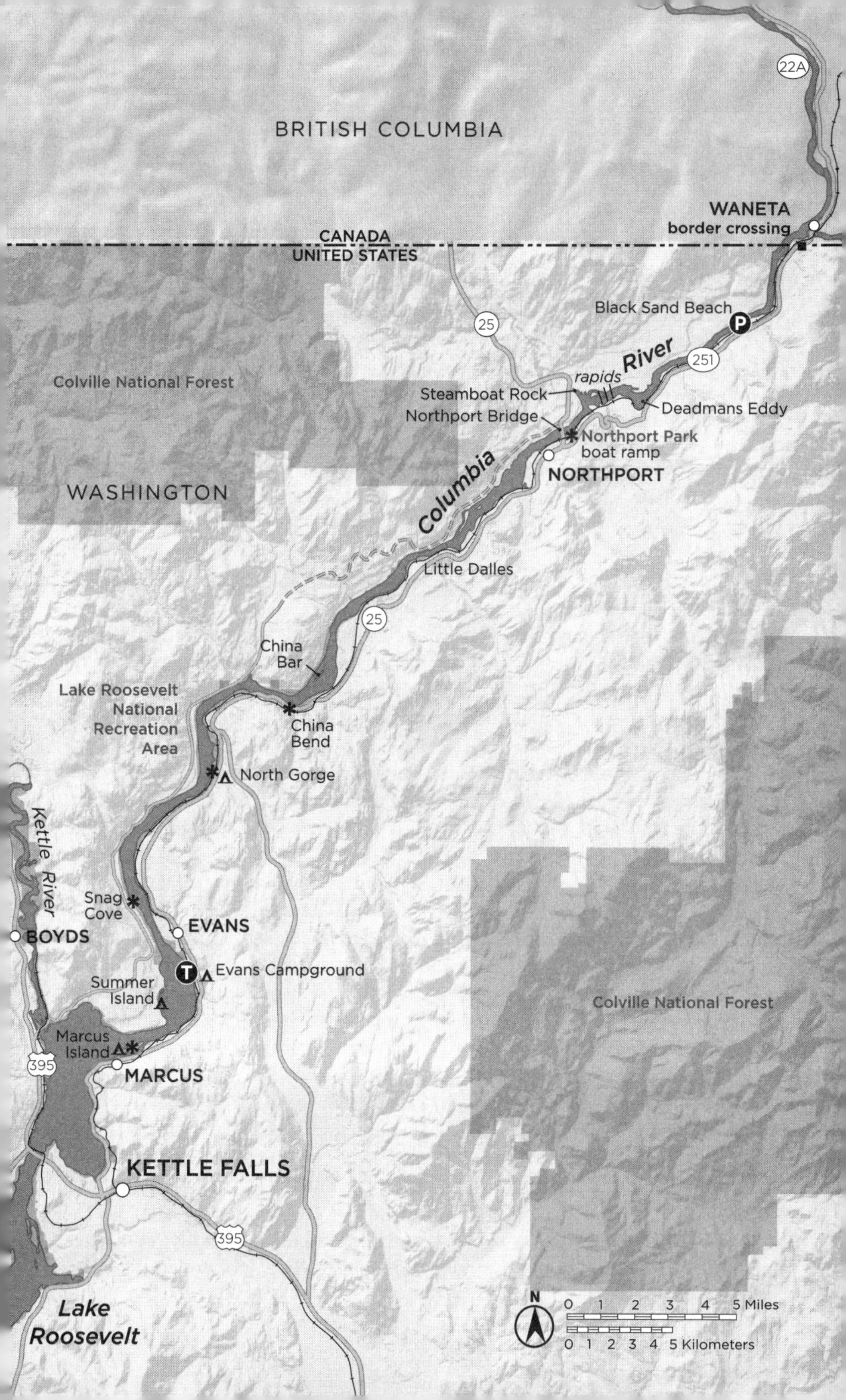

BRITISH COLUMBIA

22A

WANETA
border crossing

CANADA
UNITED STATES

Black Sand Beach

25

P

251

Columbia River

rapids

Steamboat Rock
Northport Bridge

Deadmans Eddy

Colville National Forest

Northport Park
boat ramp

NORTHPORT

WASHINGTON

Columbia

Little Dalles

25

China
Bar

China
Bend

Lake Roosevelt
National
Recreation
Area

North Gorge

Snag
Cove

Kettle River

EVANS

BOYDS

T Evans Campground

Summer
Island

Colville National Forest

Marcus
Island

395

MARCUS

KETTLE FALLS

395

Lake
Roosevelt

N

0 1 2 3 4 5 Miles

0 1 2 3 4 5 Kilometers

LITTLE DALLES

Little Dalles was a major rapid on the upper Columbia before being partially submerged in Lake Roosevelt, the reservoir of Grand Coulee Dam, in 1942. This free-flowing section of the Columbia can still be a major obstacle for paddlers because of its volume, speed, and turbulence. The rapid is no longer visible, but noticeable hydraulics in the form of whirlpools have taken its place. The entrance to the short rock gorge is located 5.6 miles (9.7 km) downriver of the Northport Bridge where the river narrows to 335 feet (102 m) for 0.3 mile (0.5 km). Little Dalles was a major hazard to boat traffic up the river prior to the reservoir, and still gives recreational boaters and paddlers problems in high-water conditions.

The first official use of the name *Little Dalles* appears to come from the 1881 report of Lieutenant Symons. He wrote, "Trees and logs 60 or 70 feet in length disappear in Little Dalles at high water; they go right down on end and do not reappear."

and sometimes treacherous. You can no longer put in at the border or paddle through. The Department of Homeland Security, the agency in charge of our borders since 9/11, will instruct you to put in "several miles downriver" at **Black Sand Beach,** located on the southeast shore 2.3 miles (3.7 km) from the border crossing.

In general, the Columbia has an average flow rate of about 100,000 cfs from April through September, with as much as 300,000 cfs in mid-July. This is an incredible amount of fast, tumultuous water moving past rock islands and snaking its way around vertical cliffs. I suggest paddling this leg at the lower water levels, either in March/April or September/October, when the river falls below 70,000 cfs.

From the 100-yard-long (91 m), narrow, sandy beach put-in, the river angles southwest. The speed of the river along this leg creates roils, boils, and big eddies even when the river is deep and wide. Stay in the center of the river for 4 miles (6.4 km) until you see the vertical rock cliffs above **Deadmans Eddy** where the river takes a dogleg right. The safest passage is river right, staying away from the eddy and around to the north shoreline.

The Columbia turns west again just after Deadmans Eddy and wraps around two rock islands, **Steamboat Rock** on river right and a smaller one just upriver in the center of the river 5.5 miles (8.9 km) from the put-in. Both channels around the islands look reasonable, but in low water, river right of Steamboat Rock has more flow and minor rapids as the river rushes downstream.

Past Steamboat Rock, the river again takes an abrupt left turn through a 200-yard-wide (167 m) neck. Enter this area more river left, and let the river sweep you to river right and away from the small rock outcrops in the center of the river. A mile (1.6 km) downriver is the **Northport Park boat ramp,** a good take-out if necessary.

From the park, the river continues southwest under the Northport Bridge (WA State Highway 25) and past the town of **Northport.** Approximately 2 miles (3.2 km) from the boat ramp, the river flows over several large underwater obstructions. Due to the power and speed of the river, the noise in the center will lead you to believe there are rapids ahead. There are no rapids, just large boulders close to the surface, which may be visible in low-water conditions. Stay river left to avoid the reverse turbulence off these rocks.

The Columbia begins to narrow, and 4.8 miles (7.7 km) from the Northport boat ramp it enters **Little Dalles,** where the river funnels through a narrow, vertical-walled rock canyon, at times less than 330 feet (100 m) wide. Set up river left to avoid the three or four large whirlpools in the center at the beginning of the canyon. The river runs smoothly along the left wall for a mile (1.6 km) before it opens up on the left into a small bay. The power of the current released from the narrow canyon creates whirlpools here big enough to suck a kayak or canoe into the river. Most whirlpools travel downriver with the flow. Find the V created by the flow through this section, and paddle hard and fast. If you are upended, hold on to your paddle; you'll need it downriver. You are now in the **Lake Roosevelt National Recreation Area.**

Black Sand Beach, a few miles from the border, is the put-in recommended by the US Border Patrol and Homeland Security.

Once through Little Dalles, the river widens and slows as it enters the back-waters of Lake Roosevelt. **China Bar,** a long and narrow manmade island 4.5 miles (7.2 km) from Little Dalles, will be along the north shoreline. If you need a rest break, **China Bend,** a boat launch site managed by the US Department of the Interior, is a short 1.5 miles (2.4 km) farther on the south side of the river. From China Bend, follow the south shoreline for 3 miles (4.8 km) in a wide arc to where the river turns south for 2 miles (3.2 km). Depending on the wind, you can angle across the river here, and after 2.5 more miles (4 km) cross back to the south-east/south shoreline again for the final 4.5 miles (7.2 km) to Evans Campground.

Hazards include big, fast-moving water; rapids, turbulence, whirlpools, and mid-river eddies; underwater objects; wind and waves; and cold water.

FLOW AND SEASON: The Columbia in this section can be running as little as 35,000 cfs in October or reach close to 300,000 cfs in June/July. Average flow is between 90,000 and 100,000 cfs. The best time to paddle this leg is in late September through October when the water level and temperature have dropped and the weather is still warm and comfortable.

PUT-IN: Black Sand Beach, 2.3 miles (3.7 km) from the US–Canada border. From the Deep Lake Boundary Rd–Northport–Waneta Rd inter-section, 0.5 mile (0.8 km) from the border crossing, drive south 1.8 miles (2.9 km). Turn right onto an unmarked, short dirt road that immediately crosses the railroad track and takes you to an unmaintained camping/RV area and beach boat launch.

TAKE-OUTS: Northport Park boat ramp, 7 miles (11.3 km), south shoreline, east of the Northport Bridge, Northport–Waneta Rd; China Bend, 19.2 miles (30.9 km), WA 25; North Gorge Campground, 23.6 miles (38 km), WA 25; Evans Campground, 30.8 miles (49.6 km), WA 25. All distances are from the put-in at Black Sand Beach.

SERVICES: Northport has a motel, small grocery store, gas stations, and convenience stores; Evans and Marcus have limited service. The nearest large community with services, other than rental and sales of kayaks, is Kettle Falls, 11.5 miles (18.5 km) south of the town of Evans.

CAMPING: There is an unmaintained campsite area at Black Sand Beach. Maintained facilities are at US Park Service campgrounds at North Gorge Campground, 6.3 miles (10.1 km) north of Evans off WA 25; Evans Campground, 11.4 miles (18.3 km) north of Kettle Falls off WA 25; and Kettle Falls Campground, Boise-Cascade Rd off US 395.

Passage

Joyce and I drove into the United States at the **Waneta** border crossing at noon in late August. For some reason, I was flagged as a potential threat to paddle through the border. I convinced them I wasn't going to do so and pointed to the kayak on top of my SUV. "Tell me where I can put in and I'll do it," I said. The officer pointed south and said several miles downriver. "Pick a spot, but not anywhere near here."

After driving back and forth several times about 2 miles (3.2 km) south of the border along the Northport–Waneta Road, I found a 300-yard-long (274 m), narrow dirt access road that led to Black Sand Beach, a sandy beach with a silvery-black hue near some large rock outcrops in the river. There were several families enjoying the weather, but otherwise it was deserted.

This section of the Columbia is one of the most polluted river drainages in the United States. The beaches and river bottom are loaded with lead, zinc, arsenic, and other heavy metals from slag, the toxic residue discharged for a century into the river by Teck-Cominco's lead and zinc smelter and refinery in Trail, British Columbia. Contractors for the smelter owners removed over 9000 tons of sediment and toxic goo from Black Sand Beach in 2010, and then established a new beach with clean fill material. But in 2011 and 2012, the Columbia showed its teeth and roared at over 270,000 cfs for days, scouring the heavy metals from slag deposits in every eddy and bay below Trail and moving millions of tons of poison downriver to be deposited again at Black Sand Beach.

I launched in a small bay, paddled through the fast eddy created by the rock outcrop upriver, and entered the flow. The river level had dropped from 122,000 cfs ten days before when I paddled below Keenleyside Dam to 98,000 cfs, so I was not as terrified of the roiling, bubbling, and whirling around me. But the river's speed and turbulence were not to be ignored. I stayed vigilant for the many whirlpools and eddies formed beyond rock outcrops, land protrusions, and small islands.

My first obstacle was Deadmans Eddy, a bowl-like feature where the river is forced to sweep 90 degrees to the right by a large rock peninsula. If a Canadian in Castlegar loses a boat or anything that floats, this is where they'll find it, madly swirling around beneath a granite wall, unable to escape. I could hear and finally see rapids on the left, so I kept mid-river until I knew I had to paddle river right to avoid getting swept into the eddy's trap basin.

I managed to stay close to the north bank in shallow water, ease around the bend, and then catch the flow from the sweep. I could see two rock islands in the center of the river with Class II rapids alongside them, so I angled to the north bank and against a dock where a lady was sunbathing. While gathering what courage I could muster to run the rapids, I chatted with the woman on the dock who gave me a few pointers to make it through the minor rapids on the right side of the islands just below me. She also said to try to stay away from the rocks in the center of the river at the bend just before Northport.

For some reason I thought this was the end of the treacherous water, but then she said, "If you go below Northport, watch yourself at Little Dalles."

"What's the Dalles?" I said, believing she was talking about The Dalles in Oregon.

"It's where the river narrows between two rock walls," she said. "There are always really large whirlpools there."

I thanked her for the advice, pushed off, and was swept through the Class II rapids right of Steamboat Rock, the larger of the two islands. I stayed with the main flow as the river narrowed and turned left around another protruding peninsula. Here there were several kayak-sized rocks breaking the surface in the center of the river. I pulled hard across the current amid the turbulent water and paddled straight along river right to avoid the two large rocks. The Northport Bridge was visible almost a mile (1.6 km) downriver, so I moved to river left and then, with a bit of hard paddling, grabbed a giant eddy with my bow near the boat launch area just upriver of Northport and pulled out to where Joyce was waiting.

I didn't want to try Little Dalles without scouting it first, so I locked my kayak to a metal post at the boat launch. Joyce and I then drove across the Northport Bridge to the north side of the river and followed the Northport–Flat Creek Road west, sometimes near the water, sometimes above it, to a farm with a ranch house on a high bluff that looked out over the river and asked the owner if we could look from his bluff. The overlook was perfect. Little Dalles was below us less than 0.5 mile (0.8 km) and, from what I could see, was wild, but doable.

My gut was telling me not to paddle that evening as we drove back to the kayak. It was late, 5:45 PM; I had 12 miles (19.3 km) to paddle to the next pullout at China Bend before dark; I was not feeling strong; and the sun was directly in my eyes. But Joyce said I could make it because the water was flowing fast to just below Little Dalles and I would only have calm water for 5 to 6 miles (8 to 9.7 km). "There's no wind," she said, "and it's not too hot right now." I think she wanted me dead.

I squeezed into my cockpit as excited as if I were getting ready to go over Niagara Falls in a barrel, and then paddled hard to get out of the eddy outside the boat launch. With a few strokes, I picked my line under the bridge to avoid the bridge abutments and set up mid-river. As I was paddling along on the quick, flat, but tumultuous water, I heard rapids, but I couldn't see them. Then I noticed the sound was intermittent and realized it was coming from the center of the river just ahead of me. As I approached the noise, I watched as the river boiled up like a cauldron of hot lava, and then moved downriver. Within a few seconds, another roller would boil up nearby. I paddled left and missed the area by a few yards (2 m), but it was the most unusual formation I'd experienced on the river.

The entrance to Little Dalles appeared at the end of a long, easy section. As planned, I entered the gorge river left, avoiding the three or four giant

The river doglegs right at Deadmans Eddy (seen here) with Steamboat Rock downriver in the narrows.

whirlpools on my right. My entrance to the neck of Little Dalles was perfect, and I glided along the vertical cliff on my left for 400 yards (366 km), adjusting with the rudder and my paddle when a boil would throw my bow or stern one way or another.

Just before the neck, I passed under a cable with large orange marker balls, possibly to give boaters an opportunity to say a few Hail Marys. Within less than a minute, I was through the turbulent neck and exiting into a larger pool area formed by huge eddies and a bay on my left. I was trying to avoid a cauldron of roiling and bubbling in the swirling eddy in the bay, when the river began to spin on my left and then moved across my bow to the right side like a small tornado. I only had a few seconds to realize a boat-eating whirlpool was forming up and then it grabbed my bow, rotated me counterclockwise, and sucked my stern into the vortex. The last thing I remember from my cockpit was watching my bow rise and point skyward, and then I sank like the *Titanic* into a bubbling hole that closed above me. It happened so fast, it was as if a giant squid had grabbed my life vest and jerked me into the depths.

I felt the bubbling all around me as I fought to get out of the kayak; it was not easy in the swirling and chaos of the pool and wondering if I had enough air to surface. Once out, though, I fought off the kayak twirling above me, grabbed my paddle, and held on. My skirt was loose under the boat, so I grabbed it and the boat and finally rose to the surface, twirling around alongside my boat as I was carried downstream.

The whirlpool started to dissipate as it went downriver and I was soon free of it, but I was moving quickly from mid-river to the 50-foot (15.2 m) vertical cliff along the north bank. I was twirled around a couple of more times as smaller whirlpools grabbed me, but I still had the paddle and boat. As I came close to the rock wall, the river carried me away and I felt relieved not to get sucked up against the wall and pulled down. One thing became very clear—there was no way to move the boat in any direction while I was floating in the water with it.

About 0.25 mile (0.4 km) downriver, the current swept me close to an eddy near the bank and I tried desperately to get into it, only to get caught in it and flushed out again upriver. The boat was like an anchor. No matter how hard I kicked with my feet and stroked with my one free arm, the current wouldn't let me move toward shore. After being carried along for just under a mile (1.6 km), I managed to mount the upside-down kayak from the rudder end, straddle the bottom of the boat near the stern, and paddle into an eddy that took me close to shore. I pulled out.

The worst was over, but my shorts and shirt were soaked and I felt a bit hypothermic from floating in the cold water. Despite all the chaos, I had only lost my sunglasses and hat. Everything else, like my foam seat, I found in swirls and whirlpools as I floated downriver, collected them, and shoved them into the cockpit under the water. Once on shore, I turned the boat over, wrung out my clothing, and then pumped the cockpit relatively dry. It was 7:45 PM, so I stored all the wet stuff in one of the watertight compartments, pushed off into the slow but measurable flow, and started paddling hard and fast the final 5 miles (8 km) to China Bend.

As the first stars dotted the evening sky, I spotted the headlights of the SUV at China Bend. Joyce couldn't see me, but she knew I was on the river and headed in her direction. In fact, she had been on the south bank overlooking the river and Little Dalles with binoculars when she spotted my kayak coming through upside down without me. I finally popped up, she said, but it didn't look good, as she watched me fight to get the boat to shore. Following the headlights for the final mile (1.6 km), I finally pulled into the launch area at China Bend as all light left the western sky and the river turned eerily quiet.

I did the final 11.7 miles to **Evans** without incident the next morning. The Columbia was like glass as I left China Bend and turned south. Without wind and waves to worry about, I cut across from one side of the river to the other in a 1.5-mile (2.4 km) crossing as the river turned southwest for a few miles before again heading south and southeast to Evans and the US Park Service campground.

LEG 15: Evans Campground to Gifford Campground

Distance: 31.6 miles (50.9 km)
Paddle Time: 7 to 11 hours

River View

The leg from **Evans Campground** to **Gifford Campground** takes the paddler almost due south on **Lake Roosevelt,** rarely taking a bend more than a few degrees. Under windless conditions, though, it is faster to take the shorter passage from one side of the river to the other, crossing miles of wide-open water, rather than follow the shoreline.

On the west is the Kettle River Range in the **Colville National Forest** and the **Colville Indian Reservation,** while above the east shore are small rural communities, such as **Marcus, Kettle Falls, Rice,** and **Gifford,** and the lower forested mountains of Stevens County. Considering how popular the **Lake Roosevelt National Recreation Area** (LRNRA) is during the summer, this area is sparsely populated and recreation is mostly seasonal.

From the Evans Campground beach, the river takes a short, but abrupt turn to the west toward Marcus, another small community on the east shoreline. Here the river widens like a big lake, as the **Kettle River** enters from the north and the Columbia pinches down to less than 1000 feet (305 m) at the US Highway 395 bridge just south of the confluence.

Under the bridge and over the course of a mile (1.6 km) is Kettle Falls, one of the Columbia's best-known landmarks prior to the building of Grand Coulee Dam. Northwest tribes spent months here at various times of the year to catch spawning salmon, dry and prepare the fish for winter, trade goods with other tribes, perform ceremonies, and enjoy life along the river. Depending on the season, there can be noticeable flow as the river squeezes through this gap, but any advantage to the paddler soon dissipates into lakelike water as the Columbia widens and pools less than 3 miles (4.8 km) from the bridge.

For most of your journey, stay close to the east shoreline. Nine miles (14.5 km) from **Evans** is the US Park Service's **Kettle Falls Park,** a full-service facility and campground. From the park, you can paddle alongside **Lions Island,** cross the 0.5-mile-wide (0.8 km) bay to the east and hug the shoreline, or, in calm weather, set your paddle line from point to point and cross the river twice on long open-water paddles to a prominent point on the east shore. The Columbia leans southwest from this point and, again, in calm weather, the paddle line is point to point in broad open water for 5 miles (8 km); but if there's any chop, keep to the east shoreline.

The west shoreline, although still part of the Lake Roosevelt National Recreation Area, is Colville Indian Reservation land to the center of the river channel and will be for the next 140 miles (225 km). Regulations among federal, state,

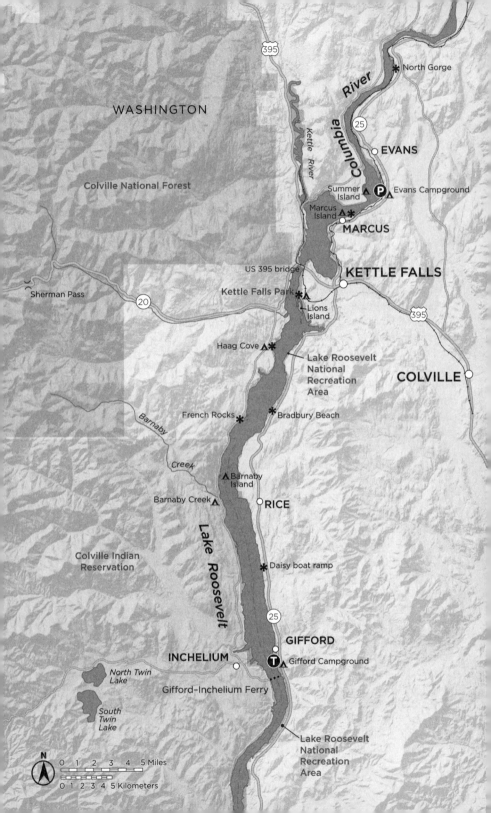

LAKE ROOSEVELT NATIONAL RECREATION AREA

The Lake Roosevelt National Recreation Area (LRNRA) was designated by the Secretary of the Interior in 1946 and put under the management of the National Park Service. The purpose is to enhance water-based recreation for a large number of people. The LRNRA is 156.9 square miles (406.3 sq km) and encompasses the 130-mile-long (209 km) shoreline of Franklin D. Roosevelt Lake, more commonly known as Lake Roosevelt.

The National Park Service lists more than 75 species of mammals, 200 species of birds, 15 species of reptiles, and 10 species of amphibians found in the LRNRA. The fish populations of today are far reduced from those prior to the building of Grand Coulee Dam, primarily through the loss of numerous salmon and steelhead runs. But other factors, such as the introduction of nonnative species, industrial pollution, the diversion and damming of adjacent rivers and streams, and reservoir drawdowns, have also had an impact.

Beneath the US Highway 395 bridge, Kettle Falls, historically one of the largest tribal gathering places and fishing grounds in the entire Pacific Northwest, is now 90 feet (27.4 m) underwater.

and tribal agencies differ, but for the most part, the US National Park Service manages the shorelines of Lake Roosevelt.

For 3 miles (4.8 km), the river makes a wide, sweeping turn to the south, passing **Barnaby Island** on the west, before the final 11-mile (17.7 km) straight shot to Gifford Campground, a NPS facility with forty-seven campsites. This is a long stretch of river without any landform to break the wind. Stay close to the east shoreline.

Hazards include big, open water; wind; and waves.

FLOW AND SEASON: Depending on the season, there can be minor flow at Kettle Falls, but Lake Roosevelt is exactly that—a lake. This paddle is best done in midsummer to late fall, but can be paddled comfortably from March through November.

PUT-IN: Evans Campground, Lake Roosevelt National Recreation Area, 9 miles (14.5 km) on WA 25 off US 395.

TAKE-OUTS: Marcus Island, 2.5 miles (4 km), WA 25; Kettle Falls Park, 8.8 miles (14.2 km), WA 25; Bradbury Beach Park, 14.8 miles (23.8 km), WA 25; Daisy boat ramp, 25.5 miles (41 km) WA 25; and Gifford Campground, 31.6 miles (50.9 km), WA 25. All distances are from Evans Campground.

SERVICES: Motels, restaurants, grocery stores, gas stations, and convenience stores are available in Kettle Falls, Colville, and, to a lesser extent, in some of the smaller communities along WA 25.

CAMPING: The US National Park Service has established nineteen tent campgrounds along the shores of Lake Roosevelt National Recreation Area, seventeen of which have trailer sites as well. They are excellent facilities and well maintained. Along this leg on the east shore are NPS campgrounds at Evans (see Put-in); Marcus Island (see Take-outs); Kettle Falls (see Take-outs); Cloverleaf, 1 mile (1.6 km) S of Gifford off WA 25; and Gifford (see Take-outs). There are also three campgrounds on the west shore that can be accessed from the Inchelium–Kettle Falls Road: Haag Cove, Barnaby Island, and Barnaby Creek.

Passage

I found my whole journey on Lake Roosevelt to be one of the most pleasant and beautiful sections along the entire length of the Columbia. The rugged scenery, white sandy beaches, and remote shorelines are captivating and enjoyable.

CEREMONY OF TEARS

On June 14, 1940, Native Americans from throughout the Northwest gathered at Kettle Falls for a three-day "Ceremony of Tears" to mourn the loss of their ancestral fishing grounds that was soon to be flooded by Grand Coulee Dam on the Columbia River in Central Washington. Kettle Falls was second only to Celilo Falls (which was inundated by The Dalles Dam in 1960) as a fishing and gathering place for Native Americans along the Columbia. Salish speakers called it *Shonitkwu*, meaning "roaring or noisy waters." It was said that salmon were once so plentiful at Kettle Falls a man could walk across the river on their backs. Huge numbers of salmon began arriving in late June, continuing through October, en route to their spawning grounds upriver. Fishermen speared and netted up to 3000 fish in a single day. The "Ceremony of Tears" also marked the end of a way of life for the First Peoples that had developed over thousands of years. Less than a year later, Kettle Falls disappeared 90 feet (27.4 m) under Lake Roosevelt.

I paddled this section in early September and besides two or three boats of fishermen, the lake was deserted. I left the Evans Campground and cut across the river to the prominent peninsula 1.5 miles (2.4 km) downriver, and then back across to Marcus. There was considerable chop as I rounded the bend at Marcus into the big bay above the US 395 bridge, but I paddled straight across the 2 miles (3.2 km) of open water anyway, rather than follow the much longer shoreline. The river narrowed at the town of Kettle Falls, and as I passed under the bridge, I could feel rather than see some water movement through this narrow gap. I'm sure in July/August there is considerable flow in this area.

Kettle Falls has a history of logging activity, and this was evident from the large log corrals along the shoreline, old steel barges, and round, bright orange buoys, 15 feet (4.6 m) in diameter, holding up the corners of the log and chain booms. These relics are not common, but I occasionally saw them scattered along the 130-mile (209 km) journey on Lake Roosevelt to Grand Coulee Dam, as they were probably used during the dam's construction in the 1940s.

As I was just getting my "sea legs," I pulled out at the town of Kettle Falls to see the park, and then continued past Lions Island, which is the low, level land south of the park. The morning chill had given way to pleasant warmth and the lake was calm, so I cut diagonally across the river for over a mile (1.6 km) to a prominent point on the west shoreline and then continued along the small bays and sandy beaches for 2.8 miles (4.5 km) as the lake leaned to the southwest. I could see the lake angled back to due south far in the distance, so after a short break on one of the many beaches, I took off on a 2-mile (3.2 km) crossing of the Columbia to Bradbury Beach, an immaculate and picturesque National Park Service (NPS) facility, where I met Joyce for lunch.

Three miles (4.8 km) farther along the east shoreline, the river takes a wide, sweeping bend to the southeast and public access along the shoreline is spotty, as the LRNRA trades ownership with private landowners. Fortunately, the better beaches are in the hands of the public and private beach access is well marked.

As I was paddling, I didn't notice the northern boundary of the Colville Indian Reservation, but from where the river starts to turn south, over 2.1 million acres west of the river from the center channel are included in reservation land. Access to the beaches and shoreline is still allowed because, even though it is tribal land, many parts of the shoreline are also included in the LRNRA.

I hugged the east shoreline around the wide sweep to the southeast, and then aimed for a point 4 miles (6.4 km) downriver where the shoreline slowly came back out. The wind had picked up, and with 10 miles (16 km) of unobstructed wide-open lake before me, the waves grew in size with every hour. I paddled hard to gain a few miles and kept close to the shoreline. With my arms feeling like lead from paddling into the wind, I reached the boat ramp at Daisy and pulled out to let the wind and waves subside.

The next morning it was calm. I put in early and made the 6.4-mile (10.3 km) paddle just in time for a great camp breakfast of pancakes and eggs at Gifford Campground.

LEG 16: Gifford Campground to Columbia Campground

Distance: 34.3 miles (55.2 km)
Paddle Time: 8 to 11 hours

River View

The leg from **Gifford Campground** to **Columbia Campground** continues the river's southern flow from the mountainous terrain of northern Washington to the basalt scablands of the **Columbia Basin,** with the exception of a 6-mile (9.7 km) jog due west.

From the Gifford Campground beach, angle 1 mile (1.6 km) across the river to the west shoreline as the river begins a slow turn to the southwest for the next 5 miles (8 km). Be sure to time your passage from the campground so that the **Gifford–Inchelium Ferry,** which crosses the river 0.5 mile (0.8 km) from the park, is not in transit (see Resources section for ferry schedule).

The route along the west shoreline will take you past several intricate hidden bays, small sandy beaches, and forested banks for 4 miles (6.4 km) before you will see the need to angle back to the east shoreline as the river turns directly

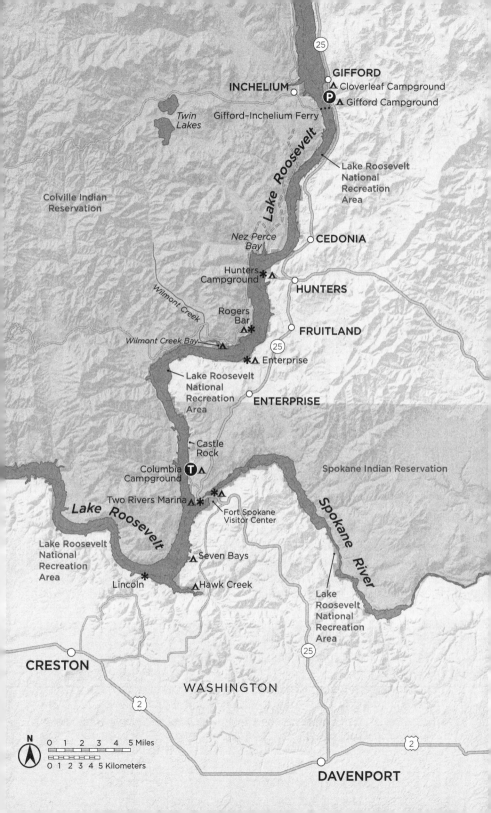

Mirror reflections of glacial mud deposits cut through by the Columbia River

south for 4.8 miles (7.7 km) at the bend. The east shore is lined in steep banks of taupe-colored mudstone and layers of fine sand and clay up to 150 feet (45.7 m) high, which makes for a geologically fascinating journey down this section of river. In calm conditions, you may want to slowly angle across to the west shoreline where the Columbia takes a short jog to the west and then back to the east side again to where the **Lake Roosevelt National Recreation Area** (LRNRA) **Hunters Campground** is located. Be aware that you will have to make at least a 0.5-mile (0.8 km) crossing to reach the campground and beach area. The Hunters Campground is another showpiece for the National Park Service, a place worth spending some time during your journey.

Upon leaving the park, stay along the east shoreline for up to 1.3 miles (2.1 km), and then past the sharp peninsula, angle across the lake for 3 miles (4.8 km) to the obvious white, sandy beaches of **Rogers Bar** on the **Colville Indian Reservation.** If the sun is out and there's no wind, you will want to stop at every tiny bay from Rogers Bar to **Two Rivers** because of the isolated and inviting sandy beaches.

The Columbia begins to turn due west at Rogers Bar. Stay along the north shoreline for 3 miles (4.8 km), just past **Wilmont Creek Bay,** before angling 1.8 miles (2.9 km) across the river to the south shoreline. After another 2 miles (3.2 km) of bays, beaches, and even an isolated island below forested shoreline, the river takes a wide, sweeping turn to the south. Once you turn south, stay to the east shoreline to cut off the slight bend in the river. Less than 8 miles

(12.9 km) from the turn is the LRNRA Columbia Campground. You can end your journey here after 30.5 miles (49 km) or paddle another 3.5 miles (5.6 km) to the **Two Rivers Marina** and boat launch at the confluence of the Columbia and the **Spokane River**.

Hazards include big, open water; wind and waves; ferry crossing; and increased recreational high-speed boat traffic on weekends and holidays.

FLOW AND SEASON: There is no flow on this section of Lake Roosevelt. To enjoy the small, isolated beaches along this leg, the best paddling time is in midsummer to early fall, but anytime between March and November is recommended. If possible, avoid summer and holiday weekends. Paddle early in the morning to avoid most motorized watercraft.

PUT-IN: Gifford Campground, 0.5 mile (0.8 km) north of the Gifford–Inchelium Ferry dock on WA 25.

TAKE-OUTS: Hunters Campground and boat launch, 12.2 miles (19.6 km), on south shore, Hunters Campground Rd from Hunters; Rogers Bar, 16.5 miles (26.6 km), on west shore, Rogers Bar Rd off BIA Rd 1; Columbia Campground, east shore, 30.5 miles (49 km), Mitre-Rock Rd off WA 25; Two Rivers Marina, 34 miles (54.7 km), WA 25. All distances are from Gifford Campground.

SERVICES: This area of the river has limited services. Davenport, 24 miles (38.6 km) south of Two Rivers on US 2, is the closest community with grocery stores, gas stations, and convenience stores, several motels, and a bed-and-breakfast. Two Rivers Resort has a casino, marina, and convenience store; Hunters has a convenience store, a bar and grill, and a restaurant, but no other facilities.

CAMPING: Vehicle-accessible camping is available at Cloverleaf Campground and Gifford Campground, just off WA 25 a short distance north of the Gifford–Inchelium Ferry (east shore); Hunters Campground (see Take-outs); Rogers Bar Campground (see Take-outs); Enterprise, an unmaintained boat launch beach camping area at the end of Emerson Road, 1.5 miles from WA 25 (south shore); Columbia Campground (see Take-outs); Two Rivers Campground and Fort Spokane Campground, both accessed from WA 25. There are also unlimited remote beach camping possibilities accessed only by boat. See the Lake Roosevelt National Recreation Area website (in Resources) for more details.

Passage

I left Gifford close to 9 AM, crossed behind the ferry *Columbia Princess* as it passed the center of the lake on its journey to the Gifford side, and continued angling across the lake to the northwest shoreline. There are a few outlying homes in the trees above the lake downriver from the ferry dock, but generally speaking the Colville Indian Reservation land along the lake is sparsely populated and both shorelines are protected by the LRNRA. Once around the first bend, I angled back to the east shoreline because the river was turning south again to avoid the grass and timber hillsides that climbed steeply off the river on the reservation side.

At the Columbia's turn to the south, I could see that the river had cut through 100- to 200-foot-high (30.5 to 61 m), light-colored mud bluffs shot through with horizontal sandy bands. The cliff swallows had burrowed into the vertical sand cliffs, well protected from predators but close to the many hatches of insects near the lake. I paddled along the shallows close to the mud cliffs near the east shore, occasionally beaching the kayak to find some shade to relax, investigate driftwood piles, and search through deposits of small mudstone formations for unusual shapes created by water erosion.

On a warm, windless day after Labor Day, the crescent-moon-shaped, sandy beach of Rogers Bar was deserted.

CONFEDERATED TRIBES OF THE COLVILLE RESERVATION

The Colville Indian Reservation was established by Presidential Executive Order in 1872. Twelve aboriginal tribes of First Nations Peoples made up the Confederated Tribes of the Colville Reservation (CTCR): the Colville, the Sanpoil, the Nespelem, the Lakes, the Okanogan, the Methow, the Chelan, the Entiat, the Wenatchi (Wenatchee), the Moses Columbia, the Palus, and the Nez Perce of Chief Joseph's Bands. These bands are of the Salish and Sahaptin nomadic tribes that, prior to western influence in the mid-1850s, followed the seasons of nature and sources of food.

The reservation is located in northeast Washington north of the Columbia River, primarily in Okanogan and Ferry counties. It is the sixteenth largest Indian reservation in the United States and second only in Washington to the Yakama Reservation. The CTCR is a federally recognized sovereign nation, and the 8434 members (2010 census) are governed by the Colville Business Council. The council oversees the tribe's business ventures, community development, and tribal police, among other government departments.

The CTCR operates forest products mills, owns a logging company, runs three gaming facilities, has an industrial park, and rents recreational houseboats on Lake Roosevelt. The tribes also hold interest and ownership stake in Grand Coulee Dam and Wells Dam. Despite the council's efforts to increase employment opportunities, unemployment can be as high as 50 percent.

After 4 miles (6.4 km) of these bluffs, the river made an easy jog to the southwest and the LRNRA Hunters Campground, located on the point where the river turns due south of this wide section of river. Directly across from the campground is the **Nez Perce Bay,** a 1-mile-long (1.6 km), narrow bay that cuts into the Colville Indian Reservation.

Joyce met me at the park's shallow mudflats for an early lunch, and then I launched from the shallows and followed the shoreline around the corner to where the river made a beeline south for 5 miles (8 km). The Labor Day weekend was over, but with the perfect summer weather continuing, a handful of fishermen, jet skiers, and pleasure boaters were still on the river, and noon seemed to be their witching hour. Along this stretch of water, I passed a large number of small beaches and bays, several of which were being used by groups of boaters and families. Some of the larger beaches had 60-foot (18.3 m) rental houseboats tied to permanent NPS and tribal cable anchors placed along the shore for this purpose.

I crossed the lake to Rogers Bar on the reservation side, one of the nicest beach areas and campgrounds on Lake Roosevelt. It was deserted despite this being one of the finest September days I could remember. Once back in my boat, I stayed along the north shoreline as the Columbia turned due west for over 6 miles (9.7 km).

At the entrance to Wilmont Creek Bay, I crossed back to the south shoreline to make the wide bend to the south and Columbia Campground along the east shore. I paddled close along the sandy shore for 3.5 miles (5.6 km), skipping across minor bays, until the lake's shoreline receded to the east and changed from beach to rock cliffs. As it receded, I paddled in a straight line into the center of the lake toward **Castle Rock,** a Rock of Gibraltar–looking rock buttress almost 800 feet high (244 m) and 2 miles (3.2 km) downriver from where the shoreline curved back toward the southwest. Two miles (3.2 km) farther, and after one of the nicest paddles on the river, I pulled out on the beach at Columbia Campground, which was deserted after the Labor Day holiday, with only Joyce there waiting with the dogs and the SUV.

LEG 17: Columbia Campground to Grand Coulee Dam

Distance: 39.3 miles (63.2 km)
Paddle Time: 9 to 12 hours

River View

The leg from **Columbia Campground** to **Grand Coulee Dam** begins the river's long journey due west and even north at times as it makes its way to the base of the eastern slope of the Cascades. The Columbia doesn't seem to know which way to turn as it snakes its way through a gorge of rock walls and steep, forested slopes. The paddle is characterized by long crossings of wide-open water; deep, rocky canyons slicing through the basalt and granite breaks over 1400 feet (427 m) high; narrow, white sandy beaches; a ragged shoreline of rock outcrops, hidden bays, and shallow coves; and inaccessible roadless areas. Only by boat can you can see this entire leg of the river.

From Columbia Campground, paddle south along the east shoreline for almost a mile (1.6 km) before angling across the river to the **Colville Indian Reservation** side. Stay along the north shoreline as the river makes a wide bend to the northwest. The shoreline is pocketed with small coves with sandy beaches amid rock outcrops and cliffs. While this shoreline is remote and untouched, the east and south shorelines at this turn in the river are relatively populated with the seasonal communities of **Two Rivers, Deer Meadows, Seven Bays,** and **Lincoln.**

Approximately 10 miles (16 km) from Columbia Campground, angle across the river for 1 mile (1.6 km) to the towering rock cliffs and paddle around the peninsula of **Sterling Point.** The river runs straight west for 3 miles (4.8 km) past the point, so if it's windy, stay to the south shoreline. In calm conditions, angle

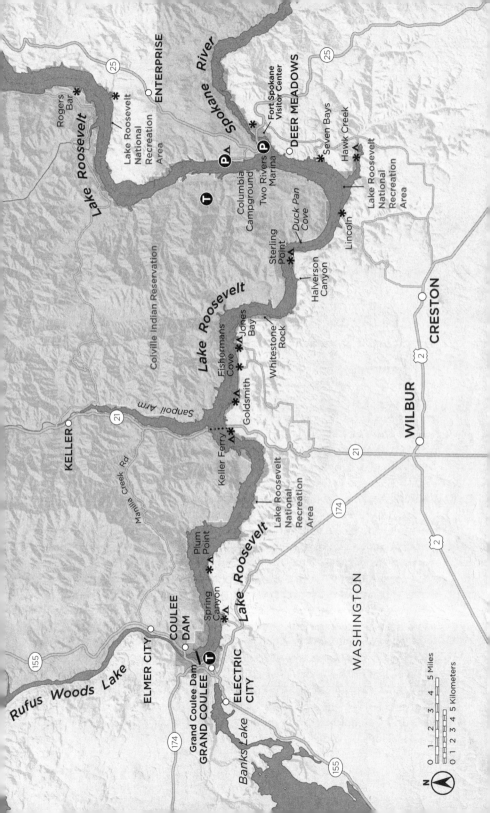

Washington State ferry *Sanpoil,* which runs on demand, crosses the Columbia River at its confluence with the Sanpoil River.

across the river again to the north shoreline and paddle along the beaches for another 2 miles (3.2 km) before making another crossing of the river to **Whitestone Rock,** one of two impressive vertical rock walls plunging into the river. Paddle around the peninsula crossing the mouths of several small bays, including **Jones Bay,** a **Lake Roosevelt National Recreation Area** (LRNRA) campground and boat launch facility located at the northern tip of the peninsula. From Jones Bay, it is 5.4 miles (8.7 km) to the **Sanpoil Arm** of the Columbia and the **Keller Ferry Campground.**

The river is not done snaking north to south and back again as it moves west to Grand Coulee Dam, but in windless conditions you can smooth the corners enough by paddling across the river several times to avoid the longer shoreline paddles. From the Keller Ferry Campground, paddle along the east-facing shore for 1 mile (1.6 km) before making the short 0.5-mile (0.8 km) crossing to the prominent rock formations on the Colville Indian Reservation side. Hug the sand-and-gravel north shore for 5.5 miles (8.9 km) to where the shoreline turns abruptly north past the last irrigated crop circle on the low-lying bar. Cross here to **Plum Point,** the tip of a sand-and-gravel peninsula 9.6 miles (15.5 km) from the Keller Ferry Campground.

Once around the tip of Plum Point, you can almost expect wind and waves because there is nothing to block the wind from the west. From here you have another 5.5 miles (8.9 km) of straight open water to the take-out at the city of **Grand Coulee** near the dam. Angle across the river from Plum Point 3.2 miles (5.2 km) to the rocky north shore, and then follow the shoreline for 1 mile

(1.6 km) before making the 1.5-mile (2.4 km) crossing in front of the dam to the LRNRA boat launch. If you choose to take out prior to the dam due to wind and waves, stay along the south shoreline to the LRNRA **Spring Canyon Campground,** 3.3 miles (5.3 km) from Plum Point.

Hazards include big, open water; wind and waves; ferry crossing; increased recreational high-speed boat traffic.

FLOW AND SEASON: There is no perceptible flow on this leg of Lake Roosevelt. This leg, like so many others on Lake Roosevelt, can be paddled any time of year, but the best time to take advantage of warm days or fall colors is March through October. As with most of the sections on the Columbia popular with power boaters, fishermen, and campers, avoid summer and holiday weekends if possible and paddle early in the morning to avoid motorized watercraft.

PUT-INS: Columbia Campground, 1.3 miles (2 km) north on WA 25 from the Two Rivers Casino turnoff then left on Mitre Rock Rd; Two Rivers Marina and boat ramp, north side of the Spokane River bridge off WA 25; NPS Fort Spokane public boat ramp, off WA 25.

TAKE-OUTS: Lincoln, 7.7 miles (12.4 km), Redwine–Canyon Rd off US 2; Sterling Point, 11.5 miles (18.5 km), on south shore; Jones Bay Campground, 19 miles (30.6 km), on south shore; Fishermans Cove, 20.8 miles (33.5 km), on south shore; Keller Ferry Campground, 24.2 miles (38.9 km), WA 21 from Wilbur; Spring Canyon Campground, 37 miles (59.5 km), Spring Canyon Campground Rd, WA 174; City of Grand Coulee boat launch, 39.3 miles (63.2 km), off WA 155 in Grand Coulee. All distances are from Columbia Campground. For Sterling Point, from US 2 east of Creston take Redwine–Canyon Rd to Sterling Valley Rd N. For Jones Bay Campground, turn on SE Brace St in Wilbur to Sherman Rd N, then take Sherman Rd E to Kunz Rd E to Hanson Harbor Rd to Jones Bay Rd N to the cutoff road and access. For Fishermans Cove, follow the directions for Jones Bay, but continue on Hanson Harbor Rd to Jones Rd E and Fishermans Cove E.

SERVICES: Services are limited in the Two Rivers area to a convenience store and gas station, but more facilities could be added in the future. The nearest "large" town with a grocery store and motel is Davenport, 24 miles (38.6 km) south on US 2. There are no services at Keller Ferry. Grand Coulee is a destination community, meaning it caters to tourists visiting Grand Coulee Dam, so there are good motels and restaurants, grocery stores and gas stations, but no paddling services.

> **CAMPING:** Camping is available in both vehicle-accessible and boat-in-only LRNRA campgrounds. Vehicle-accessible camping is at Fort Spokane Campground, WA 25; Columbia Campground (see Put-in); Hawk Creek Campground, south shore, Miles-Creston Rd N to Hawk Creek Rd N; Sterling Point Campground, (see Take-outs); Jones Bay Campground (see Take-outs); Keller Ferry Campground (see Take-outs); and Spring Canyon Campground (see Take-outs). Boat-in camping can also be found at Plum Point Campground (see River View).

Passage

I paddled this leg on a quiet, mostly wind-free day in late September. It was still too early in the year for the splash of fall colors, but the canyons and steep hillsides were pocketed with the deep green of ponderosa pines set amid the gold and tans of dry bunch grass, faded greens of sagebrush, and layers of deep, brownish-red basalt.

Lake Roosevelt was a sheet of glass as I launched off the beach at Columbia Campground, just 2 miles (3.2 km) north of Two Rivers Resort. A surface fog was dissipating in the morning sunshine and, despite the promise of a perfect

A relic from past logging along the Columbia, a wood chip burner stands along the shoreline of Lake Roosevelt at Lincoln.

ICE AGE FLOODS

Between 15,000 and 17,000 years ago, Lake Missoula was created up to 89 times by ice dams blocking the Clark Fork River. Each time an ice dam gave way, a 300- to 1000-foot-high (91 to 305 m) wave would flow toward Idaho and Washington at up to 80 mph (129 kmph) pushed by 8 to 10 cubic miles of water every hour, ten times the combined flow of all the rivers on Earth. Within 6 to 10 hours, the floodwaters would reach Wallula Gap, where hundreds of cubic miles of water were unable to squeeze through and backed up, creating Lake Lewis, swirling into a whirlpool the size of Portland.

Beyond the gap, within another hour, the flood would hit the narrows at Celilo Falls. Here, the water would accelerate through the narrow gorge, but at Beacon Rock, 60 miles (97 km) downriver, the wave would slow as it left the Cascades and widened near Portland. At 30 mph (48.3 kmph), the floodwaters would squeeze through the coastal range at St. Helens, just 2 to 3 hours from Celilo Falls. Even 75 miles (121 km) from the mouth of the Columbia, the front wave is still massive. Though it loses strength and velocity in the Pacific Ocean, it still pushes billions of tons of debris as far as 100 miles (161 km) offshore.

fall morning, not a soul was on the lake. I warmed up by angling for 2.4 miles (3.9 km) to a prominent point on the Colville Indian Reservation side and then hugged the 8-mile-long (12.9 km) curve around the peninsula lined with picturesque halfmoon-shaped sandy bays and rocky coves. In the sandy-bottomed, crystal-clear shallows just offshore, I spotted ripple marks. Since there was no flow here, they were possibly wind-made during the winter before the reservoir level was raised for summer recreation.

At the opening to **Duck Pan Cove,** a west-facing, odd-shaped 10-acre (4.5 ha) bay with a Maui-like beach entrance, I set off across the 0.5 mile (0.8 km) of river to Sterling Point, another prominent peninsula where the Columbia makes its second snakelike turn of the day to the west. At the point, I beached alongside the LRNRA dock, got out and stretched my legs, and enjoyed watching a gang of turkeys graze in the low-lying brush under the pine tree canopy.

From Sterling Point, I again angled across the river to the reservation side. There was just a slight morning breeze now, and the 3-mile (4.8 km) straight stretch of wide-open water before the river turned north was beginning to develop some chop and waves. I made the 1-mile (1.6 km) crossing to the rock cliffs along the north shore and then paddled around the bend beside a ribbon of beach shoreline for another 2.5 miles (4 km). I could see that the river was turning back to the west shortly, so at the entrance to another large bay, I angled across the river again to Whitestone Rock, a towering wall that plunges into the river near adjacent vertical rock cliffs, all of which are crowned with ponderosa pines. I found paddling beneath these walls nature's way of helping me keep my stature in this world in perspective. The rugged terrain ended and the shoreline returned to sand-and-gravel beach as I turned the corner.

Past Jones Bay I was paddling into a light breeze, so I pointed my bow toward open water, rather than follow the shoreline, and headed for the peninsula jutting out from the south shore. I was about halfway along this 4-mile (6.4 km) open-water paddle when I spotted a fast-moving dot on the north side of the peninsula just above the horizon. I stopped paddling and watched as an EA-6B Prowler, a Navy electronic warfare-and-attack aircraft from Whidbey Island, flying just under the speed of sound, finished its turn and roared over my head just a few thousand feet (610 m) above me.

I was soon to the apex of the rounded peninsula opposite the confluence of the Columbia River and Sanpoil Arm just a mile (1.6 km) short of the Keller

Rough water immediately above Grand Coulee Dam on the way to the boat launch in the city of Grand Coulee

Ferry Campground. The sixty-four-year-old *Martha S*—Washington's oldest operating ferry, put into service just three months before I was born in December 1948—was making its 1.2-mile (1.9 km), 10-minute crossing to the north shore, so I leaned into the now-windy bay and paddled through the heavy chop for the campground to finish off the first 24.4 miles (38.9 km) of the leg (the *Martha S,* which could carry only six cars, was replaced in August 2013 by Washington's newest ferry, the $9.6-million *Sanpoil,* a twenty-car ferry). Due to the wind and waves of an approaching storm front, I ended my paddle for the day at the campground.

I returned the second week in October to finish the final 15 miles (24.1 km) of this leg in somewhat better conditions. It was a short drive from Spokane to a now-deserted Keller Ferry Campground. A cool wind was circulating and the river was crowned with whitecaps. There wasn't another boat on the river except for the *Martha S,* which I would call a relic if it weren't the same age as me. I set off from the beach with a northeast wind to my back, followed the shoreline for a mile (1.6 km), and then made the 0.5-mile (0.8 km) crossing to the rocky outcrops on the north side. The river here makes a bend around a low-lying deposit of rich soil and gravel washed down from the high hills above the two rivers, the Columbia and Sanpoil. Farmland is scarce on the Colville Indian Reservation, so this flat piece of land was being irrigated by five or six circular systems.

About 7 miles (11.3 km) out, I angled across the river to the gravel beach at Plum Point, the obvious peninsula where the river turns directly west to Grand Coulee Dam. Thus far I had not had any trouble with the wind and waves, but around the point a west wind was blowing and the river, 0.75 mile (1.2 km) wide for over 5 miles (8 km) with no land forms to break the wind, had rollers and whitecaps. I couldn't see the dam, but knew it was just out of sight around the bend to the north on the opposite side of the river.

I pulled out on the beach at Plum Point, put on my spray skirt, and then launched into the oncoming waves. The river was active with evenly spaced breaking rollers as I paddled hard into the wind, angling toward the rocky shoreline on the reservation side. I kept my bow into the waves and after 45 minutes reached the protection of the jagged shoreline of small but effective rocky points and bays. I pulled into a protected cove across the river from the city of Grand Coulee to rest before setting off and paddling the final 1.5 miles (2.4 km) to the boat launch. It was an unsettling feeling paddling alone in rough water just 0.5 mile (0.8 km) from the top of one of the world's largest dams. But from my perspective on the water, Grand Coulee Dam's 12 million cubic yards (9.2 million cu m) of cement looked like a thin line across the horizon, not the concrete behemoth seen from below.

Joyce was waiting for me at the boat launch as I arrived just after noon, 3.5 hours after leaving Keller Ferry, glad to finally reach the end of Lake Roosevelt.

River View

The leg from **Grand Coulee Dam** to **Chief Joseph Dam** is one of the most remote and difficult to access on the entire Columbia. The river below Grand Coulee Dam cuts deep through central Washington's scabland basalt flows down to granite bedrock, creating a mini Grand Canyon that is difficult to reach by vehicle because of the roadless area of the **Colville Indian Reservation** to the north and multiple layers of vertical basalt and private ranch property to the south.

The Bureau of Reclamation built numerous campgrounds and boat launches along **Lake Roosevelt** but very few public facilities along **Rufus Woods Lake,** the reservoir behind Chief Joseph Dam. The river leaves the bottom of Grand Coulee Dam at 5 to 7 mph (8 to 11 kmph) and is channeled between large boulder riprap and levies 250 yards wide (229 m). The shoreline and levies are under the jurisdiction of the Bureau of Reclamation and are in the public domain, so you can launch just about anywhere downstream; however, the large riprap needed to keep the swift water and changing flow of the river in check is rough on launching a boat.

The closest public boat launch to the face of the dam is the **Seatons Grove boat ramp,** located 6.2 miles (10 km) downriver (see Put-ins) from **Grand Coulee.** A closer, but unmaintained, rough access site can be found 1.9 miles (3 km) downriver from the dam on the west shore. The water is fast and turbulent through here, but there are no rapids or whirlpools. You'll be swept along the 4.5 miles (7.2 km) to Seatons Grove in less than an hour.

Past Seatons Grove, the river slows but still has a good flow for many miles. Chief Joseph Dam, 47.2 miles (76 km) from Grand Coulee, is a "run-of-the-river" dam, meaning water released from Grand Coulee Dam to Chief Joseph Dam must be passed on to Wells Dam farther downriver at approximately the same rate. This can be a significant benefit to paddling this leg at certain times of year, mainly during spring runoff.

The Columbia from Grand Coulee flows to the north and northwest through high canyon walls on the west and low-lying floodplain areas cut by small coulees to the east for 15.5 miles (24.9 km) before taking an abrupt dogleg west. There is an unmaintained gravel boat launch just before the first fish pens at the apex of the river's turn and near Columbia River Road. Once you pass this point, plan on making the take-outs above Chief Joseph Dam. From here, the

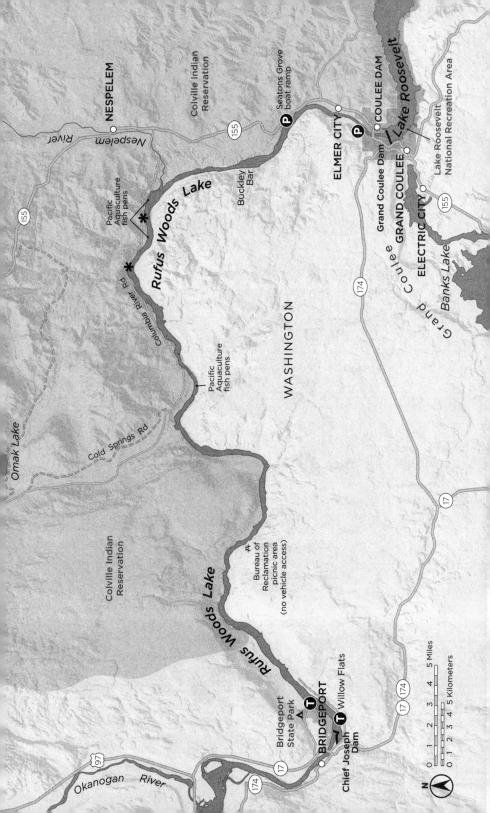

IRRIGATING THE COLUMBIA BASIN

The idea of bringing water to the dry soils of central Washington began with Wenatchee businessmen before 1920, and the proposal was picked up and promoted by their congressional representatives. Congress appropriated the first $63 million to start building Grand Coulee Dam in 1933 and funds for the Columbia Basin Irrigation Project ten years later.

Once Grand Coulee Dam was finished in 1942 and Lake Roosevelt was filled with 9.4 million acre-feet (11.6 billion cu m) of water, the irrigation project got under way. After years of work, it was finally completed in the mid-1950s. The system consisted of six 65,000-hp pumps to lift water from Lake Roosevelt 280 feet (85 m) to Banks Lake, the equalizing reservoir in Grand Coulee; two dams to hold 715,000 acre-feet (882 million cu m) of water in Banks Lake; 330 miles (531 km) of major north–south canals; nearly 2000 miles (3219 km) of lateral canals; 3500 miles (5634 km) of drainage canals for excess water; the building of O'Sullivan Dam to create the Potholes Reservoir; and 241 additional pumping plants.

The Basin project was paid for by US taxpayers and irrigates 671,000 acres (271,544 ha). Continuing operating costs are heavily subsidized by federal and state funds. The state of Washington continues to spend millions to add pumps and canals to send water to the Odessa region through the Weber Siphon even farther south, despite studies showing that extending irrigation in the Columbia Basin is a huge economic loss.

Water is pumped from Lake Roosevelt into Banks Lake, a reservoir used to help irrigate Columbia Basin farms.

river snakes its way generally west through terrain that gets more vertical by the mile (1.6 km) and less accessible. Maps and Google Earth indicate that Columbia River Road continues through to US Highway 97. It does, but it's a four-wheel-drive single track through some of the most rugged country you'll want to drive—or not.

A mile (1.6 km) past the gravel boat launch is one of Pacific Aquaculture's three floating net pen aquaculture facilities on the river. Pacific Aquaculture, a Washington State–based trout farming company and a division of Pacific Seafood, contracts with the US Department of the Interior, Bureau of Indian Affairs to raise steelhead for consumers throughout the United States. Fishermen line the banks and anchor their boats below the pens in hopes of catching an escaped monster trout and, in fact, do quite well. Eagles also frequent this area, catching as many fish as those holding a rod, sometimes more. The fishing is good on Rufus Woods Lake, so you will most likely encounter a number of fishing boats, including high-powered bass boats, along the route.

The river narrows to about 0.1 mile (0.16 km) about 24 miles (38.6 km) from the dam and just a few miles short of another fish-rearing facility. You may be able to take out here in a pinch from a gravel boat launch just upriver from the pens, but since it is on Colville tribal land and adjacent to a fish pen facility, check with the tribe beforehand.

The river here takes a wide sweep around a big bend and then turns south for almost 4 miles (6.4 km). On the floodplain below the steep bluffs on the west shoreline are several irrigated crop circles and farmhouses, but no river access. Four miles (6.4 km) farther on the same side of the river are more irrigated crops, but again, no public access. Most of the land on either side of the river along this portion of Rufus Woods Lake is privately owned and inaccessible to the public. But if you need to stretch or take a long break, at about 35.1 miles (56.5 km) from the put-in below Grand Coulee Dam and 12.1 miles (19.5 km) from US Army Corps of Engineers' **Willow Flats** take-out above Chief Joseph there is a Bureau of Reclamation–maintained boat-access-only dock and picnic area on the south shore.

The scenery in this part of the gorge is spectacular as the river flows through basalt rock walls and high plateau bluffs rising over 1300 feet (396 m). After another 5 miles (8 km) of gorge, you paddle by hundreds of acres of irrigated crops on the floodplains above the steep banks of the river. There is still no public access near the irrigated crops, although you are now only 5.5 miles (8.9 km) from the take-out at **Bridgeport State Park** on the north shore and 7 miles (11.3 km) from the US Army Corps of Engineers' Willow Flats boat launch and park, close to the dam on the south shore.

Hazards include swift, turbulent water below Grand Coulee; high-powered fishing boats; remote, inaccessible areas; and possible wind and waves in the long, straight runs of the river.

FLOW AND SEASON: The flow below Grand Coulee Dam is 5 to 7 mph (8 to 11 kmph) generally, but could be more during spring runoff. It begins to slow past Elmer City. Depending on the season, you can get a 1- to 2-mph (1.6-kmph to 3.2-kmph) flow 15 to 25 miles (24.1 to 40.2 km) downriver, perhaps more, but the backwaters of Rufus Woods Lake eventually reduce the flow to almost nothing. This leg can be paddled anytime, but April through October is the best time of year.

PUT-INS: Rough put-in 1.9 miles (3 km) north of Grand Coulee Dam, north on Columbia Ave, keep right at Y in gravel road; Seatons Grove public boat launch, 6.2 miles (10 km), north shore off WA 155 and Spirit Ridge Rd.

TAKE-OUTS: Gravel boat launch, 15.5 miles (24.9 km), north shore off Lower Columbia River Rd; Bridgeport State Park, 45.8 miles (73.7 km), north shore east of Bridgeport on State Park Golf Course Rd off WA 17; USACE Willow Flats picnic area and boat launch, 47.3 miles (76.1 km) on south shore, east of Bridgeport off WA 17 and Pearl Hill Rd NE. All distances are from the unmaintained put-in 1.9 miles (3 km) below Grand Coulee Dam.

SERVICES: The city of Grand Coulee and surrounding communities have motels, grocery stores, convenience stores, and restaurants, but no paddling services. Bridgeport has fewer services than Grand Coulee, but additional services are available at Brewster and Pateros downriver.

CAMPING: Several nice public camping areas at the beginning and end of this leg include Springs Canyon Campground on Lake Roosevelt above Grand Coulee Dam; Steamboat Rock State Park on Banks Lake south of the city of Grand Coulee off WA 155; Bridgeport State Park (see Take-outs); Bridgeport Marina Park/Waterfront Park, on the river in Bridgeport off WA 17 and 9th Street.

Passage

I paddled this relatively remote section of the Columbia during the third week of October. As I floated through this spectacular scenery, spotting rafts of ducks and geese, browsing mule deer, great blue herons fishing in the shallows along the shore, and bald eagles perched on snags waiting to take a rising trout, I kept thinking: I don't have to travel much farther to find paradise in Washington.

GRAND COULEE DAM

Grand Coulee Dam is the largest hydroelectric power producer in the United States. As of 2013, it is the fourth largest in the world behind China's Three Gorges Dam, Venezuela's Guri Dam, and Brazil's Itaipu Dam. The dam displaced 3000 people, eliminated 1100 miles (1770 km) of salmon habitat, and its reservoir, Lake Roosevelt, flooded more than 70,000 acres (28,327 ha). Besides hydroelectric power, Grand Coulee is also important for flood control and irrigation. Built on solid granite using 12 million cubic yards (9.2 cu m) of cement, the structure holds back the water in its reservoir by gravity (weight of the dam).

After paddling from Keller Ferry to Grand Coulee in the morning (Leg 17), I decided to fill out the day by beginning the 47-mile (75.6 km) paddle journey to Chief Joseph Dam that afternoon. Joyce and I drove up and down the river below Grand Coulee Dam searching for a maintained boat launch near the dam, but couldn't find one closer than 6 miles (10 km) downriver, the Washington State Department of Fish and Wildlife's (WDFW) Seatons Grove. The levy along the east shoreline has access, but the boulder riprap that armors the shore makes launching difficult.

As I was searching the east shore, I saw several fishermen at an unmaintained gravel parking area across the river, so I drove around to the west side in Douglas County, followed Columbia Avenue north, and located a rough put-in 1.9 miles (3 km) from the dam face. I alternately carried and dragged the kayak down the steep gravel to the rocky shore and launched.

The river was flowing at 93,500 cfs (2648 cms) through the narrow channel below the dam, and I was swept downriver at around 6 to 7 mph (9.7 to 11.3 kmph). I stayed to the center and paddled to keep my kayak running straight in the roiling and turbulence below me. Within a half hour, I pulled into the protected boat launch area of Seatons Grove, removed my wetsuit, and continued downriver in a slower but still powerful flow. Several miles (3.2 km) from Seatons Grove, the river widened into an almond shape, with **Buckley Bar,** a lens-shaped island, in the center. I paddled river right along 400-foot-high (122 m) white clay bluffs, avoiding the shallows near the island and a number of fishermen anchored in the far channel. From the end of the clay bluffs it was less than 6 miles (9.7 km) to the unmaintained take-out on the north side of the river where Joyce had agreed to meet me.

I put back in at this same spot a little after 7 AM the next morning. The heat of the previous afternoon was long gone, replaced by a frosty October sunrise. Launching just upriver from the Pacific Aquaculture fish pens, I met the foul smell of the fish food (distributed automatically by a machine) wafting upriver with the

The Colville Tribes contract with Pacific Aquaculture to farm steelhead in pens along Rufus Woods Lake.

surface fog. I was just settling into the seat of my kayak for the day's 33.6-mile (54 km) paddle when I passed the pens. I couldn't see the size of the steelhead in the pens, but several 8- to 10-pound (17.6- to 22-kg) monsters leapt from the open water around me as I paddled by, possibly escapees. Shore fishermen lined the gravelly bank just below the pens hoping to catch one of the big fish hanging around, while there were several boats farther out trolling slowly up and down the river. Fishing is excellent throughout the reservoir, and the Washington State record for rainbow trout has been broken in Rufus Woods Lake four times since 1998, most recently in 2002 with a fish weighing 29.6 pounds (13.4 kg).

Once I passed the lineup of fishermen near the fish pens, I was alone on the river. The surface fog was as thick as cotton and clung to the river for my first 3 hours of paddling. There were moments when I found myself too close to the shore or wondering if I should pull out and wait for it to clear. Nevertheless, I paddled hard to stay warm until the fog finally began to lift, unveiling the rugged beauty and brownish-red tones of the basalt and granite breaks on either side. The river made a quick turn to the southwest for the next 7 miles (11.3 km), so I angled across the river multiple times point to point as it dodged high rock buttresses and fingerlike peninsulas. At the river's return to the northwest, I paddled by another large tribal pen facility located just offshore of a narrow floodplain with irrigated crop circles.

I angled across the river once again, and within a few miles (3.2 km) the river made another sweeping turn to the south around a large wheat farm on a low-lying floodplain. I pulled out on a large island adjacent to the farm and watched several mule deer near the shore. They ignored me and continued nibbling on browse, but a covey of California quail decided I was a menace and

EXTINCTION SHOULD NOT BE AN OPTION

The US Bureau of Reclamation knew that without fish ladders, Grand Coulee Dam would permanently block millions of salmon migrating upstream to spawn each year from 1100 miles (1770.3 km) of rivers and tributaries in the United States and Canada. The Federal Power Act of 1920 required the builders of dams to either provide fish passage or hatcheries in compensation for the loss of passage. The bureau chose the easy and cheapest way out—hatcheries.

The justifications for allowing this mass extinction of wild salmon are as numerous as the fish that bumped their nose against the finished concrete structure in 1938—from fluctuating water level below the dam to a high cost-to-benefit ratio. At the end of the day, though, there was no significant reason for wholesale extinction of entire runs of fish. With renewed enthusiasm, better scientific knowledge of the salmon, decades of technology improvements, and a cost-to-moral-benefit ratio on the side of the fish, we need to retrofit Grand Coulee and Chief Joseph dams and the mainstream dams in Canada to allow fish passage. The salmon will return if we provide the passage.

burst from the nearby clump of trees. What little possibility there was of road access from the reservation side was now gone, although for the next 10 miles (16 km) I passed several more farms with irrigated crops on tribal land.

The jagged and armor-like basalt cliffs along the river here had turned the river northwest again, so I kept to the north side of the river for a few more miles (3.2 km) before cutting back across, as the river was forced southwest again by 1400-foot (427 m) steep and highly eroded bluffs. I found the banks along the shoreline steep along this section, and it would have been difficult to stop and take a break on the shore. Once around the corner, I could almost see the dam over 7 miles (11.3 km) downriver. I was still feeling strong, but after spending so much time in the kayak, I was also ready to end this leg.

The steep cliffs and river breaks of the past miles fell back to low rising hills, giving way to large farms growing crops on the narrow floodplains along both sides of the river. I pulled out once more at an irrigation pump station just a few miles upriver from the Willow Flats picnic area and boat ramp to massage my aching rear, and then finished strong, despite the late-afternoon heat in the stifling canyon. There I found Joyce once again patiently waiting with a cool bottle of water and a friendly smile.

SEGMENT 4

CHIEF JOSEPH DAM TO McNARY DAM

Total Distance: 224.2 miles (360.9 km)

Segment 4 has eight one-day journeys from Chief Joseph Dam, which is the first dam without fish ladders, runs south to McNary Dam where the Columbia turns west, cuts through the Cascade Mountains, and empties into the Pacific Ocean. The river wasn't powerful enough at this point in its journey to breach the hard granite and gneiss of the North Cascades, so it was forced to flow south into the basalt scablands of central Washington before finding a weakness at Wallula Gap and an exit through the more erodible basalt to the ocean. The paddling is predominantly on reservoirs, as this segment has six of the fourteen main-stem dams. But it also includes the most popular paddling leg along the Columbia and last free-flowing section before the tidal zone below Bonneville Dam, Hanford Reach. Challenges abound for the paddler along this segment, but the narrow, straight pools behind the dams; untouched desertlike terrain; basalt cliffs rising from the water; and abundant bird and wildlife sanctuaries make these legs a must for any paddler.

LEG 19: Chief Joseph Dam to Wells Dam

Distance: 21.3 miles (34.3 km)
Paddle Time: 5 to 8 hours

River View

The leg from **Chief Joseph Dam** to **Wells Dam** is an adventure through Washington's prime apple orchard country and one of the Columbia's most popular summer Chinook salmon fishing habitats. The river cuts a deep, narrow path through the area's sandy soil as it leaves the L-shaped face of Chief Joseph Dam, which produces more hydropower than any other dam in the United States other than Grand Coulee.

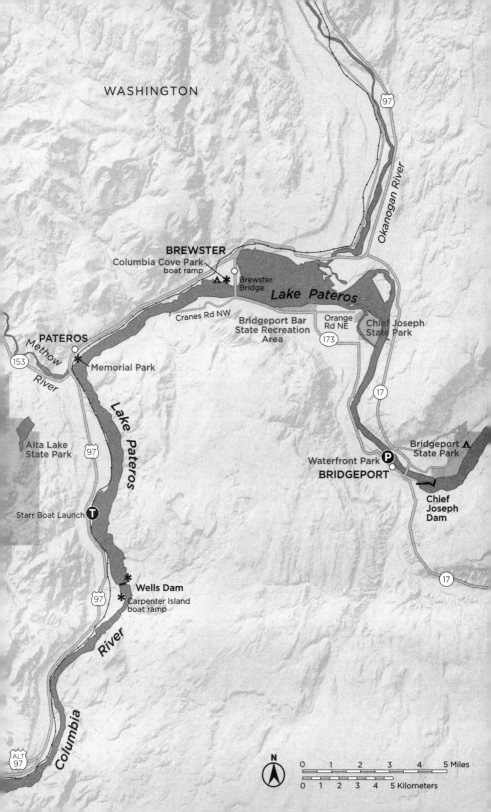

WASHINGTON

BREWSTER
Columbia Cove Park
boat ramp

Brewster
Bridge

Lake Pateros

Okanogan River

97

Cranes Rd NW

Bridgeport Bar
State Recreation
Area

Orange
Rd NE

Chief Joseph
State Park

173

PATEROS

Methow

153

Memorial Park

River

17

Lake Pateros

Alta Lake
State Park

97

Waterfront Park

Bridgeport
State Park

P

BRIDGEPORT

Starr Boat Launch

T

Chief
Joseph
Dam

Wells Dam

97

Carpenter Island
boat ramp

17

River

Columbia

ALT
97

N

| 0 | 1 | 2 | 3 | 4 | 5 Miles |

| 0 | 1 | 2 | 3 | 4 | 5 Kilometers |

Chief Joseph Dam, as a "run-of-the-river" dam, provides continuous flow and fast-moving water for around 5 miles (8 km) as the river cuts a deep swath through a bed of coarse boulders and gravel to the northwest and then turns directly north before entering **Lake Pateros,** the reservoir held back by Wells Dam. The **Okanogan River** enters the Columbia here from the north, but is swallowed up by the immensity of Lake Pateros.

At the north end of **Chief Joseph State Park,** the river continues west another 5 miles between small islands and the south shore to the **Brewster Bridge** (Washington Highway 173). A mile (1.6 km) past the town of **Brewster,** the Columbia begins its journey south, easy at first, leaning southwest for about 6 miles (9.7 km) through high cliffs to **Pateros** and the mouth of the **Methow River,** before feeling the pinch of the eastern slopes of the North Cascades and plunging directly south 5.5 miles (8.9 km) to the take-out, 2.7 miles (4.3 km) upriver from Wells Dam.

Hazards include swift, turbulent water at the put-in; weather-driven wind and waves on Lake Pateros; and rocks just below the surface offshore south of the Methow River in all water levels.

The passage through vegetated gravel islands in Lake Pateros downriver from Chief Joseph State Park

FLOW AND SEASON: Like so many sections on the Columbia, this one can be paddled just about any season, but the flow will fluctuate dramatically from a low in winter of 80,000 cfs to very big, fast-moving water in late June up to 300,000 cfs. Any portion of the river below Grand Coulee is subject to dramatic changes, so be aware of water levels, especially as more water is released in the afternoons. I paddled this leg in mid-October at around 100,000 cfs, and the river was running fast but smooth to Lake Pateros. In July, as I drove WA 17, I stopped on the bridge crossing the Columbia a mile (1.6 km) below the Chief Joseph Dam and was impressed—and intimidated—by the current, rapids, and hydraulics that 300,000 cfs can create in a narrow canyon. I chose to return in October when the river flow had dropped significantly.

PUT-IN: Waterfront Park, 2.3 miles (3.7 km) downriver from the face of Chief Joseph Dam, exit WA 17 onto WA 173 in Bridgeport, and turn right on 9th St to Jefferson Ave. Car-sized boulders and riprap lining the steep banks and private property make it difficult to launch just below the dam.

TAKE-OUTS: Brewster Columbia Cove Park, 10.3 miles (16.6 km), end of W Bruce Ave off S Bridge St, Brewster; Pateros Memorial Park boat ramp, 15.8 miles (25.4 km), left on Lakeshore Dr off US 97 and then to S Dawson Rd; Starr Boat Launch access area, 21.3 miles (34.3 km), west shore off US 97; Wells Dam, 24.1 miles (38.8 km), east side of dam, portage only, no vehicle access. All distances are from Waterfront Park, Bridgeport.

SERVICES: There are numerous motels, mainly the "no lobby" variety, located in Brewster and Bridgeport. Pateros has two high-end motels, one situated right on the river. All three of the small towns have gas, grocery stores, and several fast-food chain restaurants, but in this part of the country think burritos, enchiladas, and refried beans. Small, folksy Mexican restaurants abound in this region, and you can bet they're authentic. Boat rental and repair are available in Chelan and Wenatchee.

CAMPING: This leg of the Columbia has few campgrounds and RV parks, but there are three very nice facilities that provide all the amenities: the Bridgeport Marina and RV Park in Bridgeport (see Put-in); Bridgeport State Park on the north shore of the river above Chief Joseph Dam; and the Brewster Columbia Cove Park, Brewster. I would definitely find a controlled and patrolled facility and, for your safety, not stop and throw your bag on the ground in a convenient orchard.

Flowing at more than 300,000 cubic feet per second, the Columbia at flood stage surges past the town of Bridgeport (on the left).

Passage

It was mid-October before I was able to paddle this short section of river, which is a magnet for thousands of ducks and geese. I put in at 10 AM from Bridgeport's Waterfront Park and quickly adapted to the river's flow of 3 to 4 mph (4.8 to 6.4 kmph). There were no other boaters on this section of the river, even though there was a good run of Chinook that time of year. Once into the main channel, I moved along swiftly, scanning the water ahead for any unusual hydraulics, other than the usual roiling, but the river was flat. Despite the 60-foot (18.3 m) steep gravel banks, some of the homeowners had installed specially adapted, adjustable boat docks along the shore, which were built to rise and fall with the dam's releases.

About 3.7 miles (6 km) from the put-in, I reached Chief Joseph State Park, which is primarily an island preserve for birds and wildlife with walking access only. Don't be fooled by the obvious flow in the side channel river left coming from around the island. It looks inviting to avoid a lengthy paddle around the park, especially if there's a headwind, but it is blocked by the maintenance road less than a mile (1.6 km) from the main stem. I paddled around the park, staying inside the islands just offshore, despite the thick milfoil and other surface vegetation that was prevalent in the shallows. In the fall, pick your way through the mats of weed by finding deeper channels.

The islands are also a convenient stopping point to stretch, relax, and enjoy the abundant birdlife before paddling the long, open-water stretch to the Brewster Bridge and, if necessary because of wind and weather, Brewster Columbia Cove Park on the north shore. I found the south shoreline of this huge bay-like part of the river very shallow and weedy above the bridge and downriver to Pateros. Ducks love the weed rafts and seem to be an indicator of thick vegetation, so use their presence to avoid problem areas and paddle to deeper water.

The 10-mile (16 km) river section to Pateros from the Brewster Bridge is mostly inaccessible to vehicles due to orchards and private property, steep rocky banks, and thick shoreline and water vegetation. I pulled in at **Memorial Park,** a boat ramp and tiny park-like take-out in Pateros, for a break before turning south, picking up a light flow from the Methow River, and paddling the final 5.4 miles (8.7 km) to the Starr Boat Launch, a take-out on the west shore maintained by the Douglas County Public Utility District (PUD).

The mouth of the Methow River was speckled with trolling and stationary salmon fishermen, and along the paddle to the take-out, I was passed by migrating boats moving up- and downriver throughout this section of river. There was a minor amount of turbulence at the mouth of the Methow from the high water, but I stayed river right anyway, carefully watching for large rocks that were protruding above the water 1 mile (1.6 km) from Pateros. The shallows along the west bank were picketed with goose nests (installed by the Washington Department of Fish and Wildlife) built from large galvanized washtubs sitting atop 10-foot-high (3 m) steel pipes. Several had been used for shotgun practice by hunters—hopefully without the geese in them.

The river widened a few miles before the dam, so I paddled into the west bay to reach the Starr Boat Launch take-out above the dam. A paddler could pull out just about anywhere on the west shore along this section, if necessary, but there is a railroad track and very few vehicle access points, so try to make the distance. Another option is a gravel take-out on the east shore right above the dam. If you use this take-out, either bring your portage wheels to reach the bottom of Wells Dam or contact the Douglas County PUD's Wells Project Office at (509) 923-2226 ahead of time for assistance in portage.

You wouldn't want to be a nesting goose on Lake Pateros—too many goose hunters are looking for an easy dinner.

The put-in at the unmaintained manmade gravel beach is a stone's throw from the spillway below Wells Dam.

LEG 20: Wells Dam to Rocky Reach Dam

Distance: 40.5 miles (65.2 km)
Paddle Time: 9 to 12 hours

River View

The leg from **Wells Dam** to **Rocky Reach Dam** flows amid the grandeur of vertical granite cliffs rising into the Cascades to the west and the reddish-brown basalt walls dropping from the Columbia Plateau to the east. This is where the Columbia cuts a deep, narrow trough through the rock walls, flowing north to south in more or less a straight line. Where the gorge widens, irrigated apple and peach orchards, and the more recently planted vineyards, rise in neat rows to the base of the rock walls.

This leg is narrow with few large pools, and it meanders just enough to keep you wondering what is around the next bend. Surprisingly, the eastern side below Wells Dam is remote roadless shrub-steppe wildlife habitat, protected by rock cliffs for over 8 miles (12.9 km). Once below the dam and away from US Highway 97, this section becomes peaceful and quiet. The **Chelan River** is the

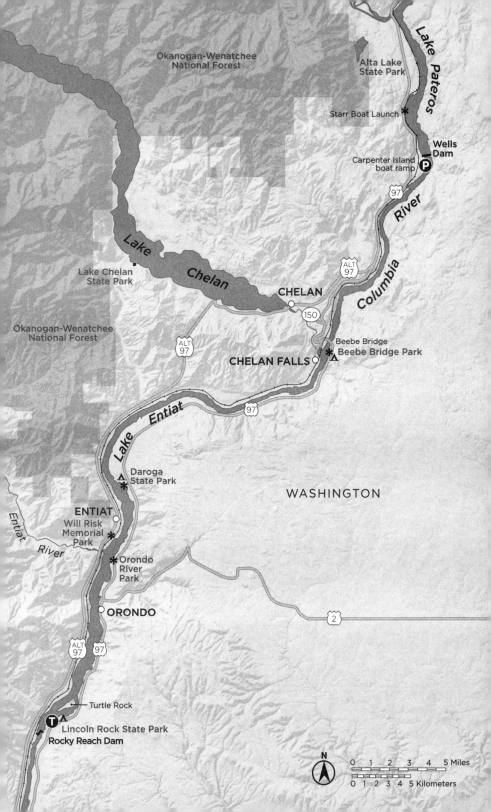

only major tributary and enters the Columbia 12 miles (19.3 km) below the dam, but it has no impact to the paddler.

From the put-in at the **Carpenter Island boat ramp** on the west shore 0.25 mile (0.4 km) from the spillway, the river twists and winds its way southwest at a good flow for the first 6 miles (9.7 km), and then it begins to slow as it widens briefly. Stay river right or center with the flow. There are no obstructions or islands, at least in the spring, so the paddle is safe and enjoyable.

Around 9 miles (14.5 km) out, the river straightens for 2.5 miles (4 km) and passes beneath the **Beebe Bridge.** You can still have a slow flow here as the river canyon narrows to 260 yards (235 m) wide just below the bridge. The Columbia passes by **Beebe Bridge Park** on river left and shortly thereafter the city of **Chelan Falls** on river right.

Fourteen miles (22.5 km) from the put-in, the river turns almost directly west for 7 miles (11.3 km) before taking a wide curve back to the southeast, but staying fairly consistent in its 0.25-mile (0.4 km) width, to **Daroga State Park** 28 miles (45 km) out. The Columbia widens in spots, pools, and is more lakelike as it goes almost directly south from the park past **Entiat,** on river right 30.5 miles (49.1 km) downriver from the put-in, and **Orondo,** on river left 34.5 miles (55.5 km) downriver.

Just 1.7 miles (2.7 km) short of the take-out at **Lincoln Rock State Park** is the Chelan County PUD–owned island of **Turtle Rock.** There's no right or wrong way around the island, and the distance to the take-out is almost the

Looking south toward the Beebe Bridge and Beebe Bridge Park

same, but the east side is quite scenic and there seem to be fewer boaters and jet skiers in the narrower channel.

Hazards include swift, turbulent water below Wells Dam; wind and waves on **Lake Entiat;** and high numbers of recreational boaters and jet-skiers, especially on weekends and holidays. The winds in this section of the river are predominantly from the south.

FLOW AND SEASON: You can paddle this leg just about any time of year, but I would advise a call to the Douglas County Public Utilities District (PUD) office or a look at its website to check the daily flow rate. A flow rate of between 150,000 and 300,000 cfs is typical in May, June, and July, and then it declines through the fall and winter months. If you like a more conventional, relaxing paddle, I suggest you put in at Beebe Bridge Park, rather than 0.25 mile (0.4 km) below Wells Dam, as the hydraulics, turbulence, and faster flow from the dam can be difficult for certain boats and paddlers.

PUT-INS: Carpenter Island boat ramp, off US 97 on the west side of river; Beebe Bridge Park, 12 miles (19.3 km), on the east shoreline downriver from Wells Dam off US 97. For Carpenter Island, turn off at the Wells Dam PUD Park exit, and then follow the asphalt road for 0.5 mile (0.8 km). Turn right and drive another 0.5 mile (0.8 km) to a marked gravel road on your left, which cuts through an orchard for 0.2 mile (0.3 km). The road descends to a manmade gravel plateau. Take the immediate left at the bottom and drive toward the dam and the launch area. There are no amenities other than a concrete boat ramp.

TAKE-OUTS: Beebe Bridge Park, 12 miles (19.3 km), east side, US 97; Daroga State Park, 28 miles (45 km), east side, US 97; Entiat Park/Silicosaska Park, 31 miles (49.9 km), west side, US 97; Orondo River Park, 32 miles (51.5 km), east side, US 97; and Lincoln Rock State Park, 40.5 miles (65 km), east side, US 97. All distances are from the put-in on Carpenter Island.

SERVICES: Wenatchee and Chelan have all services, including fine motels, restaurants, grocery stores, convenience stores, and boat sales and rentals, while Entiat and Orondo have limited services.

CAMPING: Tent and RV camping are available at Beebe Bridge Park, Daroga State Park, and Lincoln Rock State Park, all of which are off US 97. If you intend to paddle in July and August, call ahead and book a site early.

Passage

I was more than a bit worried as I put in just 0.25 mile (0.4 km) from the face of Wells Dam in early April. Just the noise of 160,000 cfs of water rushing through several open gates, the turbines, and the turbulence directly below the dam was enough for me to wonder if I should put in farther downriver. I scouted the west shoreline for a mile (1.6 km) below the dam and decided the water was flowing through the channel without any rapids or reverse bow waves, so I put on my wetsuit and PFD and launched from a gravel beach at the Carpenter Island boat ramp. The river picked up speed as I paddled into the main flow from the protected launch. Across the river, the direct flow from the dam hit a pinching shoreline and created several hundred yards of rapids, while I paddled through the roiling and boiling on the west bank without a problem as the river swept me downstream.

Two miles (3.2 km) downriver both banks converged into a bottleneck. I entered the neck in the center of the V to avoid the rough water and sped through easily. Less than a mile (1.6 km) farther, the river narrowed again, and it was obvious river right was the safest flow because the bend pushed the main flow to the center. I was surprised how fast the river carried me along.

After 4 more miles (6.4 km), the river lost most of its dam-released power into Lake Entiat, the pool behind Rocky Reach Dam, although I still needed to stay in the center flow in the bends of the river. Twelve miles (19 km) downriver, I paddled across a strong flow created by the narrowing of the canyon walls at the US 97 Beebe Bridge to Beebe Bridge Park, a full-service PUD-operated park, where I took a short break, stripped off my wetsuit, and fueled for the long, slow stretch to Lincoln Rock State Park. Although there are numerous rough put-ins and take-outs along this leg on either side of the river, these spots are usually difficult to access because of private land ownership or, in the case of the west side of the river, the BNSF railroad track and steep gravel banks.

No matter what time of year, the river from Beebe Bridge Park to Rocky Reach Dam is relaxing and easy amid the widening canyon. The river flows primarily to the southwest, but jogs to the west for over 10 miles (16 km) as the river takes a wide bend around the Entiat floodplain. There is still measurable flow in the spring/early summer at this point, so the trip proceeds quickly and there is time to watch and listen to common loons, which seem to frequent this area of the river. Expensive riverside single-family homes are being built on the east shoreline where orchards were once planted.

Eleven miles (17.7 km) below Beebe Bridge Park, I pulled out for a break on a small sandy beach downriver from a hundred-home gated community with a private boat launch, park, and swimming area, and then continued to Daroga State Park 28 miles (45 km) from Wells Dam, where I pulled out for the day because of an obligation that evening.

On Mother's Day a month later, I returned ready to finish the leg to Lincoln Rock State Park. This is an easy and pleasant 13-mile (21 km) paddle that, if not for a few slight bends, would be as straight as any section on the river. Consider this section if you are just tuning up for the summer or a beginning paddler, as this is one of the most pleasant sections of the Columbia—but not on Mother's Day or a warm, sunny weekend day after 11 AM. Close to noon seems to bring out the supercharged wake boats and jet skis to create raucous noise and water chop up and down the river. In other words, paddle early, because almost every shoreline homeowner's dock has two or three pesky jet skis ready to buzz the water, and the boat ramps are busier than New York's Penn Station at 5 PM on a Friday.

Just short of 4 miles (6.5 km) downriver from Daroga State Park is Entiat's Will Risk Memorial Park on the west bank and, almost directly across the river, Orondo River Park, a commercial facility that has a nice crescent-shaped beach during low water, a picnic area, and another boat ramp. I paddled this dam-created lake section easily in 2.5 hours. There wasn't a breeze on the river, so I took a straight line from point to point, rather than follow the curve of either shoreline. Canada geese were still nesting along the shore and slack-water eddies, and rafts of goslings and their guardian geese were in mid-river enjoying the morning calm.

I chose to paddle around the east side of Turtle Rock, which curved southwest to the Lincoln Rock State Park boat ramp. I pulled out on a gravel beach area just to the west of the boat launch, attached the kayak wheels, and towed my Necky to the car. The lineup of ski boats and mega-sized inboards was just starting.

LEG 21: Rocky Reach Dam to Rock Island Dam

Distance: 18.6 miles (30.0 km)
Paddle Time: 4 to 6 hours

River View

The leg from **Rocky Reach Dam** to **Rock Island Dam** is a short but interesting paddle on the **Rock Island Pool** between these two Columbia River dams, both owned and operated by the Chelan Public Utility District. From the unmaintained cement boat launch primary put-in 1.1 miles (1.8 km) below the spillway of Rocky Reach Dam, the river flows rapidly through a deep, straight, and narrow channel for 5 miles (8 km) before reaching the wide Wenatchee Valley floodplain and the outskirts of the cities of **Wenatchee** on the west shore and **East Wenatchee** on the east shore.

The river slows as it enters a wide bay just past **Olds Bridge** (US Highway 2), but can still have a strong current in the spring and early summer in the main channel as far downriver as Rock Island Dam. On the west shore

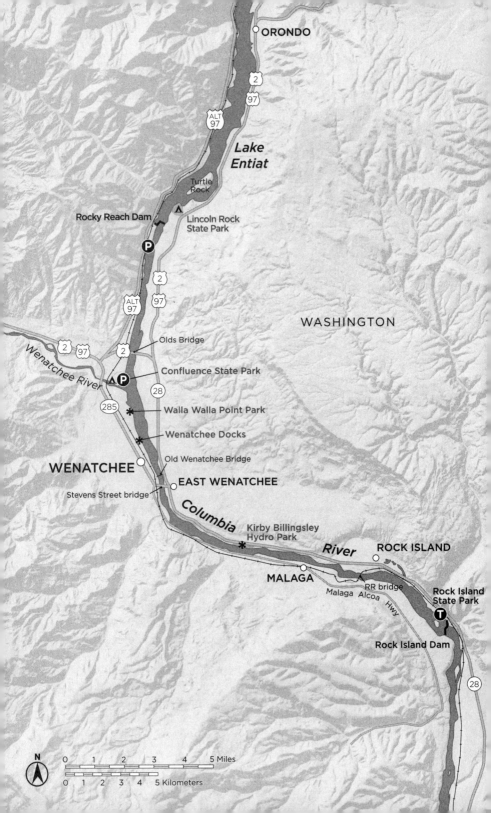

ORONDO

Lake Entiat

Turtle Rock

Rocky Reach Dam

Lincoln Rock State Park

WASHINGTON

Olds Bridge

Confluence State Park

Walla Walla Point Park

Wenatchee Docks

Wenatchee River

Old Wenatchee Bridge

WENATCHEE

EAST WENATCHEE

Stevens Street bridge

Columbia

Kirby Billingsley Hydro Park

River

ROCK ISLAND

MALAGA

Malaga Alcoa Hwy

RR bridge

Rock Island State Park

Rock Island Dam

N

0 1 2 3 4 5 Miles

0 1 2 3 4 5 Kilometers

The predominantly industrial west shoreline below Rocky Reach Dam in the Wenatchee Valley

is **Confluence State Park,** a good secondary put-in to avoid the turbulence below the dam in high-water conditions. Just below the park, the **Wenatchee River** enters from the west but does not have an impact on the flow of the river most seasons. At the **Stevens Street bridge** (Washington State Highway 285), which spans the river between Wenatchee and East Wenatchee, the Columbia narrows to 260 yards (230 m), pinching up to 300,000 cfs into a confined space. The hydraulics, even at lower water levels, can be seen and felt for the next few miles, as the river bulges and narrows through a rugged and rocky shoreline. Be aware of an occasional basalt island or submerged rock obstruction that creates turbulence and a hazard downstream.

The best take-out facility is at the **Kirby Billingsley Hydro Park boat ramp** 11.1 miles (17.9 km) from the put-in, but still 9 miles (14.5 km) from the top of Rock Island Dam. At 14.5 miles (23.3 km) from the unmaintained put-in, and in the main channel, are two noticeable unnamed rock islands, both of which can easily be avoided. There are more small rock islands 16.1 miles (25.9 km) out and directly under the last railroad bridge. In high water all of these islands should be given a wide berth to avoid downstream turbulence in fast water, especially the larger islands. Farther downriver from the islands are large industrial complexes, roadless terrain, railroad track, and private property,

BROTHER, CAN YOU SPARE ME A DIME?

What do agriculture, barging, rail, oceangoing ships, wind farms, and dams have in common besides the Columbia? They are all heavily subsidized by the government. The reason for the gifting of funds may be different, but the process is the same—a group of citizens or investors believe they are entitled to benefits, such as free water, reduced power rates, or tax breaks; they organize to support their cause with politicians; and then they work to keep these same politicians in office.

Farmers pay next to nothing for irrigation water and hydroelectric power in the Columbia Basin. Dam reservoir levels are maintained and locks are operated for free for tugs and barges. Railroad companies built their tracks on land gifted to them by Congress. The Army Corps of Engineers dredges the lower Columbia so Hanjin and Toyota and other container ship companies can navigate the river. Dams are operated for agri-business, rather than to build on a salmon fishery that was once the best in the world. And now we're subsidizing a new set of stockholders, wind farm conglomerates, with billions in federal grants, state tax credits, loan guarantees, and accelerated depreciation on federal and state taxes. There doesn't seem to be an industry on or near the Columbia River that doesn't have their finger in the federal pie or the taxpayer's pocket.

Passing beneath the US Highway 2 (Olds Bridge) bridge over the Rock Island Pool just upriver from Wenatchee

all of which discourage taking out within 4.5 miles (7.2 km) of Rock Island Dam. Fortunately, the Chelan County PUD allows paddlers to take out on river left (east side) at the floating cable barrier in front of the dam, 18.5 miles (29.8 km) from the put-in.

Hazards include swift, turbulent water in the spring and summer; bridge pilings, rock islands and subsurface rocks in the channel; high wind and waves; and high-speed recreational boats and jet skis.

FLOW AND SEASON: This leg has a strong current in the spring and summer, but very little flow in the late fall. It can be paddled in any season, but given the swift water through the narrow canyon, bridge pilings, and rock islands, the best time is in summer or early fall. I paddled this section twice: in mid-May when the flow rate was approximately 210,000 cfs, and in mid-October when the flow rate was more like 60,000 cfs. The difference in the water turbulence is dramatic. While I found it easy to avoid the hydraulics around the river's obstructions in May, the later months September and October have significantly less water and fewer jet skis and recreational boaters.

PUT-INS: Unmaintained public boat ramp (primary), 1.1 miles (1.8 km), west shore, gravel road access off US 97; Confluence State Park (secondary), 5 miles (8 km), Easy St off N Wenatchee Ave to E Penny Rd to Isenhart Rd. All distances are from the spillway of Rocky Reach Dam.

TAKE-OUTS: Walla Walla Point Park, 6.4 miles (10.3 km), N Miller St off N Wenatchee Ave to Walla Walla Ave; Wenatchee Docks, 6.6 miles (10.6 km), E Orondo Ave off S Chelan Ave to N Worthen St; Kirby Billingsley Hydro Park boat ramp, 10 miles (16 km), northeast shore WA 28 (the last maintained public access area for a take-out prior to Rock Island Dam); rough take-out, 18.5 miles (29.8 km), northeast shore, WA 28 (must cross railroad tracks to parking area next to WA 28). All distances are from the unmaintained primary put-in.

SERVICES: This paddle is in the heart of the Wenatchee Valley. All public services are available, including boat rental and repair. Motels, restaurants, RV parks, and other travel amenities are plentiful and excellent.

CAMPING: Confluence State Park (see Put-ins) and Lincoln Rock State Park (see Leg 20) are the best facilities in the area for RVs and camping. Within 20 miles (32.2 km), but above Rocky Reach Dam, are Daroga State Park, Orondo River Park, and Entiat Park.

Passage

The Columbia was running at 210,000 cfs when I launched from the beach at Confluence State Park on a hot mid-May afternoon. I had spent the morning paddling from Daroga State Park to Lincoln Rock State Park (Leg 20), and the day was so calm and cloudless I couldn't resist an afternoon paddle to Rock Island Dam. The river was running so high that I felt more comfortable launching from Confluence State Park, rather than the unmaintained boat ramp just 1.1 miles (1.8 km) below Rocky Reach Dam. (I returned later in October when the river was low and put in at the unmaintained boat ramp below Rocky Reach Dam, and continued to the barrier at Rock Island Dam for a great paddle on a fall day.)

In May, the afternoon heat brought out the sun worshippers, and the river was teeming with high-performance ski/wake-board boats, pleasure boats, and jet skis, creating water chop, motor roar, and waves I had not experienced on the Columbia since paddling on Labor Day weekend on Lake Roosevelt. I stayed river right for the first mile (1.6 km), and then paddled into the main channel where I could feel the river beginning to increase its flow, as Rocky Reach Dam began its afternoon spill and the canyon narrowed.

Soon after I passed the Wenatchee Docks, the motorized boat traffic all but disappeared, and, other than the sound of traffic over the Stevens Street bridge, I could have been on Rufus Woods Lake above Chief Joseph Dam, which is as quiet a section of the river as can be found. The strong afternoon

One of many basalt pillars and islands in the rugged canyon the Columbia cuts through the Wenatchee area.

current carried me quickly under the Olds Bridge, which is now a part of the Apple Capital Loop Trail, and the Stevens Street bridge. Both bridges are constructed with two large piers in the river to hold up their spans. I stayed in the center of the river to avoid the piers' downriver hydraulics.

Other than two short sections of turbulence, the river was smooth and fast to Kirby Billingsley Hydro Park, where I pulled out for a short break along the tree-lined bank.

I set off again, skirting the two center rock islands in the main channel 3.4 miles (5.5 km) below Hydro Park without a problem. Then, concerned about public access farther downriver near the dam, I located a rough take-out at an empty construction lot in a housing development and took out. This access point is no longer available to the public.

When I returned in October, the river was barely flowing. A few days prior to paddling the last few miles of this leg, I called the Chelan County PUD and spoke with the district's chief security officer and asked him directly about take-outs near the dam. He said the PUD's policy is to recommend paddlers take out at Hydro Park, but that taking out a kayak or canoe on the northeast shore at the floating barrier above the dam is allowed. He said it's a safety issue, but at this time of year with very little flow, approaching the dam's floating barrier is okay.

I took him for his word and set off from the primary put-in just below Rocky Reach Dam, then paddled past Confluence State Park and downriver to where I had taken out in May when the river was high and fast. I continued in the glassy water past several more rock islands 0.5 mile (0.8 km) downriver, paddled beneath the railroad bridge, and entered the wider pool behind Rock Island Dam. I stayed river left and took out close to the corner of the dam's floating barrier, a spot recommended by the security officer, 18.5 miles (29.8 km) from the put-in and just 250 feet (76 m) from the dam's floating barrier. I pulled my kayak up the short bank, through the brush, and over the railroad track to where Joyce was parked with the SUV to end a great morning on the river.

LEG 22: Rock Island Dam to Wanapum Dam

Distance: 31.6 miles (50.8 km)
Paddle Time: 7 to 10 hours from Columbia Siding Rd put-in; 5 to 7 hours from Crescent Bar put-in

River View

The leg from **Rock Island Dam** to **Wanapum Dam** is another of the remote and inaccessible areas of the Columbia River—except by boat. Access close to Rock Island Dam is limited and, in fact, the Grant County PUD website

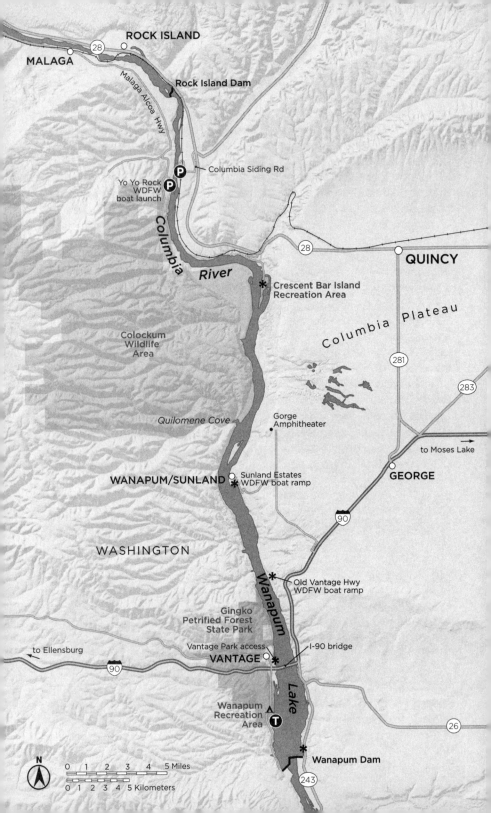

recommends paddlers put in at the **Crescent Bar Island Resort** 12.5 miles (20.1 km) downriver. However, there is a good put-in closer to the dam.

Below Rock Island Dam, the river flows through the channel at 5 to 6 mph (8 to 9.7 kmph) in the spring for the first 5 miles (8 km), but begins to slow down quickly as it pushes into the backwaters of **Wanapum Lake,** the pool behind Wanapum Dam. Nine miles (14.5 km) below Rock Island Dam, the river turns east for 3 miles (4.8 km) before passing the almost urban recreational development of **Crescent Bar.** Across the river and along the west shore is the **Colockum Wildlife Area,** a 91,603-acre (37,070 ha) wildlife and habitat preserve, which borders the Columbia on the west for the next 15 miles (24.1 km) downriver. Flow from the dam all but stops at Crescent Bar, and the real paddling begins.

There is a good reason this area of the river is called a "gorge": The Columbia slices through a deep canyon of spectacular basalt cliffs, rising in vertical steps, some over 300 feet (91 m) high, to the shrub-steppe, desertlike terrain rising to the Cascades to the west, and to the irrigated crop circles of farmland on the **Columbia Plateau** to the east.

At 7.5 miles (12 km) from Crescent Bar is **Quilomene Cove,** a popular destination with the motorboat set because of its protected cove and long, white sandy spit for sunbathing; and at 10 miles (16 km) from Crescent Bar on the east shore is the small resort town of **Wanapum,** which has a public boat launch and river access site. The **Gorge Amphitheater,** a popular Northwest concert venue, is also visible from sections of the river, perched over 600 feet above the east shore.

The Columbia exits the cliff and gorge-like terrain at **Vantage,** as the valley widens just before Wanapum Dam. There are not a lot of convenient takeouts on this leg. Be prepared for strong winds from the south, paddle early, and check the weather reports. The gorge area is virtually a wind tunnel, and

Pulling a kayak to the put-in through a PUD-restored riparian area below Rock Island Dam

afternoons can be breezy to an all-out gale. Also, avoid this leg of the journey any time there is a concert at the Gorge Amphitheater, as the pleasure and ski boats number in the hundreds, making for a very rough and noisy paddle.

Hazards include swift, turbulent water below Rock Island Dam; remote and inaccessible areas of the river; weather-related wind and waves; and high-speed recreational powerboats, particularly on weekends and holidays.

FLOW AND SEASON: There is considerable flow for the first 5 to 6 miles (8 to 9.7 km), especially in the spring, but the river pools and becomes a lake long before Crescent Bar. Although this leg can be paddled all year around, May through October is the best season to catch good weather. Avoid weekends and holidays.

PUT-INS: Columbia Siding Rd put-in, 2.7 miles (4.3 km), east shore; Yo Yo Rock WDFW (Washington Department of Fish and Wildlife) boat launch, 4.5 miles (7.2 km), Colockum Rd to Tarpiscan Rd, west shore; Crescent Bar Island public boat ramp, 12.5 miles (20.1 km), Crescent Bar Rd off WA 28. All distances are from the Rock Island Dam spillway.

For Columbia Siding Rd, drive south 3.4 miles (5.5 km) from the dam on WA 28 to Nelson Siding Rd and turn right, and then right again onto Columbia Siding Rd. Drive 1.5 miles (2.4 km) on gravel road and cross the tracks. The shoreline 0.7 mile (1.1 km) upriver and 0.7 (1.1 km) downriver is owned by either the Grant County PUD or the Washington State Department of Natural Resources, and is easily accessed across a short field from the dirt road.

TAKE-OUTS: Sunland Estates WDFW boat ramp, 20.4 miles (34.3 km) east shore, W Baseline Rd off WA 281; Old Vantage Highway WDFW boat ramp, 25.4 miles (42.2 km), east shore, Silica Rd SW off I-90 to Vantage Rd; Vantage Park and boat ramp, 29.1 miles (48.4 km), west shore at Vantage I-90 bridge; Wanapum Recreation Area, 31.8 miles (53.8 km), west shore south of Vantage I-90 bridge on Huntzinger Rd; Wanapum Dam Upper Boat Launch, 33.4 miles (56.2 km), top of Wanapum Dam off WA 243. All distances are from the Columbia Siding Rd primary put-in.

SERVICES: Same as those for Rocky Reach to Rock Island section (Leg 21). Wenatchee and East Wenatchee are full-service communities. Services at Vantage are limited to a gas station and restaurant.

CAMPING: RV and camping sites are located at Lincoln Rock State Park, Confluence State Park (see Leg 21 for details); and Wanapum Recreation Area (see Take-outs).

Passage

I put in on the east shoreline of the Columbia River, 2.7 miles (4.3 km) downriver from Rock Island Dam, just as the mid-May morning temperature was rising. This leg is one of the finest paddles on the Columbia—if there's no wind. I located a narrow strip of shoreline restoration land owned by Grant County PUD alongside Columbia Siding Road and a few hundred yards from the river. The lay of the land provided a low-angled, grassy bank to lower my kayak into the water; a small eddy to keep it in place; and a clean launch area free of jagged basalt rocks. The Yo Yo Rock boat ramp put-in was 1.8 miles farther downriver on the west shore, but my site was far enough from the dam to remove most of the turbulence.

The river was running below 200,000 cfs as I paddled into the main channel and was carried along swiftly through a narrow section 250 to 300 yards (229 to 275 m) wide and 0.5 mile (0.8 km) long, just below the launch.

There are only two small rock islands to avoid below the dam, both in the center of the river: a house-sized rock with several satellite rocks about 2.2 miles (3.5 km) from the put-in, and a smaller rock 4.4 miles (7 km) out.

At about 5 miles (8 km) from the dam, the Columbia doglegged to the east toward the Crescent Bar development and recreation area. As I approached the river's abrupt turn to the south, I paddled diagonally across to hug the west

Wanapum Lake has numerous sand beaches to stop along the paddle from Rock Island Dam to Wanapum Dam.

shoreline and the Colockum Wildlife Area. Just around the point, I found a small but pristine, light beige sandy beach and pulled out for a short break. The day I paddled this leg was perfect: the temperature was in the 90s; there wasn't a breeze on the water; and because it was a Monday, I saw only three motorized boats the entire paddle.

Once I had passed **Crescent Bar Island,** I was on my own for 8 miles (12.9 km) in one of the Columbia's hidden jewels: a deep, cliff-enclosed gorge, sparsely vegetated and richly populated with waterfowl, shorebirds, and wild-life—and without the trappings of human development. After those 8 miles, I rounded the west shoreline of an island 1.5 mile (2.4 km) long and paddled past **Sunland,** another recreational resort development located on a 1-mile-long (1.6 km) gravel bar known as Wanapum. This section of the river from the island, past Sunland, and in other shallow areas of the river to Vantage, is sandy-bottomed and weedy, a problem I encountered in most of the lakes behind the dams in late summer and fall.

Without wind and the resulting waves and rollers, I paddled diagonally across the river from Sunland to the west shore, which I paralleled as close as possible for the final 8 miles (12.9 km), passing beneath massive overhanging and vertical basalt walls. The "wow" factor from the rugged and spectacular scenery cannot be overstated. The high walls provided some much-needed shade, as the afternoon sun pounded the unusually calm gorge, and the cliff swallows dodging in and out for bugs provided the entertainment. From Vantage it was just a short 3-mile (4.8 km) paddle around the I-90 bridge riprap, along the vegetated shoreline, inside the island, and then to the Wanapum Recreation Area where Joyce and I camped for the night.

LEG 23: Wanapum Dam to Priest Rapids Dam

Distance: 16.3 to 17 miles (26.2 km to 27.4 km), depending on put-in
Paddle Time: 3 to 5 hours

River View

The leg from **Wanapum Dam** to **Priest Rapids Dam** passes through one of eastern Washington's driest shrub-steppe habitats. The contrast between the desertlike 327,000-acre (132,332 ha) **US Army Yakima Training Center** rising into the Cascade foothills from the west bank of the Columbia and the deep, lush greens of irrigated crop circles and orchards on its east bank resembles that between put-in and take-out—wild at one end and serene at the other. This short but exciting leg turned out to be one of my favorite paddles.

Depending on the season and winter runoff, the Columbia can be hell-bent on leaving **Wanapum Lake** and surging toward Priest Rapids Dam. There are

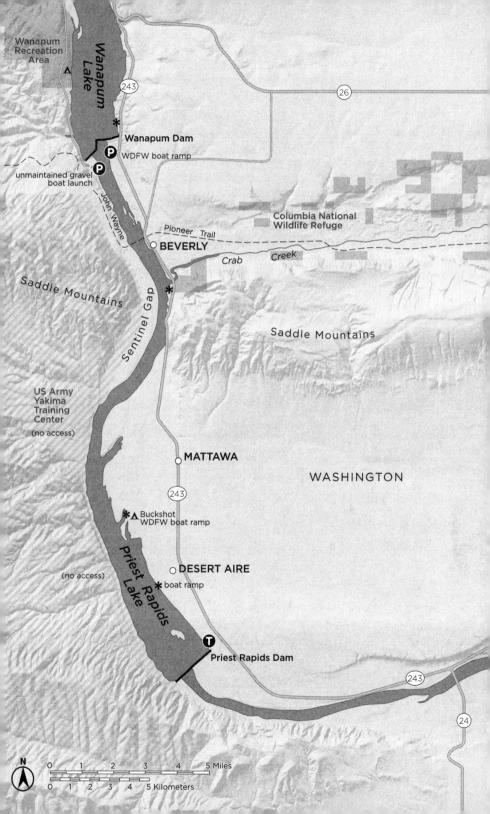

two good put-in sites. In high water, the gravel beach 0.5 mile (0.8 km) below the dam on the west side is best. When the spillway gates are closed later in the year minimizing the flow, the WDFW (Washington Department of Fish and Wildlife) public-access boat ramp directly below the earthen portion of the dam is a good put-in. The river is only 0.25 mile (0.4 km) wide as the canyon narrows below the dam. May through July provides bigger, faster water for at least 8 miles (12.9 km) before **Priest Rapids Lake,** the reservoir behind Priest Rapids Dam, begins to push back and slow the river's momentum.

From the dam, the river flows southeast for about 4 miles (6.4 km) to where **Crab Creek,** the only major tributary, enters from the east, and then the Columbia takes a long, easy sweep to the southwest. The river widens and there is shallow water with the usual water weeds along river left. Eight miles (12.9 km) into the paddle, the Columbia smacks up against the basalt hills of the Army's Yakima Training Center above the west shore, then turns south and southeast in another arc to Priest Rapids Dam for the final 8.5 miles (13.7 km).

Hazards include swift, turbulent water below Wanapum Dam; weather-related wind and waves; and rattlesnakes on shore.

Looking north from above Wanapum Dam toward the I-90 Vantage Bridge that crosses Wanapum Lake

FLOW AND SEASON: This is another leg that can be paddled just about any time of year, but to really enjoy safe, big, moving water, paddling this section when the flow rate is between 150,000 and 300,000 cfs is a must. The best time for a leisurely paddle, warmer water, and cooler daytime temperatures is in September or October.

PUT-INS: WDFW Wanapum Dam Rd boat ramp, at dam face on east bank, WA 243 (okay in low water); Wanapum Dam PUD unmaintained gravel boat launch site (primary), 0.5 mile (0.8 km) below the dam on west bank off Huntzinger Rd (best in high water).

TAKE-OUTS: Crab Creek unmaintained gravel access, 4 miles (6.4 km), off WA 243; WDFW Buckshot boat ramp, 12.4 miles (20 km), Rd 26 SW off WA 243; Desert Aire public boat ramp, 14.5 miles (23.3 km), Desert Aire Dr off WA 243; unmaintained gravel beach at the top of Priest Rapids Dam, 16.3 miles (26.2 km), WA 243. All distances are from the primary unmaintained gravel boat launch site, and take-outs are on the east shore.

SERVICES: Services are, in a word, limited. As for motels, Vantage has the Riverstone Resort, but your best bet is to drive to either Moses Lake, Ellensburg, or Richland. Mattawa has a full-service grocery store as well as a tortilla factory known also for its tasty Mexican pastries. The small towns have a number of gas stations and convenience stores.

CAMPING: Wanapum Recreation Area provides excellent camping, RV, and picnicking facilities. The WDFW also allows camping at its boat launch area known as Buckshot at the west end of Rd 26 SW off WA 243, but there are no amenities.

Passage

Wanapum Dam was releasing 230,000 cfs when I paddled this leg in late July. Just off Huntzinger Road on the west side of the Columbia River, I located a publicly accessible but unmaintained put-in on a sandy bar owned by the PUD 0.5 (0.8 km) mile below the dam. I found this launch better suited for kayaks and canoes, especially in high-flow conditions.

I launched easily from the sandy bar and, once into the main flow, stayed river right to avoid the hydraulics coming off the long, narrow islands along the east shore. The fast-moving center channel proved to be the best line as I passed under the abandoned 1909 Milwaukee Railroad bridge, now a segment

A DEFINITION OF POWER

I, Frank Buck, am sorry to say I almost didn't make it to this dedication. But I am glad to be here. I have a few words to express about white people. You are glad that this Priest Rapids Dam is finished. You are dedicating it today. We are very glad to be here with you today. This power is very important to you. This power is like food to you. The water that is making this power provides you all the food you need. Your power and my power are two different things. The things that I am showing outside of the teepees, that is the food we Indians was provided with. That food will take care of us. That food makes me strong and healthy. It is our medicine. Even what law comes against us, we don't hold it against you. We Indians are still friends with you. You white people, we Indians. It is our thoughts to go together as on this Earth. We will be taken care of.

—Wanapum Chief Frank Buck's speech
at the dedication of the Priest Rapids Dam, June 2, 1962

From Wanapum Dam's powerhouse on the right, the Columbia flows south through Sentinel Gap where the ice age floods flowed through the Saddle Mountains.

of the **John Wayne Pioneer Trail.** Four miles (6.4 km) downriver, I passed the mouth of Crab Creek on the east shore, which enters the Columbia below the unincorporated town of Beverly. As usual, I had the river to myself to enjoy as I marveled at the moonscape-like hills high above the river.

Along the west shore is one of Washington's largest apple orchards, planted on a wide bar that flanks the river from the railroad bridge south for 4.5 miles (7.2 km). The river is wide and shallow beyond Crab Creek, as it takes a sweeping turn to the southwest and cuts through the **Saddle Mountains** to form **Sentinel Gap,** a well-known ice age floods landmark. After the sweep, the Columbia turns directly south to Priest Rapids Dam. I paddled easily, closely approaching the great blue herons, geese, and ducks quietly sitting in the shallow wetlands near shore. Moving in and out close to the east shore, I enjoyed watching the small fish fry darting over the golden-colored gravel salmon spawning beds just a few feet below me.

The WDFW's Buckshot boat ramp is located up a dead-end channel 0.25 mile (0.4 km) from the river and hidden by trees, but at the mouth leading to the site, I landed on a gravel spit for a break before paddling the remaining distance to the top of Priest Rapids Dam. Once I had passed Desert Aire's crowded public park and boat launch, I was once more the sole boat on the river. I paddled close to shore and past the 0.5-mile-long (0.8 km) gravel island near the dam along the east shoreline. Joyce had located a public access road that ended 300 yards (274.3 m) above the face of the dam and was there waiting when I arrived in the afternoon heat.

LEG 24: Priest Rapids Dam to Ringold Springs

Distance: 34.6 miles (55.7 km)
Paddle Time: 6.5 to 8 hours

River View

The leg from **Priest Rapids Dam** to **Ringold Springs,** if done from the **Vernita Bridge,** runs along the longest wild and free-flowing, nontidal section of the Columbia River in the United States. If you ever decide to paddle the same leg on the Columbia twice, this should be your choice.

There are some wild and woolly places to put in along the north shoreline closer to the dam, but the usual launch area for paddlers is a WDFW (Washington Department of Fish and Wildlife) unmaintained gravel boat launch site on the east shore 0.5 mile (0.8 km) upriver from the Vernita Bridge off Washington State Highway 243. Keep in mind the US Department of Energy prohibits public access to many areas of the **Hanford Reach National Monument** on either side of the river from the bridge, including in 2013 the **Saddle Mountain**

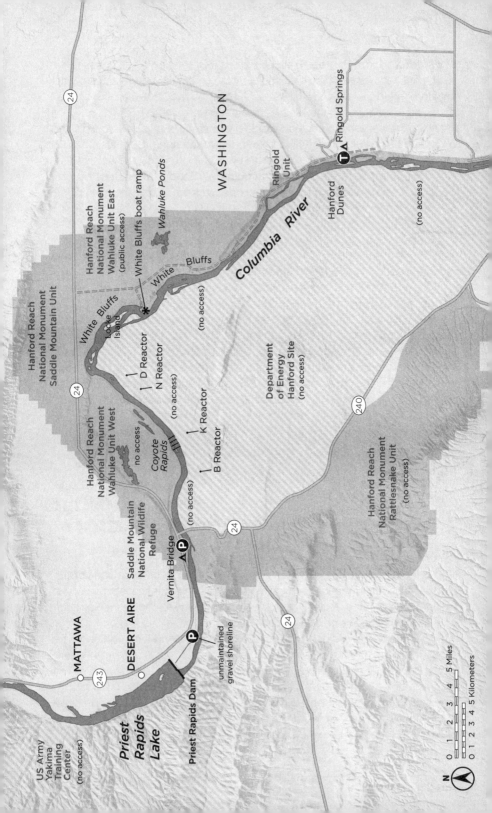

HANFORD REACH NATIONAL MONUMENT

The Hanford Reach National Monument was created in 2000 from lands of Hanford Reach, a 51-mile (82 km), free-flowing section of the Columbia River, and the Saddle Mountain National Wildlife Refuge to protect rare plants, wildlife, and remnants of human history. The 196,000-acre (79,320 ha) monument lies in one of the hottest and driest places in Washington. The lands were preserved in their natural state because they served as a security buffer for the top-secret Manhattan Project during World War II. The US Fish and Wildlife Service and US Department of Energy protect the unique habitats in the monument, which support 725 vascular plant species, 12 species of mammals, more than 200 species of birds, 9 reptile species, 4 amphibian species, 45 species of fish, and more than 1600 species of insects. The monument does not include the core nuclear reservation managed by the Department of Energy.

The Hanford Reach is known for its abundant wildlife, birds, amphibians, and unique plants. As a friend and I paddled past the sand islands near the White Bluffs, a squadron of white pelicans took off to settle farther downriver.

National Wildlife Refuge located in the **Wahluke Unit West.** The **Rattlesnake Unit** is part of the Saddle Mountain National Wildlife Refuge and is closed to the public as well. **Wahluke Unit East,** the **Saddle Mountain Unit** (north of the NWR), the **Ringold Unit,** and shorelines along the Columbia below the ordinary high-water mark are open to the public. Confusing, to say the least, but the bottom line is: either stay in your boat or close to shore, and don't land on the Hanford Site generally south of the river.

From the public launch site at the Vernita Bridge, the Columbia flows 5.5 miles (8.9 km) east and then turns northeast at the Hanford Nuclear Reservation's **B Reactor.** Another 1.5 miles (2.4 km) downriver from B Reactor and adjacent to **K Reactor** is **Coyote Rapids,** which can be noisy in big water but a minor threat to paddlers under most conditions. From Coyote Rapids, the river flows another 6.5 miles (10.5 km) past the **N and D Reactors,** located on the south shore, before taking an abrupt dogleg to the southeast at the impenetrable **White Bluffs,** an exposed 400-foot-thick (120 m) paleochannel of multiple clay-silt ice age flood deposits.

Wahluke Unit East, one of two publicly accessible areas downriver from the put-in, begins 1 mile (1.6 km) from the river's farthest point north, although as far as I could tell there is no sign or marker indicating public access. The river splits around 2.6-mile-long (4.2 km) **Locke Island,** and then takes a right-hand turn around a peninsula where the **White Bluffs boat ramp** is located.

From here, paddle another 15.5 miles (25 km) along river left to avoid numerous islands and their channels, which may be blocked, to Ringold

Bruce Hunt passes Hanford's N reactor, the last of the nine reactors built at Hanford. It was shut down in 1987.

HANFORD NUCLEAR RESERVATION

The numbers are staggering: 25 million cubic feet (710,000 cu m) of solid radioactive waste; 53 million gallons (2.1 million l) of liquid high-level radioactive waste; 177 underground tanks holding toxic goo, six of which are leaking into the aquifer; 200 square miles (520 sq km) of contaminated groundwater; 500 contaminated buildings; and 1700 waste sites with untold tons of contaminated garbage and building materials. The Hanford Nuclear Reservation is not only the most contaminated nuclear waste site in the United States, it may be the most difficult US Superfund site to clean.

Hanford was a necessary evil built as part of the top-secret Manhattan Project during World War II to create the first atomic bombs. The work done there and at Los Alamos is credited with ending the war. The first atomic bomb, "The Gadget," was exploded at White Sands, New Mexico, under the code name "Trinity" on July 16, 1945. On August 9, 1945, three days after a uranium-235 bomb was dropped on Hiroshima, the United States dropped "Fat Man" on Nagasaki, Japan. Like "The Gadget," the plutonium core for "Fat Man" was produced at Hanford.

Central Washington was an ideal location—a sparsely populated, desolate desert region, with no redeeming value except one, the Columbia River. Nuclear reactors need cold, clean water—millions of gallons a day—to cool the nuclear fissure process. Making weapons-grade plutonium-239 takes millions of megawatts of electricity, and the Columbia had Bonneville and Grand Coulee dams. The military in 1943 must have thought the location in Washington was divine intervention; but today, as radioactive contaminants leach into the groundwater and toward the Columbia, environmentalists believe it is the perfect storm.

Today, Hanford is the most serious long-term threat to the Columbia River and the livable communities along its shores. The state of Washington, the federal Environmental Protection Agency, and the US Department of Energy signed a legally binding agreement in 1989 to clean up Hanford's waste by 2018. It's already outdated, and as of late 2013 Congress continues to drag its feet on providing funding to get the job done. The Energy Department's latest schedule now calls for tank waste to be treated and contained by 2047, with groundwater cleanup and some other activities continuing through 2070.

The plutonium-239 has been removed from the site; nuclear fuel from two leak-prone pools of water near the Columbia River has been eliminated. A lot has been done, but time is not on our side. In February 2013, six of the 177 waste tanks built over fifty years ago were found to be leaking 1000 gallons (3785.4 l) a year of highly radioactive stew, possibly reaching the groundwater. Meanwhile, construction of a vitrification plant to convert millions of gallons of waste from the tanks into glasslike logs is billions of dollars over budget and years behind schedule. Members of Congress need to authorize the funds, or the cleanup will last longer than the half-life of plutonium-238—that's eighty-eight years from now.

Springs, another WDFW unmaintained boat access and gravel bar. This is a smooth, fast-moving section of water that is easily done in less than 8 hours. Mule deer, coyotes, and elk are often visible above the shores; eagles and hawks hunt the shrub-steppe habitat; great blue herons, white pelicans, ducks, and geese feed in the shallows and gravel beds; and Chinook salmon, white sturgeon, and numerous other fish species live and spawn in its waterway.

Hazards include big, fast-moving water; eddies and crosscurrents; wind; underwater obstacles; rattlesnakes on shore; and weekend jet boat traffic from Richland and WDFW boat ramp sites.

FLOW AND SEASON: The flow is a steady 5 to 6 mph (8 to 9.7 kmph), faster or slower depending on the season. Although this leg can be paddled all year round, May through October is the best time to catch good weather. The later in the year, the lower the water and the longer the paddle time. Avoid weekends and holidays.

PUT-INS: Unmaintained gravel shoreline next to barbed wire fence 5.4 miles (8.7 km) upriver from the Vernita Bridge (secondary) on the north shore off WA 243; WDFW unmaintained gravel boat ramp 0.5 mile (0.8 km) off WA 243 west of the Vernita Bridge on north shoreline (primary).

TAKE-OUTS: WDFW-maintained White Bluffs boat ramp, 19 miles (30.6 km), WA 24; WDFW unmaintained boat ramp at Ringold Springs, 34.3 miles (55.2 km). From US 395, take WA 17 to CR 170 to Basin City. From Basin City, drive south on CR 170 approx 7.8 miles (12.5 km), then turn right on Ringold River Rd and drive 0.8 mile (1.3 km) to a T intersection. Turn right, then left on the right side of the canal and drive 0.2 mile (0.3 km) to the Ringold Springs access. All distances are from the Vernita Bridge primary put-in.

SERVICES: All services, including boat repair and rental, are available in the Tri-Cities of Pasco, Richland, and Kennewick; there are very limited services at Desert Aire and Mattawa; and no services at the Vernita Bridge rest stop or Ringold Springs.

CAMPING: The Department of Energy prohibits overnight camping within the Hanford Reach National Monument. Recreational vehicles and camping are allowed at the WDFW Vernita Bridge and Ringold Springs access sites. Both sites have toilet facilities, usually in the form of a concrete vault toilet.

Passage

I paddled this leg from the Vernita Bridge to Ringold Springs through Hanford Reach with my good friend and first paddling partner, Bruce Hunt. He and I put in at the WDFW gravel bar launch site a few hundred yards upriver of the Vernita Bridge in late July around 9 AM. The sun was already high and baking the dry hills and sagebrush flats above the river. Surprisingly, despite the sunbathed, windless day, we had the river to ourselves. We lathered any exposed skin with SPF 50; put on our wide-brimmed sun hats, PFDs, and long-sleeved shirts; and launched, immediately feeling the power and flow of 225,000 cfs.

Within minutes we were past the bridge heading for Hanford's 100 Area and its infamous B Reactor, its large cooling tower plainly visible for miles. The Columbia was running high in July, and the big water swept us along quickly, showing some bottom roiling in the wide, shallow areas. Along the shoreline and adjacent to B Reactor was the facility's massive cooling-water pump station, no longer in operation but symbolic of the river's role in our nuclear history.

We paddled sparingly, just enough to keep our kayaks pointed downriver, while enjoying white pelicans, geese, and ducks feeding in the shallows. In the sagebrush, numerous mule deer does and fawns paused in their search for food to watch us float past. Within 10 minutes we could hear, but not see, Coyote Rapids as we approached K Reactor, so we moved river left to avoid the rough water. As we paddled past the rapids, the rolling waves near the shoreline were visible. Even in the center of the river in this area, there were large boulders just below the surface, which kept us busy weaving in and out of the resulting eddies.

Past the small N Reactor and much larger D Reactor complex, we eddied out and landed on the lee side of the first big island. Looking more like a low-flying bomber squadron than a flock of birds, a group of twelve white pelicans took flight from the shore. Old faded yellow metal signs in the dry brush above warned us about trespassing and "Underground Radioactive Materials." Boaters are permitted to land on shorelines within the national monument, as long as they stay below the high-water mark, so we enjoyed the sandy beach.

A few miles beyond the island, we reached the White Bluffs, layered deposits of a silt-clay mix formed from slack water during the many ice age flood events. The 400-foot-high (122 m) bluffs are home to countless cliff swallows and are exposed along the river for many miles. It's at the water-resistant White Bluffs that the river is forced to the southeast and braids through a series of six major islands, including 150-acre (60 ha) Locke Island.

In the wide pool before the river turns, we heard, long before we saw, a twenty-two-passenger tourist jet boat that frequently runs the river from Richland. The tour boat was careful to slow down and courteously skirt around us at a distance. At times, Bruce and I were tempted to take a side channel around an island, but the river's main flow soon made itself obvious and we stayed in the center channel.

We soon floated past the deserted White Bluffs WDFW boat ramp area and an hour later landed on a small sandy spit on the Wahluke Unit East side for a late lunch. Quail burst from the brush along the bank and a coyote easily loped through the shrub-steppe toward the bluffs, occasionally stopping to glance back at us to feed his curiosity. The terrain above the beaches looks inviting, but almost anything that grows, crawls, or slithers in this environment has evolved with some form of protection, such as thorns, stingers, or venom.

We set off again and immediately noticed a surge in the river's power. On schedule, Priest Rapids Dam had released more water in the afternoon and the river was now flowing at over 260,000 cfs. We were swept along for miles at a marathon pace, staying river left, before spotting the WDFW Ringold Springs gravel take-out. The river was carrying us along with such power, it was hard work angling upriver sideways in the flow to catch the eddy and end one of the finest paddles on the Columbia.

LEG 25: Ringold Springs to Snake River

Distance: 29 miles (46.6 km)
Paddle Time: 6 to 9 hours

River View

The leg from **Ringold Springs** to the mouth of the **Snake River** begins in the fast-flowing remnant of Hanford Reach, slows as the Columbia reaches the Tri-Cities (**Richland, Pasco,** and **Kennewick**), and pools as **McNary Dam's Lake Wallula** reaches north of Pasco and, at certain times of year, as far upriver as Ringold Springs.

Between Ringold Springs and Richland are ten large lenticular islands, one over 2 miles (3.2 km) in length, easily navigated on either side. There is no doubt, however, where the main river flows during high water, and it will carry you along the central channel the 11 miles (17.7 km) to the outskirts of Richland, where there is an unmaintained public access area just off 11th Street along the river on the Richland side. From 11th Street downriver for the next 18 miles (29 km) through both Richland and Kennewick, the shoreline is mostly park property and includes the 7-mile-long (11.3 km) **Richland Riverfront Trail,** picnic areas, and boat ramps. You can stop almost anywhere on the west shoreline through Richland and Kennewick, whereas Pasco's shoreline on the east shore is predominantly private property, with the occasional public day-use boat launch farther downriver.

Hazards include hidden snags within 5 miles (8 km) of Ringold Springs; swift, cold water above Richland; tugboat and barge traffic from the Snake River confluence; and powerboats and jet skis in the main channel through the Tri-Cities.

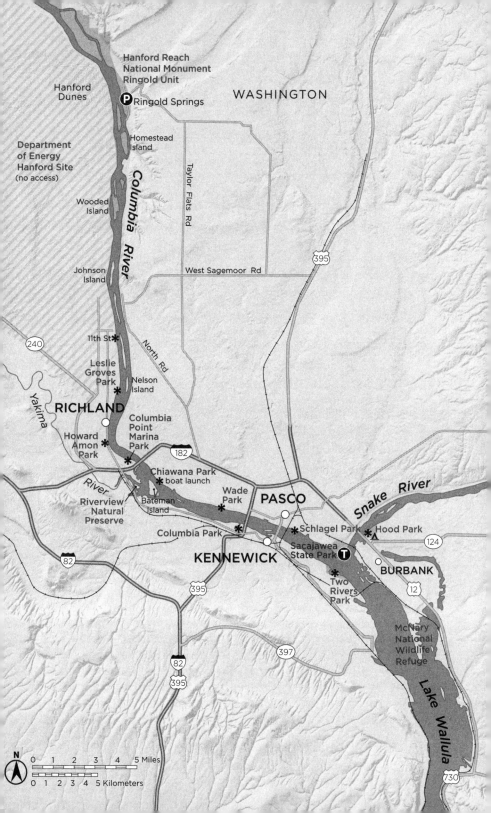

FLOW AND SEASON: The Columbia has significant flow at Ringold Springs, especially during the runoff months of May through early August. The current continues 4 to 5 miles (6.4 to 8 kmph) downriver, but eventually slows and pools as the backwaters of Lake Wallula push back. As with many sections on the Columbia, this leg can be paddled all year round, but May through October are the best months to catch good weather and high-water conditions. Avoid weekends and holidays.

PUT-IN: Ringold Springs WDFW (Washington Department of Fish and Wildlife) unmaintained gravel boat ramp (see Take-outs in Leg 24 for directions).

TAKE-OUTS: *Richland.* 11th St unmaintained boat launch, 11 miles (17.7 km); Snyder St public boat ramp in Leslie Groves Park, 13.4 miles (21.6 km); Howard Amon Park, 15.8 miles (25.4 km); Columbia Point Marina Park, 17.3 miles (27.8 km). *Pasco.* Chiawana Park boat launch, 20 miles (32.2 km); Wade Park, 22.2 miles (35.7 km). *Kennewick.* Columbia Park, 23.6 miles (38 km). *Pasco.* Schlagel Park, 25.75 miles (41.4 km); and Sacajawea State Park, 29 miles (46.7 km). All distances are from the Ringold Springs gravel boat ramp.

SERVICES: The Tri-Cities (Richland, Pasco, and Kennewick) are a full-service metropolitan area with excellent motels, great restaurants, major grocery stores, boat sales, and repair and rental services.

CAMPING: Although there are many day-use waterfront parks in the Tri-cities, none of them have RV or camping facilities, including Sacajawea State Park. Fortunately there is Hood Park, a US Army Corps of Engineers–run facility, located on the south shore of the Snake River just off US 12 and WA 124 approximately 4 miles (6.4 km) from Pasco.

Passage

The Columbia was flowing at 160,000 cfs when I put in at Ringold Springs in mid-August, 100,000 cfs less than when I paddled Hanford Reach (Leg 24). The launch area, which had been flooded just three weeks before, was now a gravel bar that extended 50 yards (46 m) into the river. I launched in a calm eddy on the downriver side of the bar and then paddled into the main stem. The mild flow and my easy paddling carried me past the large island adjacent to Ringold Springs, and I was swept by the current to the west shoreline, as the river skirted around **Homestead Island.** To my east, irrigated peach and apple

REMOVING THE ELWHA DAM WAS A GOOD START

Bruce Babbitt, US Secretary of the Interior from 1993 to 2001, made many efforts in the mid-1990s to begin the removal of the Elwha Dam and other dams throughout the United States. An essay he wrote in 2012 about his efforts was published online by Patagonia, an environmentally conscious outdoor clothing business. The removal of one of the Elwha Dams was completed in March of that year. In his essay, Babbitt thinks the four Snake River dams (Ice Harbor, Lower Monumental, Little Goose, and Lower Granite) are the main barriers to salmon and steelhead recovery in the Snake River system, a tributary to the Columbia, and should be removed. He believes the dams have changed the Snake into a "slack water barge channel" that has driven four salmon species to the brink of extinction and destroyed thousands of miles of habitat.

Preparing to launch from the Ringold Springs unmaintained gravel boat launch area

COLUMBIA RIVER BASIN: ESA-LISTED SALMON AND STEELHEAD TROUT

There are thirteen species of salmon and steelhead trout, as well as other species of fish, listed as endangered or threatened under the federal Endangered Species Act (ESA) and that occur in the Columbia River system. The ESA was passed by Congress in 1973 to protect species from extinction by protecting the environment in which they live.

Two are listed as endangered (as of the month listed): Snake River sockeye (November 1991) and Upper Columbia River Chinook (March 1999). The other eleven are listed as threatened: Snake River fall Chinook (April 1992), Snake River spring and summer Chinook (April 1992), Snake River Basin steelhead (August 1997), Lower Columbia River steelhead (March 1998), Lower Columbia River Chinook (March 1999), Lower Columbia River chum (March 1999), Middle Columbia River steelhead (March 1999), Lower Columbia River coho (June 2005), Upper Willamette River Chinook (June 2005), Upper Willamette River steelhead (January 2006), and Upper Columbia River steelhead (June 2009).

orchards lined the shore below tan-colored clay bluffs, while the desertlike Hanford Nuclear Reservation shimmered in the early-morning heat to my west.

A few hours later, I entered the outskirts of Richland. Any current was long gone, as Lake Wallula, the pool behind McNary Dam, deadened the power of the last free-flowing, nontidal section of the Columbia. Motorboat traffic was beginning to pick up as I passed the boat launch at Leslie Groves Park and stayed east of the last major island to avoid the thick surface vegetation in the shallows. The day was windless and in the mid-80s, so the motorboat crowd and jet skiers were beginning to populate the river. I paddled close to the west shoreline past Howard Amon Park and Columbia Point Marina Park, before passing under the two spans of the US Highway 12 bridge, the first of four bridges on this leg through the Tri-Cities.

At 0.25 mile (0.4 km) past the bridge, the **Yakima River** enters the Columbia and the confluence forms a wide, lakelike area with islands, wetlands, and weedy shallows. I stayed in the main channel and paddled to the east of **Bateman Island** to avoid the milfoil and other water weeds, and then hugged the west shoreline again to Columbia Park, where I took a short break. After lunch, I paddled beneath the massive **US 395 Blue Bridge** (Pioneer Memorial Bridge), and then beneath the **Cable Bridge** (Ed Hendler Memorial Bridge, WA 397), a landmark in the Tri-cities and known for its latticework "cable-stayed" design, which to me looks like two snow-capped Mount Fujis side by side over the river.

Less than 0.5 mile (0.8 km) farther is the Northern Pacific Railroad bridge, a rusty steel-beam girder structure originally built in 1887 but substantially rebuilt over the years. The bridge's vertical-lift span allows larger boats and tugs entry into the Port of Kennewick. The lift section was down for railroad traffic when I paddled underneath the operator's cabin and between the huge counterweight towers on either side of the span. As I passed by the concrete piers, I noticed a slight wake on the downriver side of the pilings indicating an increase in flow, either from the Yakima River's entry or release of more water in the early afternoon from Priest Rapids Dam.

From the railroad bridge, I angled easily from west to east across the river toward the confluence of the Snake River and Sacajawea State Park, where I paddled a short distance up the Snake and pulled out at the park's boat launch located in a shallow, weedy, protected bay, not much bigger than a housing lot. Even though this leg passes through one of Washington's denser urban areas, the city parks, orchards, and protective banks along the river eliminate much of the noise of city life, making this paddle private and enjoyable.

The symmetrical cable-stayed design work on the Ed Hendler Memorial Bridge, known locally has the Cable Bridge, resembles mirror images of Mount Fuji.

LEG 26: Snake River to McNary Dam

Distance: 32 miles (51.5 km)
Paddle Time: 7 to 10 hours

River View

The leg from the **Snake River** to **McNary Dam** is along a stretch of the Columbia rich in geologic and American history. It is in this section of the river where the mega ice age floods from the eighty or more releases of Lake Missoula 13,000 to 15,000 years ago funneled through the basalt formation called **Wallula Gap;** and where Lewis and Clark reached the Columbia at the confluence of the Snake, camped at what is now **Sacajawea State Park** on October 16 to 18, 1805, and followed the Columbia to the Pacific Ocean.

The leg begins in the protected boat launch cove at the mouth of the Snake River in Sacajawea State Park. Be alert for tugs with barges when entering the water, because the shipping channel is 100 yards (91.4 m) from the park. Tugs move deceptively fast and the barge bow waves can swamp a kayak or canoe. Cross the Columbia angling to the west shore to avoid tug traffic, and follow this shoreline for the entire journey to McNary Dam. The crossing is just over a mile (1.6 km), but you should be across before the railroad bridge, which spans the Columbia at **Burbank.**

After the railroad bridge, there are four decrepit, rusting barge hulks that are either swamped or anchored in place in a lineup 1 mile long (1.6 km). These hulks are used by Tidewater tugs to secure barges waiting for or dropping cargo. Again, be aware of tugs and barge traffic in this area.

The **McNary National Wildlife Refuge,** with over 15,000 acres (6070 ha) of sloughs, shrub-steppe uplands, river islands, delta mudflats, irrigated farmland, and riparian areas, is located along the east shoreline in various-sized parcels from Burbank south to **Wallula Gap** and **Hat Rock.** Also on the east shore along US Highway 12 is the **Boise Cascade Pulp and Paper Mill,** which spews a plume of chemicals and condensation that can be seen—and smelled—for miles, even on a windless day. On the west shoreline, and the most protected paddle route, are multiple small islands and shallows, around 5 miles (8 km) from Sacajawea State Park, which attract cormorants, white pelicans, great blue herons, and other fish hunters. Later in the summer, though, this section of shoreline is clogged with surface vegetation and should be avoided by paddling to the east of the islands.

Hover Park, a Benton County–operated park, which can be accessed by Washington State Highway 397 from **Kennewick,** is 6.7 miles (10.8 km) from the launch. If the wind suddenly picks up, this take-out will save your bacon.

Eleven miles (17.7 km) into the paddle, the river narrows to less than a mile (1.6 km) as it passes through Wallula Gap. Wallula Gap is so narrow and high, it impounded the ice age floods and created Lake Lewis, a lake more like a sea

which flooded thousands of square miles and even reached up the Snake River past the present site of Lewiston. This narrowing of the river into a gorge can create quite a wind tunnel, so be prepared to paddle back to Hover Park or face the same fate as Ulysses after his crew opened the leather bag of winds from Aeolus, the Master of Winds—you will not get to your destination.

There are no other river access points on the north side of the river from Hover Park south and west to McNary Dam. The river flows in a long, easy curve from south to west, and the paddle route stays along the north shoreline. Bays and coves to escape from the prevailing southwest and west winds are rare for almost 20 miles (32.2 km). Once around the corner, you're committed to the dam take-out, although in good weather and river conditions, you could cross the Columbia to several Oregon state park take-outs on the south shore.

Hazards include high wind and waves along this entire leg; submerged shoreline obstructions; and tugs with barges.

FLOW AND SEASON: There is little, if any, perceptible flow on Lake Wallula, even at the mouth of the Snake. This leg can be paddled all year round, but April through October is the best season to enjoy good weather. The Tri-Cities region can be the warmest area of the state, so paddlers can enjoy a springlike day, even in midwinter.

PUT-INS: Sacajawea State Park, Sacajawea Park Rd off US 12, Pasco; Two Rivers Park, E Finley Rd off WA 397, Kennewick.

TAKE-OUTS: *Washington.* Hover Park, 6.7 miles (10.8 km), Kennewick (west shore); Port Kelley Marina, 13.2 miles (21.2 km), US 730; McNary Dam boat ramp (north shore), 32 miles (51.5 km), McNary Rd off I-82. *Oregon.* Sand Station Recreation Area, 24 miles (38.6 km), US 730 (USACE); Warehouse Beach Recreation Area, 24.6 miles (39.6 km), US 730 (USACE); Hat Rock State Park, 26.2 miles (42.2 km), US 730; McNary Beach Recreation Area, 30.3 miles (48.8 km), US 730 (USACE). All distances are from the Sacajawea State Park put-in.

SERVICES: All services are available in the Tri-Cities (Richland, Pasco, Kennewick), including motels, restaurants, major grocery stores, boat sales, repair and rental services. Hermiston, on US 395, has all services except boat rental and repair, and Umatilla has several motels and restaurants, a grocery store, and convenience stores.

CAMPING: Hood Park, off US 12, Burbank; Sand Station Recreation Area (see Take-outs); Hat Rock Campground (commercial facility), off US 730, Oregon.

MEMBERS OF THE CORPS OF DISCOVERY

Military

Capt. Meriwether Lewis (1774–1809)
Sgt. Charles Floyd (Unknown–1804)
Sgt. John Ordway (1775–1817)
Pvt. Willam E. Bratton (1778–1841)
Pvt. John Colter (1775–1812)
Pvt. Joseph Field (1774–1807)
Pvt. Robert Frazer (1775–1837)
Pvt. Silas Goodrich (Unknown–1825)
Pvt. Thomas P. Howard (1779–1818)
Pvt. Jean Baptiste Lepage (Unknown–1809)
Pvt. John Potts (1776–1808)
Pvt. John Shields (1769–1809)
Pvt. Peter M. Weiser (1781–1828)
Pvt. Joseph Whitehouse (1775–Unknown)
Pvt. Richard Windsor (Unknown–1829)

Capt. William Clark (1770–1838)
Sgt. Patrick Gass (1771–1870)
Sgt. Nathaniel Hale Pryor (1772–1831)
Pvt. John Collins (Unk–1823)
Pvt. Pierre Cruzatte (Unknown–1828)
Pvt. Reuben Field (1775–1823)
Pvt. George Gibson (1780–1809)
Pvt. Hugh Hall (1772–1828)
Pvt. Francois Labiche (Unknown–1828)
Pvt. Hugh McNeal (Unknown–1828)
Pvt. George Shannon (1785–1836)
Pvt. John B. Thompson (Unknown–1828)
Pvt. William Werner (Unknown–Unknown)
Pvt. Alexander Williard (1778–1865)

Nonmilitary

George Drouillard (1773–1810)
Sacajawea (1786–1812)
York (Clark's slave) (1770–Unknown)

Toussaint Charbonneau (1767–Unknown)
Jean-Baptiste Charbonneau (1805–1866)

Passage

I thoroughly enjoyed this leg, not only for its history, but also for its rugged beauty and remoteness. I read portions of Clark's journal prior to paddling and found myself looking for the same geologic landmarks he described in his journal as he would have seen them from the river, such as **Badger Island, Twin Sisters,** and Hat Rock; and imagining the racks of drying fish, stick-built lodges, roaring rapids, and numerous islands along the Corps of Discovery's journey from the Snake River to what is now Umatilla. Obviously, the lodges and fishing racks are long gone, but I felt as though I was seeing this country for the first time as part of Lewis and Clark's party.

I put in at 6 AM to avoid the late-afternoon heat, as the day was stunningly perfect, without a cloud or a breath of wind, and the temperature was predicted to be in the high 90s by midafternoon. Once outside the cove, I angled southwest toward the west end of the railroad bridge. Having watched a Tidewater tug pushing barges turn into the Snake from the Columbia the night before, I knew I was paddling in a section of the main channel. Nearing the bridge about a mile (1.6 km) ahead, but moving quickly upriver, was another tug, so I angled abruptly to the west to clear the channel. Once I had passed the railroad bridge, I kept to the river side of four older-style barge hulks, either permanently anchored or deliberately sunk offshore from several industrial sites. I was wondering why they were there, when a tug with two barges coming upriver slowed, turned into my path, and then maneuvered its barges between the shoreline and one of the massive hulks. The tug's crew moved quickly to tie their barges to the hulk.

As the tug was working the barges into position, I slipped past on the main channel side and paddled toward a grouping of islands downriver. The shallows surrounding these islands are filled with thick mats of water weed, so I paddled on the channel side of the river, weaving in and out of acres of surface weeds, avoiding the thickest mats, which would tie up my paddle, near shore and in the shallows. The larger islands were overgrown with bushes and trees, providing safe refuge for a variety of birdlife. On one island, two dozen cormorants were perched on a dead, ivory-white, multibranched alder that had grown high above newer vegetation before becoming a crow's nest for cormorants. They noisily greeted me as I paddled by, refusing to leave such a perfect fishing spot.

As I entered Wallula Gap several miles (3.2 km) downstream, I pulled out on a rocky point for a short break near one of the many large mileage/warning placards, which line the Columbia from Pasco to the Pacific. I'm glad I did. For the next 21 miles (33.8 km) to McNary Dam, steep cliffs force the railroad tracks to line the river and even cut across bays on tall levees of basalt riprap used for fill. The railroad's steep artificial shoreline makes it difficult for a paddler to pull out. Along this section, there are few shallows with weeds along the steep banks, so the remaining journey can be done close to the shoreline in case an afternoon wind funnels through the gap.

Not surprisingly, I was alone on the river. Two fishing boats had motored by at a distance early that morning, and two tugs with barges had plowed upriver toward the Snake. But despite the perfect day, the river was calm, quiet and all mine. After 9 hours of paddling, I pulled into the WDFW's (Washington Department of Fish and Wildlife) boat launch on the north side of the dam where Joyce was patiently waiting in the intense heat of the afternoon.

The Boise Cascade Pulp and Paper Mill in Wallula uses chlorine dioxide in its bleaching process, which reduces, but does not eliminate dioxins discharged into the environment.

SACAJAWEA

Sacajawea, a Lemhi Shoshone Indian born in 1786 near present-day Salmon, Idaho, was one of the original members of the Corps of Discovery Expedition. At age twelve, she was kidnapped by a band of Hidatsa and taken to North Dakota. Sacajawea was later sold to a French-Canadian fur trapper, Toussaint Charbonneau, who claimed her and another captured Shoshone as his "wives." She gave birth to Jean-Baptiste Charbonneau in 1805, the youngest member of the expedition.

Toussaint, who spoke Hidatsa and French, and Sacajawea, who spoke Hidatsa and Shoshone, were recruited by the expedition as an interpreter team. She was the only woman to accompany the thirty-three permanent members of the party to the Pacific and back. Sacajawea was instrumental in purchasing horses from the Shoshone as the party traveled west. She was also valuable as an emissary to the many tribes and bands the expedition encountered, in collecting roots and herbs for food and medicinal purposes, and for guiding the party on their journey back through Idaho and Montana.

Sacajawea died on December 20, 1812, at Fort Manuel Lisa, North Dakota. Her two children, Jean-Baptiste and Lisette, were later legally adopted by Captain Clark.

Railroads have built their tracks on both sides of the Columbia River Gorge from McNary Dam to Portland and Vancouver. For many miles, the railway, which is built on boulder riprap dropped into the river, is the shoreline.

SEGMENT 5

McNARY DAM TO CLATSOP SPIT

Total Distance: 284.8 miles (458.3 km)

Segment 5 consists of nine one-day journeys from McNary Dam west through the Cascade Mountains and Coast Range to the Pacific Ocean. It has everything a paddler could want in an adventure—long stretches on reservoirs, big open water, desertlike heat, gale-force winds, canyons and basalt-walled gorges, rainforest vegetation, tides, current, oceangoing ships, large urban centers, sand islands, and sea lions. It's a world of extremes, yet under good weather conditions, one of the most pleasant 284 miles (457 km) along the Columbia.

With the added flow from the Snake River above McNary Dam, the Columbia is now the fourth largest river in North America and produces enough power to light the Pacific Northwest. Below McNary are the final three main-stem dams, including one of the first dams built on the river, Bonneville Dam. The river is one long and wide pool from McNary, along the scablands, into the Columbia River Gorge, and through the Cascades. Below Bonneville Dam, though, the river changes character, as the tide, current, and big ships demand the paddler adjust to new hazards and acquire a deep respect for its power and size.

LEG 27: McNary Dam to Boardman

Distance: 22 miles (35.4 km)
Paddle Time: 5 to 8 hours

River View

The leg from **McNary Dam** to **Boardman** provides a variety of scenic shoreline from white sandy beaches to heavily foliaged, inaccessible wetlands. Put-ins are on both sides of the river below the dam, but the most convenient is a gravel beach in the **McNary Wildlife Nature Area** on the Oregon side less than a mile (1.6 km) from the face of the dam.

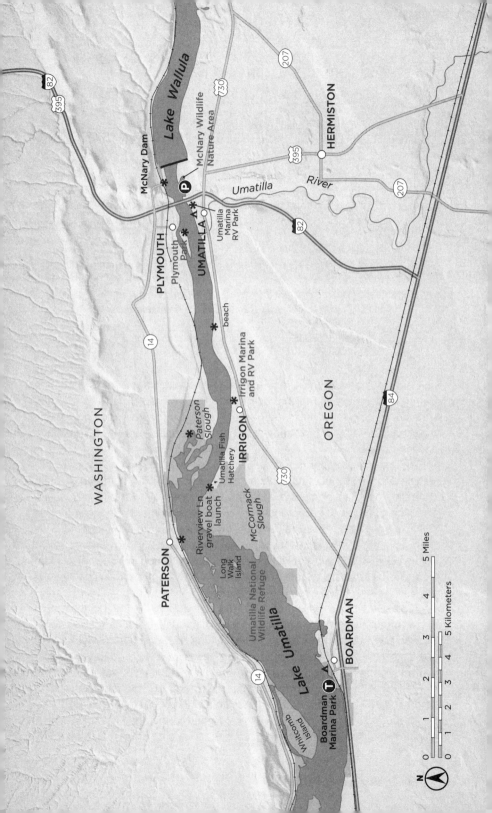

THE LEGEND OF SALMON AND WATER

The Columbia River Inter-Tribal Fish Commission (CRITFC) is dedicated to fishery management, helping tribal fishermen, protecting treaty rights, and sharing the tribes' salmon culture. The following is one of the legends about how the salmon and water helped us populate the Earth.

From a tribal legend, we learn that when the Creator was preparing to bring forth people onto the earth, He called a grand council of all creation. From them, He asked for a gift for these new creatures—a gift to help the people survive, since they would be quite helpless and require much assistance from them all. The very first to come forward was Salmon, who offered his body to feed the people. The second to come forward was Water, who promised to be the home to the salmon. In turn, everyone else gathered at the council gave the coming humans a gift, but it is significant that the very first two were Salmon and Water. In accordance with their sacrifice, these two receive a place of honor at traditional feasts throughout the Columbia Basin.

I chose to paddle the Oregon shoreline from McNary Dam to John Day Dam (Leg 29) because of the lay of the shoreline, parks, small towns, and access, but both sides make for excellent day trips. The Washington shoreline is also paralleled by railroad tracks and a two-lane state highway, but has good access as well.

The paddle begins in the fast-flowing water from the dam's spillway, but within several miles (3.2 km), it becomes lakelike, especially in the fall as **Lake Umatilla,** the reservoir behind John Day Dam, pools almost to McNary Dam. Other than an unusual chop under the Interstate 82 Umatilla Bridge, 1.5 miles (2.4 km) from the face of the dam, the paddle to Boardman is tour-like. This leg runs straight west for 10 miles (16 km), then takes a turn to the northwest before bending southwest as it passes through the **Umatilla National Wildlife Refuge.** The easiest and safest paddling line (away from the main channel and tug traffic) parallels the Oregon shoreline.

The route passes the **Umatilla Marina** after 1 mile (1.6 km) and the mouth of the **Umatilla River** at the 2.2-mile (3.5 km) mark. There are many small dune-shaped beaches along the south bank, but the best one is an obvious sandy spit 5.7 miles (9.2 km) from the put-in. This beach can also be accessed by car via Umatilla by following Oregon Highway 730 and Pleasant View Road. The river has great length and breadth on this leg, and it seems like it takes hours before the I-82 bridge finally disappears from sight as you make the turn.

At approximately 9 miles (14.5 km) is **Irrigon Marina and RV Park,** another nice take-out if wind conditions turn sour. From here it's another 5 miles (8 km) to the river's turn southwest and the Umatilla islands. There are many places to stop along the shore, but they are mostly gravel and rock, with an occasional unmaintained fishing access.

The islands of the Umatilla National Wildlife Refuge begin less than 2 miles (3.2 km) from the bend. For the most part, they are protected from unnecessary public access by weedy shallows, trees, and dense foliage. There are, however, canal-like passages that can be navigated easily through and around the milfoil and more vegetated shallows. Paddling between the islands and the mainland avoids the boat and barge traffic in the main channel and provides a unique opportunity to view flocks of white pelicans, Canada geese, and numerous varieties of ducks up close. The last small, treed island, shaped like a teardrop, is only hundreds of feet wide (61 m) but has a sand-and-gravel spit on the upriver side to pull out on. Take a break here, because it is 5 miles (8 km) in big, open water to **Boardman Marina Park,** a well-maintained facility that has a protected bay and excellent take-out at the boat launch.

Tugboats pushing barges on the Columbia River from the Pacific to the mouth of the Snake River and beyond to Lewiston, Idaho, rely on shore markers and buoys to navigate the river safely.

This area of the river is over 2.5 miles (4 km) wide in places, so if there's so much as a breeze, seek the south shoreline.

Hazards include big, open water; swift and turbulent flow below the dam; high winds and waves; and tugs with barges.

FLOW AND SEASON: McNary Dam is a run-of-the-river dam, so flow will vary with the season and spill-off to John Day Dam. Regardless, Lake Umatilla runs to the foot of McNary Dam, so any fast-moving water in the spring will be close to the dam. The best time to paddle this leg is May through October.

PUT-INS: *Oregon.* McNary Wildlife Nature Area, 0.7 mile (1.1 km) from spillway, exit 1 off I-82, 3rd St east to dam (primary); Umatilla Marina RV Park, exit 1, 3rd St to Quincy Ave (secondary). *Washington.* Plymouth Park, off WA 14 and Plymouth Rd; unmaintained gravel shoreline below dam, 0.64 mile (1 km) from spillway, exit 131 off I-82 to McNary Rd and dam.

TAKE-OUTS: Unmaintained Pleasant View Rd beach, 5.9 miles (9.5 km) on south shore, off US 730; Irrigon Marina and RV Park boat launch and park, 9 miles (14.5 km), 10th St NE off US 730; unmaintained Riverview Ln gravel boat launch, 12 miles (19.3 km), W 8th Rd off US 730 to Riverview Ln; Boardman Marina Park boat launch, 22 miles (35.4 km), N Main St off I-84 to Marine Dr NE. All take-outs listed are in Oregon and distances are from the McNary Wildlife Natural Area put-in.

SERVICES: Umatilla and Boardman, both located on the river, are small communities with limited motel facilities, groceries, and gas. Hermiston, located just off US 395 less than 7 miles (11.3 km) east of Umatilla, has numerous chain motels, grocery and convenience stores, and restaurants.

CAMPING: Umatilla Marina RV Park (see Put-ins); Sand Station Recreation Area, above McNary Dam off US 730; Boardman Marina Park (see Take-outs).

Passage

I paddled this leg in early September on a mostly calm, 90-degree day, with a slight wind to my back for the final 5 miles (8 km) to Boardman Marina Park. It took me under 6 hours at a relaxed pace. I launched off a gravel beach from the McNary Wildlife Nature Area just below the spillway on the south bank. The north shore is also accessible to paddlers, but the put-in is directly below the

IF ONLY WE HAD LISTENED

If we could go back in history and change some decisions, the building of the four Snake River dams would be high on that list. In 1949, long before the dams were constructed through the 1960s and '70s, decimating salmon and steelhead runs, the state of Washington Department of Fisheries, in an annual report, warned the governor and legislature about this serious threat to salmon. According to the report, the dams would put an unreasonable burden on the taxpayers to subsidize barging from Pasco to Lewiston and jeopardize more than half the salmon production in the Columbia River in doing so. The Department of Fisheries believed the four dams were a serious enough threat to the Snake and Columbia River's fishery that they consistently opposed the project. Unfortunately, the federal and state governments didn't listen.

At 7365 feet (2245 m), McNary is the longest dam on the Columbia River.

dam's locks and upriver from a protruding rock peninsula just a mile (1.6 km) from the dam, which could create unusual turbulence and whirlpools as you paddle to the center of the river.

Once I had passed the Interstate-82 bridge, I paralleled the vegetated, development-free shoreline, which had numerous public access points, including the Riverview Lane gravel boat launch near the Umatilla Fish Hatchery. Boat and barge traffic was almost nonexistent, but I stayed clear of the main channel. Close to the crest of where the river turns to the southwest, I entered the Umatilla National Wildlife Refuge's **McCormack Slough,** a section of the river with shallows, wetlands, and islands.

Rather than paddle in the deeper water of the main channel to avoid the milfoil and other water weeds, I chose to weave my way through the inside passage of the slough, past **Long Walk Island** and smaller islands—a good choice, as it turned out. I saw not only a significant number of white pelicans, blue herons, ducks, and geese, but also a large concentration of salmon, steelhead, and several bottom feeders. The fish were plainly visible on the light-colored sandy bottom a few feet below the surface in weed-free areas, and spooked only when I paddled close. I took a short break on the last small island before venturing out into the wide expanse of water near Boardman. After 5 miles (8 km), I paddled into the protected manmade cove of Boardman Marina Park.

LEG 28: Boardman to Arlington

Distance: 27 miles (43.5 km)
Paddle Time: 6 to 8.5 hours

River View

The leg from **Boardman** to **Arlington** marks the beginning of the river's run into the Columbia Gorge. To this point, the Columbia from its source has bounced off towering cliffs, powered its way through gaps of minor hills, and eaten into basalt flows, but here the river is forced to cut its way through the Cascade Mountains. It's as if the Columbia is finally tired of avoiding obstacles and decides to straighten like a pole and push west at all costs. The paddler's dilemma, of course, is the inevitable wind and waves from the west and through the gorge that make this section of river from Boardman to Bonneville Dam the best wind- and kite surfing in the world—and at times, a paddler's nightmare.

From **Boardman Marina Park,** the river begins to narrow to a mile (1.6 km) or less for the remainder of its journey to the Pacific. Only around Astoria does the Columbia resemble a lake again, rather than a snakelike river. Cross the

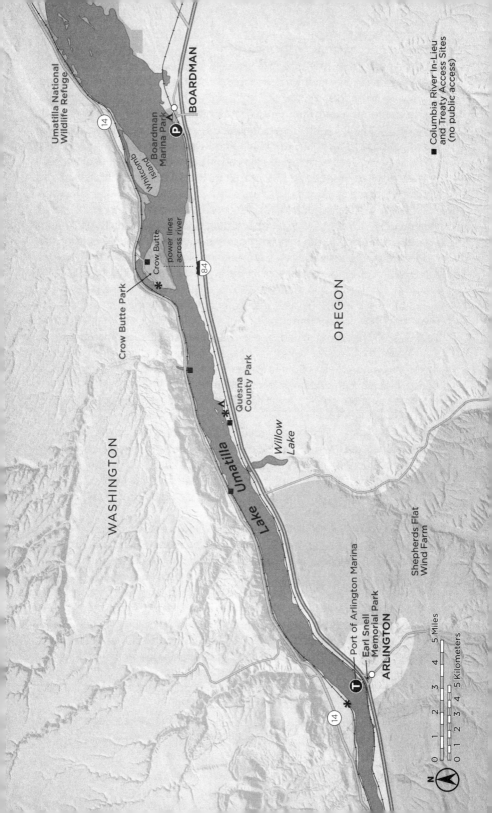

wide-open pool for 5 miles (8 km) to the rocky point where the Columbia curves ever so gently to the southwest, and then follow the rocky, bushy shoreline for the rest of the paddle to Arlington.

Be aware of underwater rock hazards offshore. Not only are there large boulders, some placed by the ice age floods and others by the railroad, but shoals of basalt flow that were submerged when John Day Dam was built. There are few places to stop along the paddle and get out of your boat because of the terrain: angular basalt boulders, short 10-foot cliffs, and thick, willowlike and thorny brush.

The first good take-out with vehicle access is **Quesna County Park,** just off Interstate-84, 13 miles (21 km) from Boardman Marina Park (Leg 27's take-out). A boat launch facility with minimal amenities, Quesna County Park is located inside a large protected bay with two entrances separated by a long, narrow, rocky spit and island vegetation. On a foggy day, you could miss the first entrance, but the second entrance is obvious. The boat ramp and parking area are at the west end of the park. Adjacent to the county park is the Columbia River Inter-Tribal Fish Commission's (CRITFC) Three-Mile Canyon treaty fishing access site, which is restricted for use by members of the four member tribes: the Nez Perce, Umatilla, Warm Springs, and Yakama nations (see sidebar). If there's any wind, Quesna County Park is a good place to exit the river, because the next take-out is in Arlington almost 14 miles (22.5 km) downriver.

From the county park, stay to the south shoreline, but again, be aware of solid rock and large boulders just under the surface. For a few miles the shoreline is short vertical cliff, the remnant of one of the many basalt flows. Pull-outs to take a break are few and difficult to access. The view of Mount Hood downriver almost 100 miles (161 km) away is spectacular, but it is a constant reminder that the next 8.5 miles (13.7 km) are straight, wide-open water without any land protrusions to break the wind, so the paddle to Arlington should only be done on a windless to low-wind day.

Three miles (4.8 km) west of the park is **Willow Lake,** which does not have public vehicle access, but the Columbia River shoreline can be accessed with difficulty by the Heppner Road exit off I-84. From Willow Lake, you will share the shoreline with the railroad, which has built its track on large-boulder riprap dropped into the river. There are a few rough pull-outs to rest, though, where small natural peninsulas stand out from the artificial riprap shoreline.

The river takes a slight bend to the southwest 3 miles (4.8 km) from Arlington. You will see the grain silos at the **Arlington Marina** and lower wind turbines from the **Shepherds Flat Wind Farm.** The entrance to the marina is on the downriver or west end past the silo. Once inside the protected bay, there are numerous places to take out along the shore, including the boat launch facility or the beach in Arlington's **Earl Snell Memorial Park.**

Hazards include big, open water; high wind and waves; tugboats with barges; and submerged shoreline obstructions.

IN-LIEU AND TREATY FISHING ACCESS SITES

The Columbia River Inter-Tribal Fish Commission (CRITFC) operates and maintains thirty-one fishing sites from McNary Dam to Bonneville Dam; twenty-six are treaty fishing access sites and five are in-lieu sites. Of the twenty-six seasonal-use treaty access sites for tribal members, four sites are shared with the public. In-lieu sites are for tribal members only, and these facilities allow year-round residency. The access sites were provided by Congress for exclusive use by the four tribes—the Nez Perce Tribe, Confederated Tribes of the Umatilla Reservation, Confederated Tribes of the Warm Springs Reservation of Oregon, and the Confederated Tribes and Bands of the Yakama Nation—to offset the loss of their traditional fishing grounds flooded by the reservoirs behind the dams. Site access and violations of laws at the sites are subject to tribal law enforcement.

Do not use any site other than the four with shared-use facilities: Sundale Park (WA), LaPage Park (OR), North Shore (WA), and Avery (WA). To contact the CRITFC enforcement office, call 800-487-3474. For information on CRITFC or access sites, call 541-296-6010.

Three Mile Canyon on the Oregon side of the river is just one of thirty-one tribal treaty fishing access sites on the Columbia River below McNary Dam.

FLOW AND SEASON: There is usually no discernible flow below Boardman. The best time to paddle this leg is between March and October. Wind and waves are the major factor on this leg, so any windless day would be ideal.

PUT-IN: Boardman Marina Park, exit 164 off I-84 to N Main St, west on Marine Dr NE.

TAKE-OUTS: Quesna County Park, 13.1 miles (21.1 km), exit 151 off I-84, Three-Mile Canyon exit; Port of Arlington Marina, 26.8 miles (43.1 km), exit 132 off I-84, Arlington; and Earl Snell Memorial Park, 26.9 (43.3 km), exit 132 off I-84, Arlington. All distances are from the put-in.

SERVICES: Services are limited to Boardman, Arlington, and Biggs Junction, all of which have motels, restaurants, gas and convenience stores, and sometimes a grocery store. There are no paddling services.

CAMPING: Full-service RV/camping along the river is available at Boardman Marina Park (see Put-in); and limited-service RV/camping is available at Quesna County Park (see Take-outs).

Passage

I chose to continue my paddle along the Oregon side of the Columbia on Lake Umatilla for the next two legs to the John Day Dam, not just because Boardman was my previous take-out but because the south shore has small bays and rocky points that offer some protection from the wind; also vehicle access along the paddle route, although limited, is convenient. The Washington side has good access to the river, but too many of the boat launch/access points are CRITFC access sites and, as such, are not usable for the general public (see sidebar on treaty fishing access sites).

I exited Boardman Marina Park in calm, flat water and pointed my bow across the large bay toward a tall, latticed transmission tower on the bank of the river 6 miles (9.7 km) away. Mount Hood boldly stood out in the distance, a small Fuji-like image on the horizon, which would be my companion for most of the paddle to Hood River. My route took me close to the main channel and possible barge traffic, but few barges seemed to be operating, and it was worth not having to follow the long inset shoreline. Besides my usual early-morning companions, paired geese and numerous ducks, the river was quiet and welcoming.

Just beyond where the transmission tower and powerlines span the river, it bends slightly to the southwest. On the north side of this bend is Washington's

SHEPHERDS FLAT WIND FARM

As of 2013, the second-largest wind farm in the United States is based in Arlington, Oregon. It has 338 turbines and generates 845 megawatts of electricity, which can power 173,000 homes. The project's total cost was $1.9 billion; developers paid $650 million, and taxpayers $1.24 billion. The developer of the wind farm, Caithness Energy, was being investigated for abuse of the energy tax credit program in 2013.

Shepherds Flat Wind Farm near Arlington is one of the world's largest corporate wind farms.

Crow Butte Park, a 1500-acre (607 ha) island connected to the main shore by a manmade road. It's owned by the US Army Corps of Engineers, but operated by the Port of Benton.

About 7.5 miles (12 km) from Boardman, I found a tiny bay with a 6-foot section of gravel shore where cattle were able to reach water. I pulled out there to stand up and stretch, and ended up waiting to avoid the multiple wave sets from a tug with barges pushing upriver. Once the waves had dissipated I took off, keeping 50 to 100 feet (15.2 to 30.5 m) offshore to avoid the rocks just under the surface. I noticed a number of other small gravel beaches, but for the most part the shoreline is inaccessible due to offshore rock and thick thorny bushes and vegetation. After 13 miles (21 km), I paddled into the well-protected

DEATH, TAXES, AND, YES, GARBAGE

As we paddle along the river deep in the gorge, we see power being generated by the numerous dams blocking the river and by the hundreds of wind turbines lining the basalt breaks. What we don't see is the green power generated by methane created by two of the largest landfills in the Pacific Northwest, located just above the river, the Columbia Ridge Landfill above Arlington and across the river the Roosevelt Regional Landfill above Roosevelt. These two landfills take all the garbage from Seattle; Portland; Guam; Oahu, Hawaii; and many other cities and counties up and down the coast. It's the railroad along the banks of the Columbia and the barging on the river that make these landfills economically possible.

Landfills are notoriously difficult to site and develop. No one wants one in their backyard, but the location and geology above the gorge makes this area ideal for landfills. The two plateaus on either side of the Columbia are remote and sparsely populated, and the landfills sit over hundreds of feet (61 m) of basalt covered by an impervious clay layer up to 300 feet thick (91 m). If the 60-mil liner ever leaks its toxic goo, studies estimate it would take 15,000 years for the groundwater to reach the Columbia.

The more recently established Roosevelt Regional Landfill takes in more than 2 million tons of garbage a year, of which 97 percent is delivered by two BNSF trains a day with 125 to 150 containers filled with garbage. Roosevelt produces 37 megawatts of electricity, enough to power 30,000 homes, while Arlington's Columbia Ridge presently produces 6.4 megawatts, enough for 5000 homes. With the region's hydroelectric power, wind turbines, and methane, the Columbia River Basin produces more green energy than almost any other place on Earth.

bay of Quesna County Park, pulled up on the gravel beach alongside the boat launch, and had lunch.

To this point the river curved away from I-84 and the railway and had been relatively free of noise, but that changed within 2 miles (3.2 km) of the park. Leaving the flat farmland stretching out from the river, I was now entering into the steep, basalt-walled gorge. The sound of truck traffic and the numerous trains on both sides of the river reverberated off the towering walls and over the water. This leg was not going to be the quiet and peaceful paddle that many of the legs along the river had been, but the scenery made up for the noise.

I paddled out of the park and hugged the shoreline, passing the opening under the tracks and freeway to Willow Lake 2.5 miles (4 km) out. I knew that Lewis and Clark paddled this section from Umatilla to Arlington, almost

208 years before, on October 19, 1805 on a river that was churning with rapids through basalt islands lined up like bowling pins, and only 0.25 mile (0.4 km) wide near Arlington. Their passage was most likely noisy as well, but from the natural sound of water rushing through a constricted gorge and cascading up against rock, rather than the artificial sound of commerce and vehicles. But even though through time we have changed the Columbia's character and drowned many of its challenges, it was still mine alone on that day and for most of my journey from the source.

The shoreline didn't change much to Arlington, although along this section the railroad paralleled the shoreline. Where the track came in contact with the river, the railroad had built its track on large basalt riprap that fell steeply into the water. I pulled out once more on another gravel beach to ease the soreness in my back, and then made the turn more southwesterly to Arlington, which I could see 3 miles (4.8 km) away. As I approached the Port of Arlington Marina entrance, a large raft of coots and mallards separated, and then finally flew off. Inside the bay, I paddled over to a gravel shore just before the boat launch and took out to end a great day on the river.

LEG 29: Arlington to John Day Dam

Distance: 25.4 miles (40.9 km)
Paddle Time: 5.5 to 7.5 hours

River View

The leg from **Arlington** to **John Day Dam** has one of the longest straight sections of river along the entire Columbia. After a short 3.5-mile (5.6 km) paddle to a slight bump along the shoreline, you can see over 11 miles (17.7 km) downriver to a towering cliff where the Columbia curves northwest. Given the lack of access to the river and this lengthy basalt-walled wind tunnel, paddle this leg only in calm conditions.

Here the Columbia continues its journey from the desertlike grasslands and sagebrush where even rattlesnakes have to hide in the summer, deeper into the snow-capped Cascades, exposing multiple vertical layers of volcanic basalt flows in every thickness. In the spring, the hillsides and canyons are shades of green grasses dotted with wildflowers in as many colors as a crayon pack, while in midsummer through fall all the light yellow and brown pastels of dried plants dominate, highlighting the reddish-browns of the basalt, sunlit pillars, and deep, shaded clefts in the walls.

This leg has an abundance of wildlife. On the rolling farmland and shrub-steppe above **Blalock Canyon,** pronghorn antelope can be found grazing on wild grasses, mule deer browse along the slopes and canyons, and Rocky

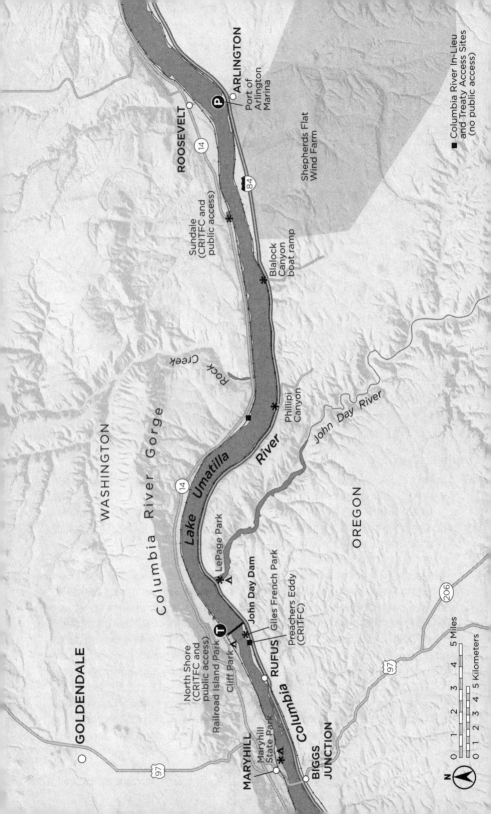

Mountain bighorn sheep make their home in the transition zone between the grassy slopes and vertical walls, easily spotted between Arlington and John Day Dam. Other wildlife spottings might include coyotes, beavers, chukars, eagles, and waterfowl.

The paddle begins at the **Port of Arlington Marina** and in calm conditions leaves the shoreline for a 3.5-mile (5.6 km) beeline to a broad peninsula. The railroad tracks parallel the river, while Interstate 84 takes a straight route onto a high bench and then down again past the peninsula. For over 6 miles (9.7 km) there's very little truck and car noise, but one or two trains rumble by every hour. With the tracks near the shore and sometimes creating the shoreline, it's difficult to find good take-outs. For much of the leg, the shoreline is artificial riprap dumped into the river by the railroad as ballast for its track. Always be aware of boulders under the surface near the railroad tracks.

Eight miles (12.9 km) from Arlington is a rock jetty that marks the boat entrance to a concrete tunnel under the railroad tracks, which leads to a gravel boat launch on the other side of the tunnel. The boat launch is accessed off the Blalock Canyon exit, and the gate to the launch area is usually open. You can at least take a break here before tackling the next 6 miles (9.7 km) to **Phillipi Canyon,** an exit off I-84 with a rough take-out if necessary. These two exits off I-84 are the only vehicle-access points on the Oregon side before **LePage Park,** at the mouth of the **John Day River,** or the **Railroad Island Park boat launch** area next to the dam's locks on the Washington side. Just before the northwest bend in the river and the Phillipi Canyon exit, there is exposed bedrock in the shallows 300 yards (274.3 m) offshore. This is the "tip of the iceberg," with a lot more rock just below the surface than above, so be careful paddling near this hazard.

Phillipi Canyon would be a rough take-out over railroad riprap, but possible if the weather turns sour. From Phillipi Canyon the river takes a wide 9-mile (14.5 km) bend to avoid spectacular basalt cliffs on its journey to LePage Park. The paddle follows the shoreline, which is again primarily railroad riprap but also short vertical cliffs that plunge into the river.

You will start to see many more foam floats anchored to the river bottom at various distances from shore and corresponding polypropylene rope attached to boulders and cliffs on the shoreline. These are permanent markers for the tribal fishermen, and they have spray-painted their initials or a number on the rock to let others know whose salmon fishing waters these belong to. During spring Chinook season, the fishermen attach gill nets to the floats and shore to catch the salmon going upriver to spawn. These floats and nets increase in number the closer you get to Bonneville Dam.

At the apex of the bend, the shoreline has more vegetation, including a few large shade trees. Three miles from the dam, the **Columbia River Gorge** opens up before you and, as if sitting on the top of the dam, there is Mount Hood. It's a surreal sight on a clear day and well worth the paddle.

You can take out at LePage Park, a beautiful public facility owned and operated by the Corps of Engineers, or paddle 2.5 more miles (4 km) across the river to the Railroad Island Park boat ramp (also known as **North Shore treaty access site**) on the Washington side, located in a protected bay. To find Railroad Island Park, which is not visible from **Lake Umatilla,** paddle through a massive culvert under the railroad tracks just 0.5 mile (0.8 km) from the dam's locks, and then left around a rocky point. The crossing from LePage Park in front of the dam to Railroad Island Park can be windy. Be aware of tugs with barges entering or leaving the locks before paddling along the north shore near the dam. The tugs travel close to the shore here, and you don't want to be between a tug and barge and the rock walls.

FLOW AND SEASON: As in Leg 28, there is usually no discernible flow in this section of the river, and the best time to paddle this leg is between March and October. Wind and waves are the major factor on this leg, so any windless day would be ideal.

PUT-INS: Port of Arlington Marina or Earl Snell Memorial Park, both in Arlington and accessed off I-84, exit 137 into Arlington (see Leg 28).

TAKE-OUTS: Blalock Canyon boat launch, 8.4 miles (13.5 km), exit 129 off I-84; Phillipi Canyon, 14.6 miles (23.5 km), exit 123 off I-84 (unmaintained and rough take-out); LePage Park, 23.5 miles (37.8 km), exit 114 off I-84 (shared tribal and public access); Railroad Island Park (North Shore CRITFC and public access site) boat ramp (Washington side), 25.8 miles (41.5 km), off WA 14 to John Day Dam Rd and public access area. All distances are from the Port of Arlington Marina boat ramp.

SERVICES: Services along this section of the river are limited. Arlington has one motel, several restaurants, a grocery store, and a convenience store. Biggs Junction has several motels, truck stops with restaurants, and convenience stores. For more comprehensive services, The Dalles is 25 miles (40.2 km) downriver from John Day Dam on I-84.

CAMPING: There are numerous opportunities along the river for RV/trailer camping, but limited tent camping outside of designated campgrounds. *Oregon.* Quesna County Park, exit 151 off I-84; Port of Arlington Marina (RV only), exit 137 off I-84; LePage Park, exit 114 off I-84; Giles French Park, exit 109 off I-84; Deschutes State Park, exit 104 off I-84. *Washington.* Maryhill State Park, US 97 bridge below John Day Dam; Cliff Park, primitive campsites accessed off WA 14 and John Day Dam Rd.

The Arlington Marina is well-protected from the wind and waves commonly found along this stretch of the river.

Passage

I paddled this leg on the last day of March, and both the weather and scenery were stunning. As I launched from the Port of Arlington Marina, the temperature was just a few degrees above freezing, and the giant windmill blades looming over Arlington and standing sentinel on the horizon downriver, like a forest of white trees, were not adding a kilowatt to the region's grid. Joyce shoved me away from the gravel beach, waved good-bye, and hurried back to the SUV for warmth and an additional hour of sleep. As I left the marina, the sun peeked over the gorge walls and landed on my back. This took the chill off the early-morning departure, and I was soon too warm in my lightweight paddling jacket.

I followed the shoreline, which for the most part was large-boulder riprap built up along the river by the railroad. Although trains went by regularly on the half hour, and I could hear the reverberation off the canyon walls from I-84 traffic as it moved away from the river, these sounds did not detract from the overall experience. This section of the Columbia River Gorge is very similar to Tibet—its beauty is in the expanse of the scene and the desertlike terrain amid so much water. With each stroke of the paddle, I felt enriched by my isolation on the river and the vistas around me. Those who were traveling through at a high rate of speed, locked in their cars, trucks, and trains, were missing the purpose of being in this incredible place.

JOHN DAY

There's a town of John Day, a John Day River, a John Day County Park, a Best Western John Day Inn, a John Day Dam, and more than likely, a few young John Days running around the Lower Columbia Basin, all named after a . . . fur trapper? Not just an ordinary fur trapper, though, but best known for being robbed and stripped naked by Indians near the river that now bears his name.

John Day was born in Virginia in 1770. He traveled west in 1810 with John Jacob Astor's Pacific Fur Company. Day became ill while trapping in the Snake River country of Idaho and was left to recuperate by the Astor party in the company of Ramsey Crooks, another trapper. The next spring, Day and Crooks made their way to the area of the John Day River, where they were assaulted by the Indians. In desperate condition, they were rescued and taken to Astoria by Robert Stuart and friends.

Day is said to have eventually suffered a mental breakdown or severe depression. Nevertheless, he continued to trap throughout the region until his death in 1820.

The National Park Service archive website can't explain his notoriety, except to say, "With scant historic documentation to explain it, trapper John Day became a legend in the region." At least he wasn't another politician.

Pronghorn antelope in the open fields above the canyon's vertical basalt walls near Phillipi Canyon

At Blalock Canyon, I located the cement tunnel under the railroad track just before the rock jetty, paddled through, and went to the rough gravel boat launch for a break. This is a US Army Corps of Engineers public access point in an area of the river that can be exceptionally windy. There were no gill nets strung between the numerous foam floats I had seen along this leg, so I knew the spring Chinook season had not started. The public access area was empty except for Joyce, who was still in her down coat despite the radiant warmth off the gorge walls. I hydrated and ate a snack, and then put back in for the stretch to Phillipi Canyon, clearly visible 6.3 miles (10.1 km) downriver.

I-84 joins the railroad tracks again along this section of the river, and the vehicle noise off the vertical, sometimes overhanging 900-foot (274 m) walls sounded as if I was sitting next to a Los Angeles freeway. But again, I ignored the sound and enjoyed the glassy water and incredible views. My next stop was alongside the railroad riprap below the Phillipi Canyon exit. It's a rough take-out because of the riprap, if you have to pull out, but I was just taking a break. There were much easier (though not vehicle-accessible) take-outs farther downriver on small rock beaches.

Past Phillipi Canyon I paddled directly offshore, watching closely for boulders just under the surface. For the most part, the 9 miles (14.5 km) to LePage Park follow the railroad sitting atop large-rock riprap, but occasionally short vertical natural cliff areas, with rickety tribal fishing platforms, provided brief though interesting distractions from the miles of manmade railroad line. I passed a small natural cove, potentially a nice rest stop (although bushy), 4.6 miles (7.4 km) from Phillipi Canyon, and pulled out onto an even smaller cove's gravel bar, 6.7 miles (10.8 km) out, to stretch. I avoided walking into the brush above the take-out because of ticks, which are common in this area this time of year.

With I-84 high on a plateau and separated from the river by rock buttes, I found the paddling close to shore and along the cliffs quiet and pleasant. At the apex of the bend in the river, I rounded a rock cliff, paddled under the canopy of several shore trees, and looked out over a picturesque view of Mount Hood, 56 miles (90.1 km) to the west, sitting on the top of John Day Dam and the river, more like a Japanese landscape painting than real.

My intended take-out above the dam was on the Washington side of the river, but I chose to paddle less than a 0.25 mile (0.4 km) up the John Day River to LePage Park first before crossing the Columbia to Railroad Island Park near the dam's locks. Just as I was leaving LePage Park and making the 2.7-mile (4.3 km) paddle to the take-out, a tug with barges came around the bend upriver. I waited in the center of the river for it to begin slowing down as it approached the dam, and then paddled 0.5 mile (0.8 km) behind it as it approached the locks, taking the four sets of bow waves and engine turbulence at a right angle. I then found the boat tunnel, a large steel corrugated culvert, under the tracks and paddled around a rock island to the Corps of Engineers' Railroad Island Park boat ramp, a shared facility with CRITFC.

The tugboat *Hurricane* pushes four barges as it leaves the John Day Dam locks for Portland.

LEG 30: John Day Dam to The Dalles Dam

Distance: 25.4 miles (40.9 km)
Paddle Time: 5 to 7 hours

River View

The leg from **John Day Dam** to **The Dalles Dam** is one of the most pleasant paddles through the **Columbia River Gorge** and still on the desertlike side of the Cascades. The Columbia leaves John Day Dam and continues its journey west past **Maryhill State Park** and **Biggs Junction.** It is then split by the 2-mile-long (1.6 km), kidney-shaped **Miller Island** before being turned by an armored basalt wall rising beyond the mouth of the **Deschutes River,** which flows through a treed marshy area into the Columbia from the south. Then the Columbia makes its way around the massive basalt wall on the south and turns southwest, passing on the Oregon side the Yakama and Warm Springs **Celilo Village**; the US Army Corps of Engineer's **Celilo Park**; and a CRITFC tribal access park.

Prior to 1957 and the construction of The Dalles Dam, this 12-mile (19.3 km) section from Celilo to the dam was well known to David Thompson, Lewis and Clark, and other travelers who ventured upon the Columbia for the river's 82-foot (25 m) cumulative drop at high water and its plunging cascades, tumbling rapids, and boat-eating whirlpools. Celilo and other native settlements and fishing camps are known to have been located in this area for the past 15,000 years,

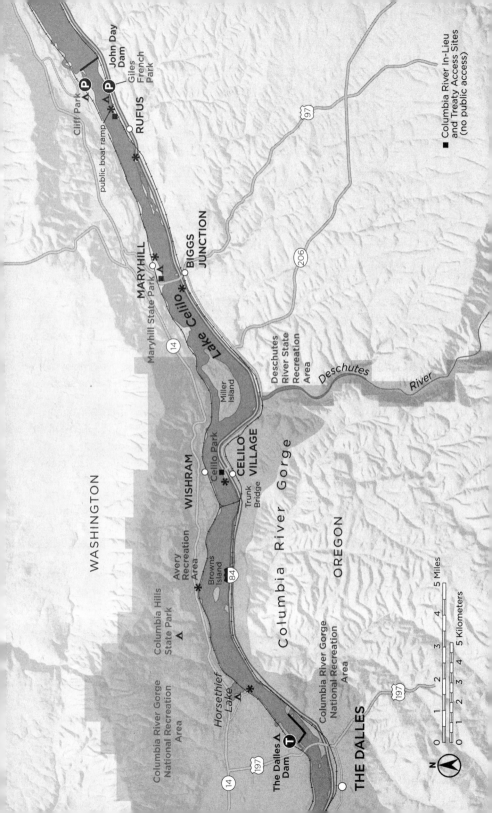

WY-KAN-USH-PUM: SALMON PEOPLE

The Columbia River Inter-Tribal Fish Commission (CRITFC) has four goals, one of which is to share salmon culture and the importance of salmon—not only to the tribes but to everyone who lives in the Pacific Northwest. This is what they believe:

Salmon are the icon of this place. They are valued as food, as a resource, and as a representation of the wildness and wilderness for which the Pacific Northwest is known. They shape our land use policies and power grid. Whether they realize it or not, every single person in the Northwest is Wy-Kan-Ush-Pum. We are all Salmon People. Let us work together to protect and restore salmon—this fish that unites us.

making Celilo the oldest continuously inhabited community in North America until it was flooded by **Lake Celilo,** the reservoir behind The Dalles Dam.

In the spring, when the dams are releasing snowmelt, there is still some flow through this area, but scarcely noticeable. Downriver from Celilo and the **Oregon Trail Trunk Bridge,** a 1912 railroad bridge spanning the Columbia, the river widens and flows directly west for 4 miles (6.4 km) and then bends southwest for another 4 miles to The Dalles Dam.

Browns Island is in the center of the river 2.5 miles (4 km) from the railroad bridge and blends into the shorelines so well it looks as if it's part of the bank. The main channel is to the north of the island. The Tidewater and Shaver tugs move fast in this area, so if you decide to cross the river, clear the channel as quickly as possible. Depending on your route around Miller Island upriver, you may want to cross under calm conditions to slice a few tenths of a mile off the bend of the river and back across again to the take-out. I stayed along the north shoreline and found this path to be simple and safe, although a bit longer. This 8-mile (12.9 km) stretch past the railroad bridge can be windy because the canyon is in line with the prevailing winds.

There are two good escape take-outs on the north shoreline downriver from the railroad bridge in case you need to cut your journey short: **Avery Recreation Area,** a shared-use facility with the tribes; and a boat ramp at **Columbia Hills State Park** at **Horsethief Park;** both have convenient vehicle access. The take-out above The Dalles Dam is located at a public boat launch area in a protected cove next to the dam's locks.

Celilo Park, exit 206 off Interstate-84, is the only good take-out with vehicle access on the south shore. This US Army Corps of Engineers facility has a boat ramp and campsites. The south shoreline from Celilo Park to The Dalles Dam is a rough take-out at best because of railroad and highway riprap, but doable in a pinch.

Hazards include swift, turbulent water below the dam; high wind and waves; and tug and barge traffic in the main channel and close to the put-in and take-out at the dams.

FLOW AND SEASON: There is good flow from the put-in to Miller Island in the spring and early summer. The best time to paddle this leg is between March and October.

PUT-INS: *Washington.* Cliff Park (primary), 1 mile (1.6 km), gravel access, off WA 14 and John Day Dam Rd. *Oregon.* Giles French Park, 2 miles (3.2 km), maintained boat launch, exit 109 off I-84. All distances are from the John Day Dam spillway.

TAKE-OUTS: *Washington.* Maryhill State Park boat ramp, 6.5 miles (10.5 km), off US 97; Avery Recreation Area, 17 miles (27.4 km), off WA 14; Columbia Hills State Park boat ramp, 21 miles (33.8 km), off WA 14 at Horsethief Lake; and The Dalles Dam Locks boat ramp, 23.2 miles (37.3 km), at the dam with access off US 197 and The Dalles Dam access road. All distances are from the Cliff Park put-in. *Oregon.* Celilo Park boat ramp, 12.3 miles (19.8 km) from Giles French Park upriver from the tribal treaty access–only boat ramp).

SERVICES: The Dalles is a full-service community with motels, restaurants, grocery stores, and gas stations. Biggs Junction has gas stations and several nondescript motels and truck stop restaurants, while Rufus has very limited services. There are few services on the Washington side of the river along this leg.

CAMPING: There are numerous established and rough camping areas along this leg on both sides of the river. Cliff Park below John Day Dam has few amenities other than a good view of the river and a chemical toilet, but lots of flat open ground for either a tent or RV. Giles French Park has shade trees, flat ground, and a flush toilet, but no electricity, water, or wastewater disposal. Maryhill State Park has twenty campsites and fifty RV or utility sites, and is one of Washington's showcase state parks complete with all the amenities. Columbia Hills State Park (Horsethief Lake Campground) has a number of campsites and RV sites with one large toilet/shower facility. Celilo Park has free camping, lots of shade trees, and flush toilets, but no showers or RV amenities. Windsurfers like this section of river and use Celilo Park for access, so finding a camping spot can be a challenge. The take-out at The Dalles Dam Locks boat ramp has a few rough campsites and RV parking, but no amenities.

Mount Hood is visible to kayakers from McNary Dam well into the Columbia Gorge, such as in this area below John Day Dam.

Passage

This leg has everything a paddler would want—fast-moving water, protected bays, spectacular islands and cliffs, and numerous species of birds. I vacillated as to whether to put in on the Oregon or Washington side, but finally decided on Cliff Park on the north shore because I wouldn't have to cross the river; the put-in was less than a mile (1.6 km) from the dam; and there were good take-outs strategically placed along the paddle should the wind suddenly pick up—which it did that afternoon.

I slid off the pea-gravel beach easily into the shore eddy, and then paddled into the fast-flowing current below the dam. Besides the usual roiling and boiling associated with moving water, it was enjoyable to move along just out of casting range of the many fishermen trying to catch a spring Chinook. Mount Hood, lit up by the early-morning sunlight and framed by the dark basalt cliffs, looked as though it were bursting from the river. It was mid-April and surprisingly the day was as still as if I was sitting indoors. I knew this side of the river had the main channel, thus tug and barge traffic, so I stayed close to the shoreline just out of eddy range as I was swept past the many fishing spots on this side of the river. Within the hour I passed Maryhill State Park, 6 miles (9.7 km) from my put-in, and then paddled under the **Sam Hill Memorial Bridge** (US Highway 97). There was still a 2- to 3-mph (3.2- to 4.8-kmph) current under the bridge.

The river widened beyond the bridge, and I stayed with the current away from the shoreline, heading for a narrow passage north of Miller Island. As I rounded a prominent rocky point 2 miles (3.2 km) downriver, I turned due west into a circular bay with a grouping of mini rock islands river left and just upriver of Miller Island. There was a sizable seagull rookery on the largest of the five

THE COLUMBIA RIVER GORGE

The Columbia River Gorge is the only passageway through the Cascade Range for the Columbia River, which drains 259,000 square miles (670,800 sq km) of the Pacific Northwest watershed. The gorge, as defined, is 80 miles (129 km) long and begins at the Deschutes River east of the Cascades and ends at the Sandy River just upriver of Portland on the west side.

Ranging from 4000 feet (1219 m) to almost sea level and cutting a deep path through the Cascade Range, the river, and everything about it, is extreme, including the ecosystems. Near the Deschutes on the Columbia River Plateau, the annual precipitation is 10 inches (25.4 cm), only enough moisture for grasslands, cactus, and other shrub-steppe vegetation to thrive without irrigation. At the Sandy River in the Lower Columbia, the land and mountain slopes are lush and green, covered by bigleaf maple, Douglas fir, and western hemlock, the result of an annual precipitation of more than 100 inches (254 cm). The gorge has 800 species of wildflowers, 15 of which exist nowhere else on Earth.

Through this gorge, wind and water flow in great volumes. Atmospheric pressure differentials east and west of the Cascades create a wind-tunnel effect through the deep, narrow gorge, generating more than 35-mph (56-kmph) steady winds, while the average volume of water discharged at the mouth of the Columbia throughout the year is 265,000 cubic feet per second, the fourth-largest discharge by volume of any river in the United States.

Tribal fishermen mark their gill net and platform sites on the rocks along the shoreline with their initials or a tribal number.

small islands, and several blue herons were working the weedy shallows near the islands for fish fry.

The main channel of the Columbia flows southwest of Miller Island to where the Deschutes River enters, and then doglegs abruptly northwest to avoid an impenetrable wall of layered basalt near Celilo before turning west again, but some of the flow is captured and funneled through a narrow passage near the east end of Miller Island. This funnel effect increased the flow rate like it was being sucked through a straw, and I felt the river quicken through the 600-foot-wide (183 m) neck of the channel between the island and the mainland. For almost 2 miles (3.2 km) I was swept along as if the Columbia had regained some of its power before the dams pooled the river into one gigantic lake.

Once I was past Miller Island, I paddled into the main channel for a short distance past the village of **Wishram** and pointed my bow toward the north end of the Oregon Trail Trunk Bridge. Underneath me was Celilo Falls, lost to the rising waters of the dam. For the next 12 miles (19.3 km), the rapids, whirlpools, and falls that had given the Corps of Discovery more than enough trouble were no longer a threat, but I could imagine the terror some of those voyageurs must

Past Miller Island and the tribal fishing platforms, Lake Celilo broadens with Celilo Village to the south and Wishram to the north.

A DAM OF TEARS

In 1957, 10,000 people gathered to watch as Lake Celilo, the new reservoir behind The Dalles Dam, rose from the closed spillway gates and covered 11,000 years of tribal history and one of the greatest fisheries known to man, Celilo Falls. Tribal members were displaced and moved; the primitive, early village sites of Wyam and S'kin disappeared; and a place of trade, fishing, socializing, and culture for many tribes drowned—for another dam. Lewis and Clark knew only that this was the section of river they called "The Great Falls."

The tribes, commercial fishermen, noncommercial fishermen, and those opposed to another dam on the river testified against building The Dalles Dam, but Congress decided in 1950 that the electricity and flood control were just too valuable. The four inter-local tribes, the Nez Perce, Yakama, Warm Springs, and Umatilla, were compensated $26.8 million for their loss of culture and tradition, but many tribal members argued no amount of compensation could overcome the loss of their heritage.

have had as they were swept along in a cauldron of raging river, dodging rocks and whirlpools that would grab a man knocked overboard and take him into a graveyard of flotsam and river debris. I considered stopping at Celilo Park for a break, only a short 0.5 mile (0.8 km) off my route across the river, but decided against it as the wind seemed to be increasing.

There was still a slight current under the railroad bridge, but as I entered the big, open water the wind increased and I had to paddle hard to make any headway. I stayed close to the north shoreline, passing a gravel mining operation 1.5 miles (2.4 km) from the bridge. Several men were monitoring a long conveyor belt, which was being used to load a large barge attached to a tug. I paddled under the conveyor belt complex, much to the surprise of the men on the dock, but it was easier than paddling around the barge in the wind and waves now charging upriver.

Within a half hour, a 25–30-mph (40.2–48.2-kmph) wind had come up and the river was now in chop and turmoil with waves large enough to splash into my cockpit. I paddled into the wind for another mile (1.6 km) before reaching Avery Recreation Area, where I pulled out to wait out the storm, but by late afternoon the winds had increased and I knew my day was over.

I returned a few days later and put back in at Avery late that afternoon. There was a stiff northeast breeze sending water over my stern, but it certainly beat wind in my face. With the wind at my back, I paddled the 6 miles (9.7 km) to The Dalles Dam locks in an hour, staying close to the north shoreline. Only one tug and barge moved upriver near me, sending a series of bow and motor waves that seemed to die in the wind-driven chop moving downriver with me.

see the locks on the north side of the dam as I made my way along a -high (6.1 m) vertical basalt wall. There were few places to hide from any waves created by exiting tugs for the final 2 miles (3.2 km) to the take-out, which is in close proximity to the boats leaving the dam's locks, but I knew the next tug would be hours downriver. I had a pleasant paddle pushed by the wind to the boat ramp where Joyce was parked and waiting.

LEG 31: The Dalles Dam to Bonneville Dam

Distance: 44 miles (70.8 km)
Paddle Time: 10 to 13 hours

River View

The leg from **The Dalles Dam** to **Bonneville Dam** fulfills every paddler's dream: isolated, white sandy beaches; manicured parks with canopies of deciduous trees; a slight but obvious current; rocky points and bays; ospreys, eagles, and great blue herons; and even sea lions.

The put-in to **Lake Bonneville,** the reservoir behind Bonneville Dam, is at The Dalles **Riverfront Park,** less than 2 miles (3.2 km) from the spillway of the dam. The park opens Memorial Day and closes November 1, but the gravel beach launch area for kayaks and canoes can be accessed from the **The Dalles Marina Park** parking lot in the off-season. The river has lost a lot of its turbulence this far from the dam, but it still moves along through the narrow gorge at 4 to 5 mph (6.4 to 8 kmph). A rough put-in above Riverfront Park is possible at **Seufert County Park** across from the fish ladder, but the steep rocky bank and excessive turbulence through the rock islands so close to the dam make this a risky option and not recommended.

The river narrows quickly from the launch and within 1.7 miles (2.7 km) turns to the north. Stay along the Oregon shoreline to avoid tug traffic. Four miles (6.4 km) downriver are the two small **Squaw Islands** in the center of the channel and the much larger **Rocky Island** on the west side. There's not much room through the main channel west of the Squaw Islands, so if you spot a tug and barge entering this section, wait in the bay before Rocky Island or paddle the eastern channel around the island, which is less than 60 feet (24.4 m) wide in places.

Downriver from the three islands the Columbia begins to return to its normal width and the current all but disappears as it takes a bend to the northwest. Overlooking the river at the bend is a high promontory known as **Crates Point,** which some consider the upper end of the Columbia River Gorge, although the mouth of the Deschutes River (Leg 30) is judged by most to be the real start of the gorge. Just past the bend and as far as **Rowena** and **Mayer State Park**

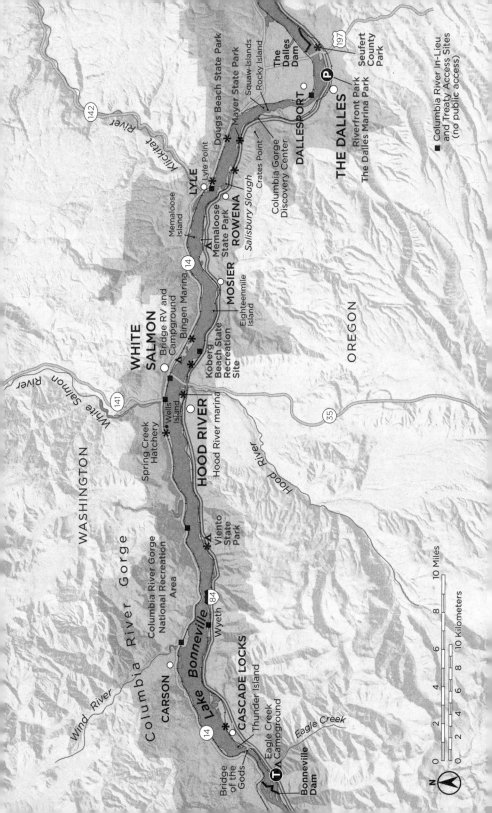

WASHINGTON

OREGON

Columbia River Gorge
National Recreation Area

Columbia River Gorge

Lake Bonneville

Wind River

White Salmon River

Klickitat River

Hood River

Eagle Creek

142

14

141

141

14

84

35

197

CARSON

WHITE SALMON

HOOD RIVER

CASCADE LOCKS

MOSIER

ROWENA

LYLE

DALLESPORT

THE DALLES

Bridge of the Gods

Bonneville Dam

Eagle Creek Campground

Thunder Island

Wyeth

Viento State Park

Spring Creek Hatchery

Wells Island

Hood River marina

Koberg Beach State Recreation Site

Bingen Marina

Bridge RV and Campground

Eighteenmile Island

Memaloose State Park

Memaloose Island

Lyle Point

Doug's Beach State Park

Mayer State Park

Squaw Islands

Rocky Island

Salisbury Slough

Crates Point

Columbia Gorge Discovery Center

Riverfront Park

The Dalles Marina Park

The Dalles Dam

Seufert County Park

■ Columbia River In-Lieu and Treaty Access Sites (no public access)

0 2 4 6 8 10 Miles

0 2 4 6 8 10 Kilometers

N

are shallow sandbars that reach well out into the river; paddle several hundred yards offshore to keep from hitting bottom. Mayer State Park, located in **Salisbury Slough,** is a well-maintained, first-rate facility 8 miles (12.9 km) from the put-in at The Dalles Riverfront Park and protected from the prevailing winds. But the term "slough" says it all—the approach to the park is shallow in places, but these areas can be identified by dead limbs rising from the water and several small vegetated islands toward the main channel.

From the gravel beach at Mayer State Park, paddle along the treed shoreline of the bay and enter the river's channel through a narrow passage between the mainland and a vegetated island. Across the river 300 yards (274 m) to the north is **Lyle Point,** a traditional tribal meeting and fishing grounds for the past 10,000 years. After fifteen years of negotiations, 33 acres of the point were purchased by the Confederated Tribes and Bands of the Yakama Nation in 2007 to prevent a high-end condo development and to preserve tribal fishing rights.

The river continues northwest from the park for 1.5 miles (2.4 km) before making a broad turn to the west. At the center of the river 12.4 miles (20 km) from the put-in is **Memaloose Island,** which takes its name from the Chinook word *memaloose,* meaning "dead, to die, expire, decay, become rotten,

Tugs with barges have three bow waves and an engine wave, which can swamp a kayak or canoe in shallow water. Point your bow into them and ride them out.

extinguish." Originally named Sepulchre Island by Lewis and Clark, the island was noted by the two explorers in their journals as originally having been a burial place of the dead for the local tribes.

Continue along the Oregon shoreline around the prominent peninsula with sandy coves to where the river widens again and runs west for a short distance. You can paddle straight across to **Eighteenmile Island** (recognizable by a cabin and dock) and a small satellite island 16.4 miles (26.4 km) from the put-in, but be aware that you will be in the tug channel for a short distance. You'll possibly feel a strong current near the islands, as the river is shallow here and the dam releases more water later in the day.

Koberg Beach State Recreation Site is 19.4 miles (31.2 km) out and has a small, sheltered sandy beach to stop on just past the basalt cliffs downriver from the tribal treaty access site. A short distance from the beach is a clean restroom facility with nearby picnic tables, green grass, and shade, a good place to relax before paddling to **Hood River.** The fishing platforms hanging from the vertical basalt walls and gill nets at the waterline are evidence that this area is a prime fishing spot for the tribes.

From Koberg Beach, it is 1.2 miles (1.9 km) to the Hood River Bridge. I haven't emphasized the potential for wind in this area because there are many calm, windless days, but there is a reason the Columbia around Hood River is considered the wind- and kite surfing capital of the world. A standard rule of thumb: if the wind- and kite surfers are having a great day on the water, you shouldn't be paddling.

Just 1.5 miles (2.4 km) from the bridge is the Hood River spit, a boat-stopper of sandy-bottomed shallows where the river is only inches deep. To avoid bottoming out and having to pull your boat to deeper water, paddle toward the main channel markers just after the bridge and turn downriver when you can no longer see the sandy bottom. The channel used by the tugs is close to the end of the spit and they have little wiggle room to avoid way-ward paddlers, so clear the spit area quickly and point your bow toward **Wells Island** 1.1 miles (1.8 km) downriver to get out of the channel. There are shallow sandy areas around the island and all along the Oregon shoreline, so watch for stumps, old pilings, and submerged rocks as you make your way downriver to **Viento State Park,** 29.2 miles (47 km) from the put-in.

From Viento State Park, it is 14.7 miles (23.7 km) to the **Eagle Creek take-out** less than a mile (1.6 km) from the Bonneville Dam locks. The Columbia, after a short 1.5-mile (2.4 km) stretch to the southwest, turns west for 6 miles (9.7 km) before making a broad turn again to the southwest and Bonneville Dam. The shoreline is primarily jagged rock points and buttresses and railroad riprap, with the odd small, sandy beach. Beware of underwater rock hazards near the shore. The route follows the Oregon shoreline, occasionally cutting across small bays.

A bit over 5 miles (8 km) from Viento is the **Wyeth** CRITFC treaty fishing access site with a protected boat ramp facility. The facility looks inviting, but it is a tribal-only facility and not open to the general public due to continuing vandalism and other criminal activities. If you decide to pull out here, you may be cited by tribal police for trespassing. Unfortunately, there are no public take-outs with vehicle access because of the railroad until the Wyeth Road exit, 8.8 miles (14.2 km) from Viento State Park, where there is a rough take-out on the nearby peninsula.

The bay here has multiple rows of rotten pilings known as wing dams parallel to the flow of the river. The best approach is to go around these obstructions rather than through them. A gap in the visible pilings usually has a submerged piling or an old fence-like railing holding them together just under the surface. There is also a current, which can trap your boat up against the pilings and turn you over. Wing dams are dangerous obstacles, so stay clear of them.

Paddle around the short rock jetty past the wing dams to the main channel side to avoid the rocks, and then parallel the shoreline 2.5 miles (4 km) to the **Cascade Locks Marina** beach. The next 3 miles (4.8 km) are as interesting a section as there is on the lower river. The Columbia River at Cascade Locks is dropping in elevation, so there is a strong current in the river and through the old locks. You have two choices: run the cement enclosure of the Cascade Locks or paddle around **Thunder Island,** the island created by the locks. Past the locks and under the **Bridge of the Gods,** paddle close to the south shoreline. Watch for rock hazards and one large grouping of pilings on the way to Eagle Creek, which enters the Columbia above Bonneville's locks. The take-out is under the Interstate 84 freeway on a sandy beach.

Hazards include strong wind and large waves; tug and barge traffic in the main channel; submerged shoreline rocks and stumps; wing dams; swift,

It is not a good day to paddle on the Columbia when windsurfers and kite surfers are having a great wind day.

turbulent water below The Dalles Dam, through the Cascade Locks, or around Thunder Island; and sandy shallows near the shoreline. As usual, put in early to avoid the afternoon winds.

FLOW AND SEASON: There is a strong current below The Dalles Dam for approximately 5 miles, but I also found a measurable flow throughout my paddle in late April. This leg can be paddled from March through November, although the spring runoff months of April through July provide a more powerful current.

PUT-IN: The Dalles Riverfront Park, exit 85 off I-84 to Brewery Overpass Rd.

TAKE-OUTS: *Oregon.* Mayer State Park, 8.1 miles (13 km), exit 76 off I-84 to Rowena River Rd; Koberg Beach State Recreation Site, 19.4 miles (31.2 km), exit westbound only off I-84; Hood River Marina, 20.8 miles (33.5 km), exit 64 off I-84 to E Port Marina Dr; Hood River Event site, 21.8 miles (35.1 km), exit 63 off I-84 to N Second St; Viento State Park, 29.2 miles (47 km), exit 56 off I-84; Eagle Creek confluence, 44 miles (70.8 km), exit 41 off I-84, eastbound only. *Washington.* Dougs Beach State Park, 6.7 miles (10.8 km), WA 14; Lyle Point boat ramp, 9.5 miles (15.3 km), WA 14 to 7th St in Lyle to Depot Road and then Cove Rd; Bingen Marina boat ramp, 19.4 miles (31.2 km), WA 14 to Maple St to E Marina Way; Spring Creek Hatchery, 23.7 miles (38.1 km), WA 14 to Spring Creek Hatchery Rd. All distances are from The Dalles Riverfront Park.

SERVICES: The Dalles and Hood River are both full-service communities and include excellent motels and dining facilities, gas stations, and grocery stores. Hood River has exceptional restaurants, specialty coffee shops, and paddle shops, and it is just a fun place to visit.

CAMPING: *Oregon.* Columbia Hills State Park (Horsethief Lake Campground), WA 14; Memaloose State Park, I-84; Viento State Park, I-84; and Eagle Creek Campground, I-84. *Washington.* Bridge RV and Campground, WA 14 (privately owned).

Passage

This was a long but fascinating leg, which I completed in two separate early-spring trips because of fierce winds west of Viento State Park, but it is doable in a long day.

I unloaded my kayak in The Dalles Marina Park parking lot, pulled it down the Riverfront Park access road to the gravel beach, then launched into the river. I couldn't have picked a better day—there wasn't a breeze on the river or a cloud in the sky. I paddled out of the shore eddy, found the fastest current near the center of the river, and quickly shot through town, but not before spotting a hungry sea lion making its way to the fish ladder a few miles upriver for an easy meal.

As I approached the narrows between the larger Rocky Island along the Oregon shoreline and the two smaller Squaw Islands in the center of the channel 4 miles (6.4 km) downriver, a tug with barges was making its way through the narrow passage, so I paddled to the rocky cliffs in the bay and waited as it moved upriver. The three sets of bow waves off the barges and tug and a motor wave were minimized in the current and broad bay, but in the narrow confines of the canyon between the islands, the waves bouncing off the vertical basalt walls and back into the river may have been a bigger problem.

Once I was past the rock islands, the river widened and I paddled near the shore as the river turned west until the sandy bottom just under the surface forced me farther out into the river. The sandy shoals along the Oregon shoreline keep the tugs in the main channel, which is near the Washington shore. The shoals continued for several miles (3.2 km) beyond the bend of the river almost to Mayer State Park, where I stopped and took a short break. The park beach and boat ramp are in a protected slough on the lee side of the prevailing gorge winds, a great escape point if the winds come up.

The slough has several vegetated, low-lying islands near the main channel, and it looked as though I'd have to paddle around them, but I found a kayak-width passage between the mainland and its nearest island in which to reenter the main river channel. The Columbia is only 300 yards (274 m) wide between the Mayer State Park peninsula and Lyle Point, one of the narrowest points on this section of river. I paddled past the park heading for Koberg Beach 10 miles (16 km) downriver, again staying clear of the shallows near the small peninsula, and then paralleled the railroad's riprap shoreline and noisy I-84 past Mema-loose Island. The bend where the Columbia takes a jog southwest has the entrance to the original 1882 railroad tunnel, which is still open. I didn't stop to investigate, but several hundred yards beyond I did pull into a tiny bay to enjoy a sliver of beach pocketed between two rock outcrops, just one of many isolated, yet inviting, places to stop along this leg.

I rounded the bend in the river and reconnected with the railroad and I-84 where the river widens. I could see Eighteenmile Island across the big bay, so rather than follow the shoreline, I set out across the 2 miles (3.2 km) of open water, using the island as a guide. It was only when I passed close by Eighteen-mile Island, the only remaining privately owned island on the Columbia River, that I realized there was still a good current helping me along and would for the rest of the day.

THE CASCADE LOCKS AND CANAL

The Cascade Locks and Canal were built in 1896 by the Army Corps of Engineers to eliminate the need to portage goods around the Cascade Rapids. It was the first lock on the Columbia River and served the shipping community for forty years before the rapids and the lock were submerged by Lake Bonneville, the reservoir behind Bonneville Dam. The lock had a lift chamber carved in solid rock 460 feet long (140 m), 90 feet wide (27.4 m), with a draft of 8 feet (2.4 m), and could lift a vessel 14 feet (4.3 m) at high water and 24 feet (7.3 m) at low water. There were three sets of gates 56 feet (17.1 m) wide and 90 feet (27.4 m) high.

Paddling in swift current through Cascade Locks immediately upriver from the Bridge of the Gods

With the spring Chinook season in progress, the tribes had their gill nets stretched perpendicular to the shore, which were clearly marked by foam floats and thus easily avoided or paddled over without damaging the nets. On the vertical basalt cliffs just short of Koberg Beach were wooden platforms hanging out over the water attached by cables and polypropylene rope. I'm sure more than one tribal member has taken a bath in the river given the state of the platforms. I landed on the clean, white sand, pulled the kayak above the wave zone, and walked up the trail to the parking lot. As I did so, I spotted a small fox in the brush just ahead of me. His curiosity led me to believe it was a kit, but even he quickly darted into the brush as I approached.

After a quick lunch at Koberg Beach, I paddled the 2 miles (3.2 km) to Hood River. The day was still windless and there wasn't a kite or surf boarder on the entire river. Just past the bridge, I ran aground on the sandy Hood River spit, which sticks out into the river for almost 0.5 mile (0.8 km). The spit is a great place for boarding, but not for boats. Once free of the sand, I paddled directly toward the main channel buoys in the center of the river to find deeper water, and finally turned the spit for Wells Island.

Thickly foliaged Wells Island, just offshore and west of Hood River, was created by the rising floodwaters behind Bonneville Dam, so it too has sandy shallows, rocks, and snags near its shoreline. I was tiring in the late afternoon sun, so I pulled out several more times on small beaches prior to finally reaching Viento State Park, 29.2 miles (47 km) from the put-in. Joyce had our tent set up in the park, so I ended the day right there.

The next morning was a great day for surf and kite boarders, but not for a kayaker. The wind on the beach at Viento State Park was gusting at 30 to 40 mph (48.3 to 64.4 kmph) and holding steady at 15 to 20 mph (24.1 to 32.2 kmph). The Columbia runs straight west into the wind from Viento and widens to over a mile (1.6 km), so I couldn't put in and finish the leg that day.

A week later I was back. The wind had blown all week, but the forecast for light winds was good—and when kayaking the gorge, light winds is a good forecast. I put back in at the beach at Viento State Park and set off for Eagle Creek 14.8 miles (23.8 km) downriver. I followed the railroad track close to shore, but also cut across three bays to save time. The wind began to pick up within the hour, so I hugged the shoreline, trying to hide behind small peninsulas to break the wind and avoid bigger swells and rough water offshore. This worked, and I finally pulled out on the beach east of the Cascade Locks Marina, 11.6 miles (18.7 km) from Viento, for a short break.

I left the beach and paddled by the stern-wheeler *Columbia Gorge,* which was moored in the river near the marina. The current was strong and fast at the entrance to the old Cascade Locks and, having scouted the exit, I was wary of the turbulence, eddies, and small whirlpools in the bay below. I lined up dead center between the concrete walls and started drifting through. I had just entered the funnel-like walls when I spotted a powerboat pull out from the boat ramp below the locks, turn into the locks, and speed toward me. I back-paddled in the current using my rudder to keep in line with the flow, while still allowing the boat to drift forward slightly. This kept my bow pointed downriver. The powerboat roared through the locks under full throttle, saw me in the upper channel, and swerved to miss me. The current washed out most of the motor wave, but I still got a good rocking. I then stroked hard to get control of the bow as I shot under Joyce, standing on the bridge, to the island and went through the locks. As I exited into the small bay, roiling and boiling water kicked my boat around as the current pulled me along toward the main channel. I passed several sea lions working the turbulence for salmon, and was soon under the Bridge of the Gods and headed toward Bonneville Dam.

The 3-mile (4.8 km) section below Cascade Locks has steep banks and few places to pull out and rest, but it is like a rainforest, as the forest is dense, the shoreline heavily vegetated, and thick mats of dark green moss cling to the rock along the shore. This is the first opportunity for the tribes to gill-net salmon coming upriver, so there are numerous fishing platforms and nets on both sides of the river. I stayed just offshore, but as I approached the spillway, I was aware that the main current was flowing to the right to feed the generators in Bonneville's power plant 0.5 mile (0.8 km) downstream. This was no place to get cocky, so I stayed close to the shoreline past some pilings, paddled around the point to the mouth of Eagle Creek, and took out on the beach directly underneath the railroad bridge to end another fine day on the river.

LEG 32: Bonneville Dam to Kelley Point Park

Distance: 43 miles (69.2 km)
Paddle Time: 9 to 13 hours

River View

The leg from **Bonneville Dam** to **Kelley Point Park** is a major change from the Columbia's placid flat water above the dams. Below Bonneville Dam the river is free-flowing and there are new variables to consider: changing tides; a steady current; seagoing container ships; wing dams and pilings; and far more industrial and recreational activity.

There are a number of excellent resources available concerning paddling on the lower Columbia from Bonneville Dam to the Pacific. The websites listed in the Resources section provide safety recommendations, launch site locations, tidal charts in specific areas, up-to-the-moment weather predictions, paddle routes, RV and campsite information, important agency contact numbers, and just about anything else you need or should know before putting in. Take the time to do your homework to ensure a safe and successful trip.

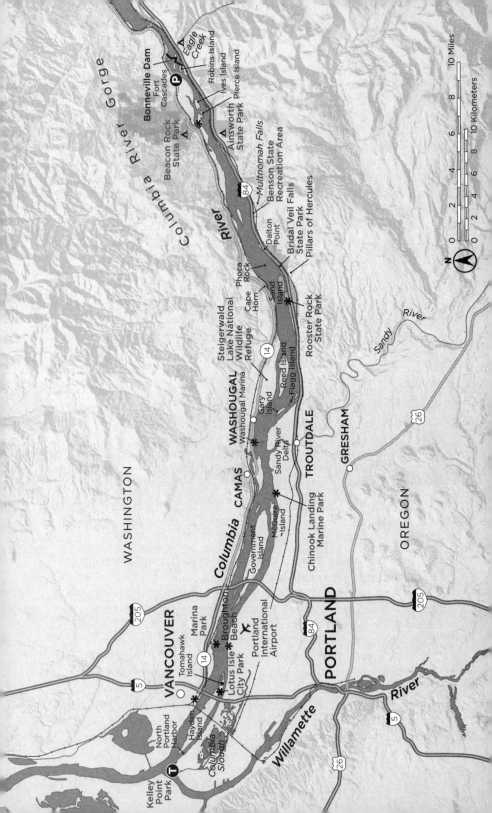

BONNEVILLE: THE COLUMBIA'S FIRST DAM

Bonneville Dam, named for Captain Benjamin Bonneville, an early-nineteenth-century army officer and explorer, was the first dam to be built on the Columbia and is located at the farthest reach of tide 145 miles (233.4 km) from the Pacific Ocean. President Franklin D. Roosevelt stepped in to ensure that the 2690-foot-long (820 m), $752-million dam would be a public source of power and kept out of the hands of energy monopolies. He signed the Bonneville Project Act in 1937, giving the dam's power over to the public and creating the Bonneville Power Administration (BPA), a federal marketing agent for electric power and to construct facilities to transmit that power.

The 1.3 miles (2.1 km) of river directly below Bonneville Dam's spillway is off-limits to boaters. The boating boundary is clearly marked by signage and includes the entire river northwest of the juvenile fish bypass tubes and Smolt Monitoring Facility located on the Washington side of the river to the spillway. The southwest shoreline of **Robins Island** is the boundary line on the Oregon side. The closest and best put-in near the dam is the **Fort Cascades WDFW (Washington Department of Fish and Wildlife) boat ramp** a few hundred yards below the bypass tubes. The ramp is clear of the lock traffic, which is across the river, and there are no big eddies, or turbulence, directly offshore.

One mile (1.6 km) downriver are two sand islands partially covered in vegetation, **Ives Island** to the east and **Pierce Island** to the west. The channel around Ives and Pierce will take you underneath **Beacon Rock** and past the alternative put-in, the boat launch at **Beacon Rock State Park.** This channel may be dry and impassable in the fall and winter because of sandy shoals and gravel beds, but in high water it is a pleasant paddle and an alternative to the fast current in the main channel.

Several miles (3.2 km) downriver, begin thinking of crossing over to the Oregon side. There is a clear line of sight to look for tugs, but also watch for salmon fishermen in small boats powering upriver, as this section of river up to the locks is a hotspot for fishing. Once you cross over, follow the shoreline, but keep several hundred yards away to avoid shallow sandy areas and underwater hazards. The main shipping channel is very close to the Oregon shoreline in this area, so move over for the tugs and barges. The river is flowing southwest and 9 miles (14.5 km) from the put-in and past the falls is the rocky point at **Benson State Recreation Area.** Stay well off the point to avoid hitting one of many hidden boulders or bottoming out in the shallows just past the rocks.

Less than a mile (1.6 km) downriver from the rocks off Benson and an equal distance upriver from **Dalton Point** is the first major wing dam, a row of old pilings perpendicular to the river. These old decaying structures are widespread along both sides of the river from Bonneville Dam to the Pacific and present a hazardous challenge to kayakers and other paddlers. Go around them, not through them, as any opening between visible pilings can have a hidden stump or a cross board just beneath the surface. As the tide and current combine to create a stronger flow farther downriver, these pilings can be deadly obstructions, so do not take them lightly.

The overall scenery in this section of the river is spectacular, as the lighter-colored broadleaf forest near the shoreline gives way to the dark green pine trees growing in steep gullies and clinging to cliffs of basalt rising thousands of feet into the Cascades. On the Oregon side of the river, waterfalls, such as **Bridal Veil Falls** and **Multnomah Falls,** cascade off cliffs or freefall hundreds of feet (61 m) into deep pools; and well-known basalt columns and cliffs, such as the **Pillars of Hercules,** Crown Point, and **Rooster Rock,** rise from the valley floor. To the north and across the Columbia are other prominent landmarks mentioned in the journals of Lewis and Clark, such as **Phoca Rock,** a small island in the center of the river; and the Bastille-like **Cape Horn,** a vertical basalt wall hundreds of feet (61 m) high that forced the railroad to build a 2382-foot (726 m) tunnel to get around the Columbia, the longest tunnel on the north bank of the river.

Several miles (3.2 km) past Dalton Point is **Sand Island.** As the name implies, the island is sand, but vegetation has covered most of it. Upriver and downriver of the island for at least a mile (1.6 km) each way are very shallow sandy shoals that in low water will force you toward the main channel on the Washington side of the river. The stretch of beach along the north shore rivals any sandy beach in Hawaii or Mexico.

The Columbia makes a lazy turn to the northwest around 19 miles (30.6 km) from the put-in. Cross the 2 miles (3.2 km) of open water to Flagg Island, north of Chatham Island 19.4 miles (31.2 km) out. At the north end of Flagg Island, leave the main channel and paddle into the waterway west of **Gary Island.** Both islands are part of the **Sandy River Delta,** so vegetation growing in seasonally flooded areas can prohibit navigation. The Columbia turns west again 21.7 miles (34.9 km) out. The water in this entire area is hand-deep, so stay several hundred yards offshore and outside of the thick reeds, brush, and other vegetation near the delta, especially later in the year. The **Sandy River** confluence is 23.3 miles (37.5 km) downriver from the put-in, and the shallow mouth is littered with old trees, limbs, and other obstructions. Once across the Sandy River, the shoreline becomes urban with all the unattractive elements that come with shoreline industry, commercial activity, and urban dwelling.

Chinook Landing Marine Park, with its 67 acres (27.1 ha) of wetlands and wildlife habitat, picnic areas, restroom facilities, and six boat-launching lanes, is 26 miles (41.8 km) from the put-in. It is one of the busiest boat launch facilities on the Columbia and reflects this in the number of powerboats leaving and

WING DAMS

A wing dam is a row of wooden pilings driven into the bottom of the river and running perpendicular to the flow. These old, sometimes rotten structures stretch hundreds of feet (61 m) from the shoreline into the river, and the pilings can be connected by thick horizontal planks. The Columbia from Bonneville Dam to the Pacific has hundreds of them of various lengths on both sides of the river. They direct the flow of the river to the middle and cause the sand to accumulate on the banks. Wing dams are obstructions and hazardous to paddlers—paddle around them, not through them.

Wing dams are a common hazard along the shorelines in the tidal zone below Bonneville Dam to the Pacific.

entering the boat ramps. There is an impenetrable wing dam near the entrance to the boat launch area that sticks out 100 yards (91 m) from the shore just upstream from the entrance to the boat launch. The current during the outgoing tide is strong here, so go around this obstacle.

From Chinook Landing, paddle through the gap between wing dams off **McGuire Island** and the mainland, and then along the rows of houseboats. Past

Beacon Rock, named by Lewis and Clark in 1805, is an 848-foot (258 m) basalt pillar that marks how far the tidewater extends upriver.

CALIFORNIA SEA LIONS

They're big, they're hungry, and they eat tons of adult and juvenile salmon below the dams. Tourists love them, commercial and tribal fishermen want them gone, and the US Fish and Wildlife Service (FWS) spends millions trying to mitigate the animals' damage to salmon recovery. But it's all good fun to the California sea lion, an eared carnivore capable of staying submerged for 10 minutes and swimming like a 25-mph (40.2-kmph) torpedo.

Like walruses and seals, sea lions are pinnipeds, mammals with four flippers that can eat an Indian fish basket of sockeye for breakfast. An adult male can weigh more than 800 pounds (362 kg), grow to 8 feet (2.4 m) in length, and collects smaller females into his harem during the breeding season. Sea lions used to spend most of their time along the Pacific coast hanging out on docks, rocks, and offshore islands, but thanks to the Army Corps of Engineers (which built the dam) they've been more than willing to belly-up to Bonneville's fish ladders for a meal.

According to a 2002 study by the government, fishermen took at least ten times more salmon out of the river below Bonneville than the sea lions, but that wasn't enough for the fishermen. The Columbia River tribes, recreational and commercial fishermen, and FWS staff haze the animals with cracker shells and seal bombs, capture them in pens, and are authorized to kill ninety-two a year. Twelve were given a lethal injection in 2012.

The sea lions are "unhazed" though. Other than making their mealtimes noisy, the estimated 300 to 500 sea lions in the Lower Columbia, and the few at the dam, know there's no free lunch—except at Bonneville. The FWS needs to spend more time chasing poachers and less time and money chasing pinnipeds.

the houseboat community, the shoreline is free of development and follows the levee. Thirty-one miles (49.9 km) out is the Interstate-205 bridge, which crosses over to **Government Island.** The noise from low-flying commercial jets landing at **Portland International Airport** on the other side of the levee is constant, especially in the morning. At 34.7 miles (55.8 km) is **Broughton Beach** and the recently remodeled **M. James Gleason Memorial boat ramp** and public facilities, a good alternative take-out to the weekend madness at Chinook Landing.

Almost 2 miles (3.2 km) downriver from the Gleason Memorial boat ramp is a gauntlet of houseboats and businesses floating between the mainland, **Tomahawk Island,** and the east end of **Hayden Island.** The river channel is very narrow through the houseboat community, but at 38 miles (61.2 km) out the harbor widens. On the south shore of Hayden Island, hidden from view by a slew of houseboats, is **Lotus Isle City Park,** with a sliver of sandy beach and a nice grassy treed area at the top of the bluff to take a break. As of 2013, there are no public restrooms, but it's a short distance to a shopping center nearby for restroom facilities.

Back on the river, it is only a few hundred yards to the I-5 bridge and another mile (1.6 km) to the BNSF Oregon Slough railroad bridge. After the railroad bridge the channel doubles in width and accommodates oceangoing container ship traffic and specialized ships carrying vehicles. This is a congested area, and paddlers need to be cautious approaching moored ships when tugs are preparing to bring a ship to dock or pull one out.

The Kelley Point Park beach is 43 miles (69.2 km) from the start. If you have wheels for your kayak, you can take out on the beach and wheel your boat to the parking lot 250 yards (229 m) inland. If not, a short 1.3-mile (2.1 km) paddle around the northwest tip of Kelley Point and up the **Willamette River** to a take-out in the **Columbia Slough** is an easy alternative. The northwest tip of Kelley Point, the confluence of the Willamette and Columbia, is blocked by a 260-yard-long (238 m) wing dam. Be sure to go around this hazard.

Hazards include swift, turbulent water below Bonneville Dam; high wind and large waves; tidal and river current; tug and barge, and oceangoing container ship traffic; sandy shallows; submerged rocks near shore; wing dams and pilings; and recreational boats moving at full-throttle near Chinook Landing Marine Park. As usual, put in early to avoid the afternoon winds and recreational boat traffic, and if possible, stay clear of the main channel.

FLOW AND SEASON: There is a steady current in the river below Bonneville Dam, although under low-water conditions and in the wider sections of the river it is almost imperceptible. Runoff can be as high as 500,000 cfs in midsummer, while in late fall and early winter flow can drop to 60,000 cfs. Below Bonneville Dam, the flow is 4 to 6 mph (6.4 to 9.7 kmph) but loses this speed quickly 7.5 miles (12.1 km) downriver where the Columbia widens. The season to paddle this leg is March through November, but for a stronger current, paddle during the spring runoff months of April through July.

PUT-INS: Fort Cascades boat ramp (Hamilton Island), 1.5 miles (2.4 km) from Bonneville Dam's spillway, WA 14 to Dam Access Rd, and then follow the signs; Beacon Rock State Park boat launch, 5 miles (8 km) from the spillway, WA 14, cross Woodward Creek Bridge to Moorage Rd. Both put-ins are in Washington.

TAKE-OUTS: *Oregon.* Dalton Point, 10.5 miles (16.9 km), exit 29 off I-84; Rooster Rock State Park beach, 14.8 miles (23.8 km), exit 25 off I-84;

Rooster Rock State Park boat ramp, 15.8 miles (25.4 km), exit 25 off I-84; Chinook Landing Marine Park, 26 miles (41.8 km), exit 17 off I-84, westbound to NW Frontage Rd to Northeast Marine Dr; Broughton Beach, 34.7 miles (55.8 km), same approach as Chinook Landing Marine Park or eastbound on Northeast Marine Dr off northbound I-5; Kelley Point Park, 43 miles (69.2 km), exit 307 off northbound I-5 to N Marine Dr. *Washington.* Captain William Clark Park, 19.8 miles (31.9 km), S Index St and S 32nd St off WA 14, Camas; Port of Camas Marina, 22 miles (35.4 km), Front St off WA 14; Wintler Park, 33.6 miles (54.1 km), Beach Dr off WA 14. All distances are from the Fort Cascades WDFW boat ramp put-in.

SERVICES: In Washington, Stevenson and North Bonneville both have limited services, such as small restaurants and convenience stores. In Oregon, Cascade Locks has a major chain motel and several motels without lobbies, convenience stores, a grocery store, and a few restaurants. Portland, Vancouver, and the outlying communities along the I-5 and I-84 corridors have every service, including all classes of motels, world-renowned restaurants, fast food, shopping centers, grocery stores, gas stations, and a number of quality paddle shops.

CAMPING: *Oregon.* Eagle Creek Campground, exit 41 off I-84 (eastbound only); Ainsworth State Park, exit 35 off I-84. *Washington.* Beacon Rock State Park, Moorage Rd off WA 14.

Passage

Before launching at the Fort Cascades boat ramp, I called a paddling shop in Portland to speak with one of the local experts who was familiar with the river and the paddle through the Portland/Vancouver area. He emphasized that the Columbia River below Bonneville Dam was not for beginners. "You're not only dealing with wind and waves, you're now dealing with a steady current, strong tides, and big boats. Stay clear of the main channel and avoid the pilings."

Armed with this new knowledge (and fearing I was one of the beginners he was referencing), I launched into the river just 1.5 miles (2.4 km) downstream from the spillway of Bonneville Dam, which was releasing over 275,000 cfs. The river was swift, even along the north bank. Just downstream, I left the main channel and took a side channel around Ives and Pierce islands to get a better river view of Beacon Rock. I was soon swept past the Beacon Rock boat ramp and back into the main channel where I maneuvered my boat to the center of the river to catch the fastest flow. I didn't know exactly where the main channel was, so I angled toward the Oregon side, staying just far enough offshore to enjoy the fast water, but out of the turbulence.

Six miles (9.7 km) downriver the Columbia doubled in width and lost most of its power. I stayed close to the lightly populated shore and a few miles farther along enjoyed the same view of Multnomah Falls seen by Lewis and Clark and mentioned in Lewis's journal entry of April 9, 1806.

Past Dalton Point the river had created a 2-mile-long (3.2 km) shallow bay of sand clear to Sand Island, and in some places I thought I would high-center. I reached the north shoreline of Sand Island and pulled out on the pristine beach near the west end. Signs above the waterline indicated this was a "clothing optional" beach and, sure enough, there was one lonely soul working on a full-body tan nearby. Public nudity didn't surprise me, but the great beaches did. From Sand Island, I stayed offshore several hundred yards past Rooster Rock State Park to avoid more of the sandy shallows. A 5–10 mph (8–16.1 kmph) wind was now blowing in my face, and I briefly considered taking out for the day at the Rooster Rock boat ramp because of the lack of take-outs past this point, but decided to continue a few more miles (3.2 km) to where the river turned northwest in hopes that the mainland and trees alongshore blocked the wind from the southwest. I set off from the shoreline near the Corbett exit off I-84 and crossed the almost 2 miles (3.2 km) of open water to Flagg Island. The waves were into my bow, but not over it, and as I got closer to the mainland, the waves almost disappeared. Out in the main channel and away from land, though, it was a different story. The river was frothing with whitecaps, what one paddler termed "little white flags of surrender."

I paddled the east shoreline of Flagg Island and then entered the shallow-bottomed channel between Flagg and Gary islands. The wind picked up again over the open channel, so I paddled a short distance along the west shoreline of Gary Island and then crossed the 300-yard-wide (274 m) channel to the protection of the mainland. This is a shallow area and probably not passable in low water. Thick reed beds and bushes grow offshore, as if the land is flooded only in the spring and summer. I noticed a small bay ahead of me choked with vegetation, connected to a low-lying, almost-submerged vegetated island that in low water would have been high and dry. I could have paddled past the north end of Gary Island and around this island-like area to the main channel, but decided to follow the strong current into the choked-up bay and see if there wasn't a hidden passage. Sure enough, just when I thought I'd reached the end, I wove around some reeds and bushes and found a kayak-width channel just deep and wide enough to take me to the main channel. It was a keyhole only a canoe or kayak would fit through, and it was fun to find an escape through the vegetation.

As I came around the north end of the Sandy River Delta and lost the protection of the trees, I faced a more determined headwind that was continuing to strengthen over the main channel. I paddled across the mouth of the Sandy River with its enormous delta and numerous dead tree parts sticking out of the sand without a problem, despite the high wind and waves. In the fall or at a low tide, though, this same crossing would be impossible. The large delta shallows that I skimmed across on either side of the mouth would be exposed, which would force a paddler far out into the channel. Once clear of the mouth, I passed gravel pits, a barge-building company, and rafts of logs tied to pilings and reached the sandy beach at Chinook Landing. Rather than take out on the beach, I chose to go around the old wing dam sticking into the river and fight the current, outgoing tide, and water chop from the big-wake boats near the ramp area. It was like paddling in a washing machine. Five minutes later, I entered into the calm water of the cove at Chinook Landing, beached my boat alongside a muddy tidal flat where Joyce was standing, and ended the day. The wind, waves, and countless recreational boats were just too much to paddle through.

I launched the next morning just after sunrise from Chinook Landing. A light rain had fallen during the night and the temperature was cool near the water. Other than two fishing boats launching near me, the park was empty of the masses from the day before and the river dead calm. I left the cove and caught the current moving swiftly with the outgoing tide. Within minutes, I was inside the channel between the Oregon shoreline and McGuire Island paddling by a large houseboat community.

With the current and tide in my favor, I steamed past the houseboats and McGuire Island and into the main channel with a tall levee to my south and Government Island less than a half mile (0.8 km) offshore. The river parallels the

Although it is lined with hundreds of houseboats and industrial complexes, Portland's urban shoreline is easy to navigate and fun to paddle.

runways at Portland International, and as I approached and passed the I-205 bridge, early-morning flights were noisily coming and going close by. It may be noisy in this area, but the levee's bank is clean of any urbanization for over 5 miles (8 km) north of the airport, making this section one of the most pleasant to paddle in the Portland/Vancouver area.

I took a short break at Broughton Beach, which has a boat ramp and public beach area, before putting back in and paddling through the east end of the **North Portland Harbor** south of Tomahawk Island. The harbor is sprawling with houseboats of every size, shape, expense, age, and condition. Halfway through this urban water world, I passed a floating coffeehouse/restaurant with a sign on the dock that read, "Motorboats Only—No Kayaks Or Canoes," so I continued paddling and had my morning chai a short walk from Lotus Isle City Park just down the harbor.

Lotus Isle City Park is on Hayden Island 12 miles (19.3 km) from Chinook Landing. The park has a bluff that overlooks an array of houseboats, boat docks, and Portland International. I found the small, out-of-the-way sandy beach by skirting an upstream wing dam and passing beneath an aerial walkway from the park's bluff to the lower houseboat community nearby. The park's beach is hidden behind the houseboats, but worth finding if you need to get out and relax.

A quarter mile (0.4 km) from the park, I passed beneath the I-5 bridge and was officially south of Hayden Island. The tide was turning, but I still had a reasonable current to move me along and past the several hundred houseboats floating off Hayden Island between the I-5 bridge and BNSF's Oregon Slough railroad bridge a mile (1.6 km) downriver and now in the west end of the North Portland Harbor. A short distance past the railroad bridge, the industrial, commercial, and urban slough ended. I stayed close to the mainland side of the river, although both the mainland and Hayden Island had small but beautiful beaches lined with shade trees.

Just 1.5 miles (2.4 km) short of Kelley Point Park I paddled past an ocean-going container ship being loaded, its huge diesel engines idling near the stern. This was my first encounter with these metal monsters, but not my last. From Kelley Point Park to the ocean, at least twenty-five container ships or car-haulers passed me on their way up or down the river. The rolling waves they send toward the shore are easily navigated in deep water, if you turn your bow into them, but these same waves can be a big problem in shallows or near shore. What caught me off guard was how quiet they are. I'd be paddling along, and suddenly one would be going by me in the main channel. These ships have the right-of-way by law, and not just because of their size. Anytime I was near the shipping channel or thought I was there, I developed eyes in the back of my head to ensure I had time to paddle out of trouble.

I was not so lucky at the next loading facility. One of the two large container ships was loaded and set to leave port. Two tugs were maneuvering alongside

Container, grain, and vehicle-carrying oceangoing ships use convenient shipping ports built along the Columbia and Willamette rivers near Kelley Point.

and at the stern. I didn't know how long this process was going to take, so when the tugs started maneuvering the ship, I angled out into the channel and around the activity as fast as I could paddle. Paddling farther into the channel was not easy, as the wind had picked up between 15 and 20 mph (24.1 to 32.2 kmph) and I was no longer protected by Hayden Island from the big waves developing in the 0.5-mile-wide (0.8 km) main channel at the confluence of the Willamette and Columbia rivers. Toss in the turbulence kicked up by the two tugs nearby and recreational boater and barge traffic out in the river, and this area turned into a cauldron of whitewater.

Once around the container ships and through the froth offshore, I reached the beach at Kelley Point Park. I could have taken out on the beach, but the night before Joyce and I found another alternative, a close-to-the-car take-out at the entrance to the park along the Columbia Slough. The slough's channel was 1 mile (1.6 km) up from the mouth of the Willamette River.

I fought through the choppy water to the far end of the Kelley Point wing dam, skirted around the big marker piling, and then entered the Willamette. This is a major thoroughfare to the Columbia for Portland's salmon fishermen, wakeboard boats, and cruisers, and they're all traveling at top speed. I stayed close to shore, but the rollers, waves, and chop made the mile (1.6 km) to the slough an arm-burner. I entered the calm waters of the slough and a few minutes later pulled up next to a couple of older fishermen tossing bait into the murky water for catfish. Joyce was there with the SUV just as I manhandled the kayak to the parking lot.

LEG 33: Kelley Point Park to Mayger Beach

Distance: 44.2 miles (71.2 km)
Paddle Time: 8 to 11 hours

River View

The leg from **Kelley Point Park** to **Mayger Beach** has miles of the finest sandy beaches found anywhere in the Pacific Northwest, many of which can only be accessed by boat. On this leg, the shoreline is the paddler's sole domain. Container ships and tug and barge traffic follow the main channel close to the center of the river, while recreational boaters and fishermen stay well offshore to avoid hitting sandy shallows, rocks, pilings, wing dams, and all sorts of boat-bottom and prop eaters hidden under the surface. This is a journey well worth paddling.

The leg begins either from the Kelley Point Park beach on the Columbia River or from the **Columbia Slough,** a mile (1.6 km) up the **Willamette River.** Beach access on the Columbia is 250 yards (229 m) from the park's main parking lot, while the slough can be reached from a small parking lot close by the entrance to the park. The Willamette is a pathway to the Columbia not only for Portland's recreational boaters, but for many container and bulk carrier ships, so watch for these vessels when crossing the Willamette River to **Belle Vue Point** at the confluence.

The paddle continues along the beaches of 26,000-acre (10,500 ha) **Sauvie Island,** the largest island along the entire Columbia River. Lewis and Clark's Corps of Discovery landed here on November 4, 1805, naming it Wappato Island for the arrowhead plant that was the staple root vegetable of the local Indians' diet. The name was later changed to Sauvie Island for a French-Canadian employee of the Hudson's Bay Company who settled there.

For the first 6 miles (9.7 km) from the Columbia Slough, public access to the beaches is limited to boats below the high-water mark because of private landholdings, but just past a long, protruding wing dam is 7 miles (11.3 km) of public beach. You can sunbathe on sections of this beach and never see another soul. The beach can be reached by vehicle by crossing the NW Sauvie Island Road bridge off US Highway 30, the only bridge onto the island, and then finding and following NW Reeder Road. **Collins Beach,** almost 5 miles (8 km) along the public section of the beach, is clothing-optional and, as far as I could tell, the most popular beachfront on the island.

In addition to the picture-perfect sandy beach along this section, the shoreline is canopied with huge trees and thick foliage. Great blue herons are as common as ducks, most likely because of a huge rookery on the island, and

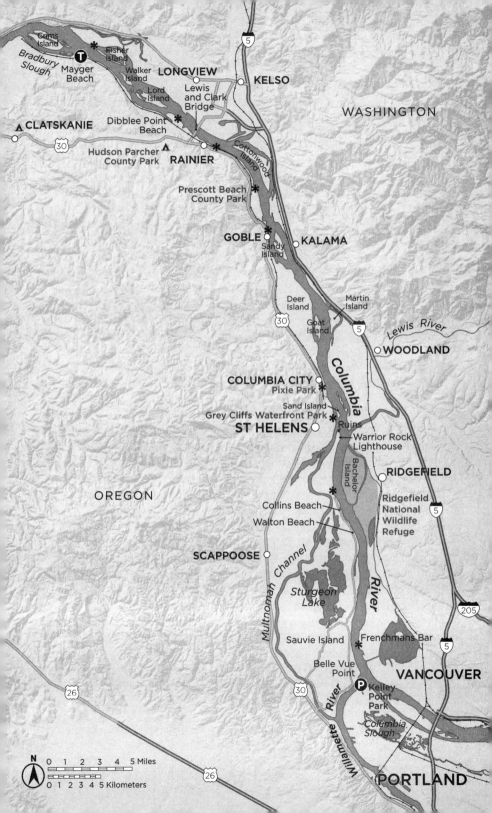

Walton Beach is 5 miles (8 km) of Maui-like sandy public beach on Sauvie Island.

almost every grouping of high wooden pilings and metal marker posts offshore used for navigation by the big boats has an active osprey nest.

Half a mile (0.8 km) upriver from the north end of Sauvie Island and 15.2 miles (24.5 km) from the put-in is **Warrior Rock Lighthouse,** a concrete two-tiered structure 28 feet (8.5 m) high that was built in the 1930s. The only remaining lighthouse on the Columbia upriver from the mouth, it guided ships until damaged by a barge in 1969. Another large structure, possibly a former salmon cannery known on the shipping charts as the "Ruins," was built at the tip of the island, but all that remains are a few partial and decrepit structures, and hundreds of old pilings rotting near the surface of the river. It's a shallow area, so stay well offshore and away from the pilings.

From the tip of Sauvie Island, cross the mouth of the 21-mile-long (33.8 km) **Multnomah Channel,** which borders the island on the west. On the St. Helens side of the channel, paddle 1 mile (1.6 km) along the city's waterfront to **Grey Cliffs Waterfront Park,** just past the marina and boat ramp. In windy conditions, this is a good take-out 16.2 miles (26.1 km) from the put-in. Across from **St. Helens, Sand Island Marina Park** has great beaches and attracts a swarm of boaters. On a warm weekend, this area is as busy with recreational boat traffic as any city west of Portland.

Less than 2 miles (3.2 km) downriver is **Columbia City** with **Pixie Park,** a short and narrow public beach between several big expensive homes. This section of river, open to the main river channel, can be windy and rough, and the beach is a good spot to take out in a pinch.

From Pixie Park, the shoreline takes on a more industrial look for over 2 miles (3.2 km) with loading dock facilities for gravel and lumber. Near the docks and downriver are a number of wing dams, one of which extends 300 yards (274 m) into the river. Paddle around these structures, as the tide and current are strong here.

Just past Columbia City is the south end of 3000-acre (1200 ha) **Deer Island** and much smaller **Goat Island.** The north end of Deer Island ends at the channel between the mainland and **Sandy Island,** a large, uninhabited island in the center of the river. It is very shallow at the south entrance to the channel around Sandy Island, so stay offshore toward the center of the channel for a short distance before regaining the shoreline to **Goble,** a tiny road stop with a fee-for-use boat ramp, a marina, and a dozen or so trailers and fifth-wheels. Goble is 27.6 miles (44.4 km) from the put-in.

From Goble, you're back in the main shipping channel without any islands to protect you from wind, waves, or ships. The shoreline is heavily foliaged and rocky in places. Just 0.5 mile (0.8 km) from Goble is a rocky point that juts out into the river. Approach this area with caution because the current is unusually strong around the point and there is a catch-basin upriver against the point fronted by a house-sized rock island. Once around this point, it is a pleasant and interesting paddle along the beachfront at **Prescott Beach County Park** and more tree-lined rocky shoreline; past a container ship anchorage area; between several monster seagoing barges that seem permanently moored near the **Rainier Marina;** and then to **Rainier City Park beach,** 34 miles (54.7 km) from the put-in at the Columbia Slough.

Rainier is a good take-out if the wind is blowing, but this leg continues downriver and leaves the heavily industrialized section of Rainier and Longview for the ships, tugs, and traffic. Downriver from Rainier and **Longview** the river actually flows backwards twice a day, so time your paddle to Mayger to coincide with the outgoing tide.

From the Rainier City Park beach, the route follows the Oregon shoreline and crosses under the massive span of the **Lewis and Clark Bridge** just after a log loading facility, and then along **Dibblee Point Beach,** a wide sandy beach 3 miles (4.8 km) west of the bridge. Downriver is **Lord Island,** recognizable by two wing dams protruding out into the main channel; stay river left and follow the shallow channel southwest of Lord Island.

On the Oregon shoreline just inside the channel entrance the *USS Washtenaw County,* a 384-foot LST-1166, Terrebonne Parish–class tank landing ship commissioned in 1953, is moored. The rusty hulk, or what's left of it, was originally destined for the maritime museum in Astoria, but since being moored in this backwater channel since 2003, it has been too badly damaged from vandalism to reconstruct, and all plans to do so are presently on hold.

This is a quiet and pleasant journey along the wetlands, tidal flats, and shoals near Lord and Walker islands, and the steep, timbered slopes above the railroad track on the mainland. The slough around the islands is a paradise for bald eagles working the river for fish. There's a full-length wing dam stretching between the two islands, so stay in the channel and follow the mainland shoreline; even though it looks like a cul-de-sac, it isn't.

Once you pass **Walker Island,** you are back in the main shipping channel for 2.6 miles (4.2 km) to Mayger Beach just as the river starts to make a wide, sweeping turn from northwest to southwest. The tiny community of Mayger is located a mile (1.6 km) inland, so you may not recognize the take-out, just a small beach among cottonwoods. The beach is 0.25 mile (0.4 km) past an old cannery building and beyond the next private dock and a few pilings. When the tide is in, the beach will almost disappear.

Hazards include bow waves from seagoing ship traffic; wing dams and pilings; submerged shoreline obstructions; strong tides and currents; wind and waves; and sandy shallows near islands.

FLOW AND SEASON: The flow along this leg is increased significantly by the Willamette and Lewis rivers, although neither has any direct impact on the paddler. The tidal flow and current increase the closer you get to the Pacific, and an outgoing tide can increase your speed 1 to 2 mph (1.6 to 3.2 kmph). The current is stronger with the spring and summer runoff and dam releases. The best time to paddle this leg is between March and July, but for those who are looking to enjoy the many beaches, June through October are prime months.

PUT-INS: Kelley Point Park, Portland, at the confluence of the Columbia and Willamette rivers (put in either off the north beach on the Columbia River or in the Columbia Slough from the parking lot at the main gate to the park), I-5 to N Marine Dr to N Kelley Point Park Rd.

TAKE-OUTS: Sauvie Island Beach, 6.6 miles (10.6 km), unmarked road to beach off NW Reeder Rd; NW Reeder Rd parking lot, 11.8 miles (19 km), end of NW Reeder Rd; Grey Cliffs Waterfront Park, 16.2 miles (26.1 km), Columbia Blvd, off US 30, St. Helens; Pixie Park, 17.8 miles (28.6 km), I street off US 30, Columbia City; Goble boat ramp, 27.6 miles (44.4 km), US 30; Prescott Beach County Park, 30.3 miles (48.8 km), Graham Rd off US 30, Goble; Rainier City Park beach, 34 miles (54.7 km), E 3rd St off US 30, Rainier; Dibblee Point Beach, 36.8 miles (59.2 km), Mill St off US 30, Rainier; Mayger Beach, 44.2 miles (71.2 km), N Nebraska St off US 30 in

Clatskanie to NW 5th St, then Beaver Falls Rd to Quincy–Mayger Rd, then Mayger Rd to Mayger Fill Rd to beach. All take-outs are in Oregon, and all distances are from the Columbia Slough put-in.

SERVICES: Portland is in a league all by itself with every service from world-class motels and restaurants to yurts and fast food, grocery stores to gas stations, and a number of quality paddle shops. St. Helens is a mid-sized community with a major chain motel and a few other nice motels. Columbia City, Rainier, and Clatskanie have nonchain motels, good restaurants, grocery stores, and other standard amenities.

CAMPING: It's as if Oregon forgot to include this area in its state parks and recreation plan. There are four parks off US 30 from Scappoose to Mayger that allow overnight camping, and two of them are not anywhere near the Columbia River: Scaponia Columbia County Park, 13 miles (20.9 km) on Scappoose–Vernonia Rd from Scappoose; Big Eddy Park, 7 miles (11.3 km), north of Vernonia on OR 47; and Hudson Parcher County Park, 0.75 mile (1.2 km) on Larson Rd off US 30 1 mile (1.6 km) west of Rainier; Clatskanie City Park, downtown Clatskanie. Boat camping is available at Sand Island Marina Park across from St. Helens; on Goat Island; and on Sandy Island across from Goble. Self-contained RVs have a big advantage along this leg because they can park near any of the vehicle-accessible beaches without charge.

While Longview's industrial shoreline is difficult to access, Rainier on the Oregon side has several nice beach areas for a paddler to take out or rest.

Passage

Given the distance of 44.2 miles (71.2 km) from my put-in at the Columbia Slough in Kelley Point Park to Mayger, I launched at daybreak. This leg took me two days because of headwind, but on a good day with a strong current and outgoing tide the distance is doable. The congested boat traffic around Kelley Point the afternoon before was now down to a few sportfishing boats. I didn't see any large ships coming down the Willamette, so a short distance downriver from the slough I angled across the 0.25-mile-wide (0.4 km) river, cleared the main channel quickly, and then rounded Belle Vue Point into the main stem of the Columbia.

The shoreline is gravel and sandy beach with private ownership above the high-water mark for the first 5 miles (8 km), except for Belle Vue Point County Park, a small county park with a gravel beach along the river that can only be accessed by boat. This section of river to **Walton Beach** has wing dams every quarter mile, so I stayed well offshore until I passed an especially long protruding row of pilings with no more homes above the beach or wing dams in the distance.

Beyond the largest of the wing dams are 7 miles (11.3 km) of public beaches. I saw less than a handful of early-morning risers on Walton Beach, by far one of the longest fine sandy beaches along the Columbia, but by the time I got to Collins Beach the sun was hot and the beach was showing the first signs of a busy day of nude sunbathing.

There seemed to be an unmarked line where the bare-buns activities ended and the more prudent beach began. I paddled another mile (1.6 km) to be sure and then pulled out on the last sandy beach to stretch and relax. Reeder Road ended in a parking lot close by. I continued past the occasional beach and heavily foliaged shoreline for 3 miles (4.8 km) to Warrior Rock Lighthouse, an obvious landmark on a small point.

The wind had picked up on the river as I was paddling by the beaches, but I was partially protected by the northwest shoreline. Once I rounded Warrior Rock, though, I faced a long stretch of whitecaps over wide-open river. Unfortunately, I still had a long way to go. A short time later, I reached the north end of Sauvie Island and at the tip stayed right of the hundred or more perfectly spaced columns and rows of pilings charted as "Ruins." From the Ruins, I paddled through the quickly building waves across the short width of Multnomah Channel to St. Helens, and then followed the rocky shoreline past the marina to Grey Cliffs Waterfront Park. The wind had a clear path upriver, creating a frothing mess of whitecaps downriver. I pulled ·out on the park's tiny gravel beach and carried my kayak up a short trail to the parking lot. I wasn't ready to give up for the day, so I had a late lunch and waited to see if the 10–15-mph (16–24.1-kmph) wind and gusts up to 25 mph (40.2 kmph) would die down in the afternoon.

Around 4 PM, the wind slowed to a breeze and the river looked inviting. I took off from the park and followed the shoreline past Columbia City's urban and

Derelicts and parts of boats abandoned along the shoreline of the Columbia can be a hazard for other boaters and a huge expense to state and federal agencies, which have to clean up hazardous material left on board.

industrial shoreline, and then around three long wing dams, one sticking out into the river almost 300 yards (274 m), to the south end of Deer Island.

A bit over 9 miles (14.5 km) from St. Helens, I left the main river channel and paddled the smaller of the two channels west of Sandy Island, a low-lying island between **Kalama,** Washington, and Goble, Oregon. The marshy, vegetated areas along the shoreline were filled with birds, and at least three blue herons squawked their annoyance at me for disturbing their hunt for dinner. Eagles seemed to know this section of river was loaded with fish as well, for they were plentiful in the old-growth trees and numerous snags overlooking the river. I ended the day's paddle at Goble just before twilight.

I was in the water early again the next morning to catch the outgoing tide. The tide had been unusually high that night and with the current carried me along the rocky shoreline downriver from Goble at a good pace. A half mile (0.8 km) into the paddle, the river's immense flow hits a rocky point like a hammer, sending the strong current to either side of the rocks and back upon itself, creating a turbulent mess that has to sort itself out and somehow send the water back into the main river. Once I was past the rocky point, I raced along miles of tree-lined shoreline; through an established anchorage area for big ships and barges; and finally to the beach just past the Rainier City Park beach, 34 miles (54.7 km) from the Columbia Slough put-in. Looking over at Longview and its busy ports, I was glad to be on the Oregon side of the river in the quiet town of Rainier.

After a brief rest on the beach, I continued through the busy port district of Longview and Rainier, where at least a dozen ships were being loaded and offloaded with logs, grain, and other commodities, or anchored nearby.

The take-out at Mayger is a few hundred yards downriver from the century-old Mayger fish-packing ware-house, a relic of a bygone era.

Two miles (3.2 km) past the Lewis and Clark bridge and just past Dibblee Point Beach, I entered the channel south of Lord Island, passing an old hulk ship I later identified as a 1950s US Navy LST (Landing Ship Tank) that had been moored in the slough since 2003. This ship, like hundreds of others abandoned along the river, looked like another *Davy Crockett* environmental disaster waiting to happen. During illegal scrap salvage near Camas in early 2011, the 431-foot *Crockett,* a former navy ship later converted to a flat deck barge, broke apart and leaked fuel oil and diesel into the river. The cleanup effort took eight months and $22 million. The owner, Bret A. Simpson, was later found guilty of two criminal violations of the Clean Water Act and sentenced to four months in prison, small fines, and home detention—another slap on the wrist by our judicial system. Abandoned boats and ships on the Columbia are a major problem for the two states' environmental agencies and the federal government. Enforcement is expensive for the taxpayers, while scofflaws get away with a pittance of the cleanup costs.

From my kayak low in the water, the channel ahead looked like a dead end, as it seemed to be an impassable slough blocked with vegetation. But there was a narrow, almost-too-shallow channel that seemed to reach the main channel of the river just 0.5 mile (0.8 km) away. I took the chance and found myself in tidal flats with a wing dam blocking my exit between Lord and Walker islands. With less than a foot of water, I paddled and pushed myself through another channel and again reached open water, this time with a clear view that showed me the slough was passable.

The almost vertical terrain along the mainland shoreline climbs 150 feet (46 m) above the river. It's hard to believe the immense old-growth Douglas firs can cling to it. There's a railroad track near the river, so the shore is rugged and built up from railroad riprap. The track doesn't take anything away from the beauty of this north-facing slope of rare old-growth fir, shoreline cottonwood, and thick brush.

A little over 2 miles (3.2 km) from the tip of Walker Island, I passed the historic Mayger fish-packing warehouse, built on pilings in 1910. Despite its decrepit appearance, it was evidently still being used in 1998. A few hundred yards downriver was my lodestone for the day, Mayger Beach. I went around a private dock sticking into the channel and a row of pilings before paddling over to Joyce who was parked on the beach that was quickly disappearing under the incoming tide. With the strong tide against me and the wind blowing hard upriver, Mayger Beach was a great place to end the day.

LEG 34: Mayger Beach to Astoria Marina

Distance: 42.4 miles (68.2 km)
Paddle Time: 9 to 13 hours (shorter time reflects outgoing tide and strong current)

River View

The leg from **Mayger Beach** to the **Astoria Marina** follows the Columbia's final journey as a freshwater river. As the Columbia approaches **Tenasillahe Island** and the 35,000-acre (14,000 ha) **Lewis and Clark National Wildlife Refuge,** it begins to slow and braid around and through numerous sand islands in **Cathlamet Bay** and becomes the Columbia River Estuary where the river's fresh water begins to mingle with the ocean's salt water. Every turn while you are on the river, in a side channel or near a slough, is another opportunity to see a different species of bird, spot an otter or beaver along the shore, or be startled by a sea lion bigger than your boat rising near your bow.

From Mayger Beach, follow **Bradbury Slough** south of **Crimms Island** 3.7 miles (6 km) to **Port Westward** and the former Cascade Grain ethanol plant, which went bankrupt in 2009 and is now being used by the new owners to store and ship North Dakota crude oil obtained by the fracking process. Enter the main shipping channel and stay along the Oregon shoreline to **Wallace**

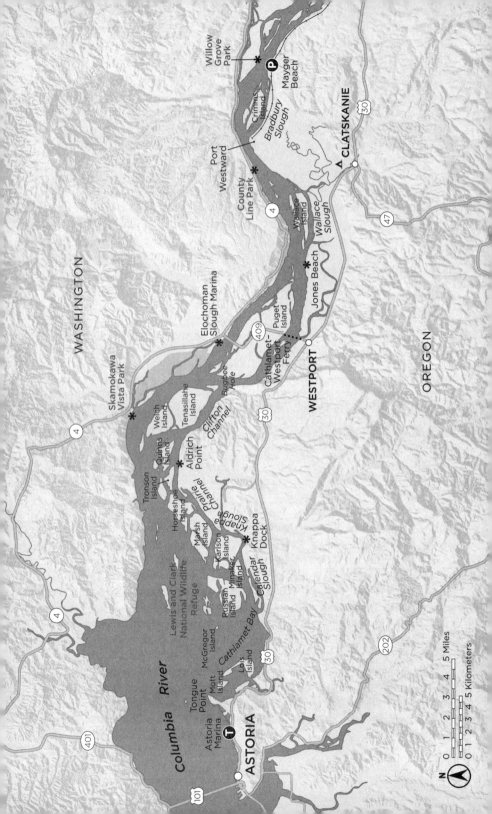

CAPTAIN ROBERT GRAY: DISCOVERING THE COLUMBIA

The Columbia River was named by Robert Gray, an American merchant ship captain born in Rhode Island in 1755. Gray is best known for being the first American to circumnavigate the globe between 1787 and 1790 on the ship *Columbia Rediviva* and, during his second trip to the Northwest coast in 1791, discovering and naming the Columbia River. During the second voyage, Gray wintered on Vancouver Island and then set sail on April 2, 1792, to follow the Washington coastline south. He was searching for the large river near the 46th parallel he had tried to enter in 1788, but was turned back by the tides. Gray found the opening again when he noticed muddy waters flowing from shore.

In the evening of May 11, 1792, Gray's men found a safe channel into the mouth of the large river. He and his crew sailed upriver 13 miles (20.9 km), where they traded with the local natives and named the river "Columbia" after his ship.

Slough south of **Wallace Island,** 7.5 miles (12.1 km) from Mayger. The slough looks as though it ends in a bay, but it continues around Wallace Island to **Jones Beach,** a kite-boarding mecca known for its steady and frequent wind. The alternative is to paddle north of Wallace Island and between several sandy satellite islands, but if it is blowing from the west, you will have a difficult paddle around the west end of the island in very rough water.

Jones Beach parallels the main channel, and ship traffic is close to the shore. If you stop for a break, pull your boat above the high-water mark, because the bow and engine waves from the big ships in the channel come out of deep water and break high on the beach. West of Jones Beach is 4 miles (6.4 km) of straight, wide-open channel for the wind and waves to build, so paddle early and with the tide to avoid this problem. Also 4 miles (6.4 km) from Jones Beach is the last ferry on the Columbia before the Pacific, the Cathlamet–Westport Ferry, which runs from 5 AM to 10:15 PM from **Puget Island,** Washington, to **Westport,** Oregon, every 15 minutes. Be alert, as the ferry enters the Columbia from **Westport Slough** and can be in your path in minutes.

Continue paddling along the south shoreline past the Georgia-Pacific pulp mill, which closed its doors early in 2013. (It may start up again under new ownership or when the market improves, but for the foreseeable future there are a lot of local folks out of work.) A few miles past the plant, the shipping channel narrows to less than 600 yards (549 m) and deepens to 60 feet (18 m) in an area known as **Bugbee Hole.** Hug the west shoreline and hope no monster oceangoing ships pass by. Within 1 mile (1.6 km) the shipping channel widens and continues north; the paddle route, on the other hand, turns northwest and follows **Clifton Channel** southwest of Tenasillahe Island, with no tugs or big ships nearby until **Tongue Point** just east of Astoria.

The paddle route through the Lewis and Clark National Wildlife Refuge and Cathlamet Bay to Astoria is simple—stay river left. Clifton Channel ends at **Aldrich Point,** the northernmost point in the state of Oregon. Lewis and Clark named this bluff Point Samuel, after Samuel Lewis, a relative of Meriwether Lewis, but by intent or accident many of the original names given to landmarks along the river by the Corps of Discovery expedition seem to have been changed by later explorers or early landowners.

From Aldrich Point, 25 miles (40.2 km) from Mayger, paddle west and then southwest in **Prairie Channel** for 4.5 miles (7.2 km) past **Tronson, Horseshoe,** and **Marsh islands**. Be aware that all the channels and sloughs are very shallow in places and especially at low tide. Stay left at **Karlson Island** and paddle into the narrow **Knappa Slough,** which runs directly south for 1.3 miles (2.1 km) to **Knappa Dock**. If the tide changes or the wind picks up, there is a pebble beach take-out with a short drag or carry to your vehicle. Knappa Slough turns to the northwest from the dock and ends just east of **Minaker Island**. Stay left again and paddle through **Calendar Slough** south of the island, but in the deeper water near the island shore to avoid sandy shoals against the mainland. Calendar Slough puts you back into Prairie Channel south of **Russian Island**. Just past Russian Island, Prairie Channel turns north. Follow Prairie Channel past the west shorelines of Russian Island and tiny **McGregor Island.**

The marine charts warn boaters that "Prairie Channel is subject to frequent change." To avoid towing your boat over sandy shallows, keep paddling north until you pass all the sand islands to your west. When you are just about directly east of Tongue Point, paddle toward the point. If in doubt, look for the heads of harbor seals and sea lions, which watch you and occasionally try to spook you by splashing surface water near your boat. They know where the deeper channel is even if you don't.

Tongue Point protrudes into the Columbia for almost a mile (1.6 km) from the mainland and is an obvious landmark from quite a distance. From the sandy islands of Cathlamet Bay, finish the day's paddle by rounding the rock point, keeping in mind this is one of the deepest areas of the entire lower Columbia at over 90 feet (27 m) deep with a strong current and tidal flow just offshore. Paddle this area when the tide is going out, or you'll be in a desperate fight to reach the eddy along the point's shoreline and Astoria. Once around the point and out of the main channel, it is a 2.6-mile (4.2 km) paddle to the Astoria Marina just past Pier 39.

Hazards include strong tides and current; shallow sandy shoals; seagoing container ships; ferry crossing; potentially high wind and large waves in the channel; submerged rocks near shore; wing dams; tidal marsh; and reduced visibility in certain months.

Jones Beach, a lower Columbia windsurfing and kite-surfing destination because of its steady winds, is on the main shipping channel, as can be seen from this ship passing kite surfers.

FLOW AND SEASON: River flow from Mayger Beach to Astoria depends on the time of year and the daily tide change. There is a current at Mayger, but it varies from standing water to 3 to 5 mph (4.8 to 8 kmph) with the tides. As the river widens and braids into the islands of the Lewis and Clark National Wildlife Refuge and Cathlamet Bay, actual river current seems almost nonexistent, but the tidal flow closer to the mouth and in the deeper channels makes up for any loss. As they say, go with the flow. Paddling against an incoming tide in Cathlamet Bay will take you more time to complete the journey. The best months to paddle this leg are April through June, when the dams are releasing spring run-off and the tides are strong. But this leg is doable throughout the year, and it would be especially fascinating in February and March during the migration season, when 3000 tundra swans, 5000 Canada geese, and 50,000 ducks gather in Cathlamet Bay and throughout the Lewis and Clark NWR.

PUT-IN: Mayger Beach, US 30 on to N Nebraska St and NW 5th St, then to Beaver Falls Rd, to Quincy–Mayger Rd to Mayger Rd.

TAKE-OUTS: Jones Beach, 11.2 miles (18 km), Woodson Rd off US 30 to Riverfront Rd; Aldrich Point, 25 miles (40.2 km), Ziak Gnat Creek Ln off US 30 to Aldrich Point Rd; Knappa Dock, 30.6 miles (49.2 km), Old

US 30 off US 30 to Knappa Dock Rd; Astoria Marina boat ramp, 42.4 (68.2 km), 36th St off US 30, Astoria. All distances are from the Mayger Beach put-in.

SERVICES: Clatskanie has a very nice motel, along with several restaurants, a grocery store, and convenience stores; Astoria is a full-service community with excellent motels and restaurants, coffee shops, bakeries, grocery stores, gas stations, and paddling shops.

CAMPING: Camping is limited along this leg, but there are two nice facilities: Clatskanie City Park, in Clatskanie; and Fort Stevens State Park, East Harbor St off US 101 to OR 104 to Pacific Dr (see Leg 35). RVs have many more options, including Jones Beach and Aldrich Point.

Passage

I set off down Bradbury Slough from Mayger Beach at daybreak with a light wind blowing into my face. It wasn't enough to keep me on shore, but I was certainly aware of sections of the river ahead of me that could be worse. I had to start. There was a strong outgoing tide with the current, and I needed the tide to make the long distance to Astoria.

I paddled with the flow of the river, feeling as though I was under sail. At the end of the channel, I came to the crude-oil shipping port at Port Westward and gained the main stem of the Columbia and its powerful flow. The huge pier and loading area along the shore was circled with yellow oil-containment booms. As I sped by, two sea lions came up behind me for a closer look and then disappeared into deep water off the pier, at 60 to 70 feet (18 to 21 m) one of the deepest holes in the river.

Past the pier, the wind picked up speed as it raced up the river from the southwest. I paddled along the shoreline for 3 miles (4.8 km) to avoid the bigger waves and then crossed the mouth of Wallace Slough to the east end of Wallace Island to get out of the wind. I didn't know where I was, so rather than paddle in the slough south of Wallace Island, which looked like a dead end, I took the narrow channel north of the island, protected from the wind and waves by the curve of the shoreline and two low-lying vegetated islands between me and the main stem of the river. This worked until I reached the sand spit at the western end of Wallace Island, which protrudes into the main channel.

The wind was howling 20 to 30 mph (32.2 to 48.3 kmph) in the shipping channel, and the river was a frothing mess. After pulling the kayak across the east sand spit, I launched along the shallow sand beach and stayed as close to shore as possible for a few hundred yards, but finally decided to pull out again, drag my kayak across the farthest sand beach on the windward side of the island, and launch across Wallace Slough—no easy task in waves going over my bow.

The distance was only 400 yards (366 m) across the narrow Wallace Slough channel to Jones Beach, but the effort to paddle into the wind and waves of the full-blown gale made it feel like 4 miles (6.4 km). I paddled hard to the beach and along the shoreline for another 100 yards (91 m) before spotting Joyce parked in the shade of the trees at the entrance to the beach area. I beached the boat and pulled it up to where I could get to it with the SUV. Jones Beach was only 12.1 miles (19.4 km) from Mayger, so I hung out at the beach for hours watching the expert kite boarders rip across the main channel and back again waiting for the wind to die. Later in the day the steady wind increased and gusts were in the 40-mph (64.4 kmph) range. We left in hopes of better conditions in the morning.

The river was without a ripple at sunrise the next day, and was flowing 3 to 4 mph (4.8 to 6.4 kmph) with the tide and current. I launched off Jones Beach and within 45 minutes passed behind the Cathlamet–Westport Ferry on its way to Puget Island. The river turned northwest past the ferry route and narrowed to less than 600 yards (549 m) to avoid an almost vertical bluff on the Oregon

The Lewis and Clark National Wildlife Refuge is a short distance upriver from Astoria in Cathlamet Bay.

shoreline. I didn't want to share this 1-mile (1.6 km) section with one of the many ships moving out with the ebb tide, so I paddled quickly past Bugbee Hole to reach Clifton Channel, which is south of Tenasillahe Island. I was lucky. Just after reaching Clifton Channel, the 67,000-ton container ship *Hanjin Paris* quietly came up behind me at 14 to 17 mph (22.5 to 27.4 kmph) and continued north up the main channel, sending 4-foot (1.2 m) rollers into my stern for an unexpected boost into the Clifton Channel.

Paddling through Clifton Channel was peaceful and enjoyable. Five eagles, two adults and three juveniles, were flying between the cottonwoods above the river, sometimes swooping down low on the water after a fish, but their success was limited to one catch before I was out of sight and around the bend to Aldrich Point. Joyce was there, and I stopped briefly for a bite to eat before pushing off into the tidal current and the beginning of Prairie Channel. I was now within the Lower Columbia River Estuary, part of the Lewis and Clark National Wildlife Refuge.

I had to be careful and locate the deeper water, because the estuary is known for its tidal marshes, mudflats, and sandbars that come and go as the tide ebbs and falls. As I turned southwest along the Devils Elbow off Horseshoe Island in Prairie Channel, what looked like a good passage near the bend suddenly became a sandbar under 3 inches of water. I backed up using my paddle as a pole, found deeper channel water, and continued, but wary of the underwater terrain.

At Karlson Island, the channel splits into Prairie Channel to the northwest and Knappa Slough to the southwest. I couldn't remember which one to take to avoid the sand islands and shoals in Cathlamet Bay, so I stayed river left and paddled toward the deeper southwest channel and was glad I did. Knappa Slough had navigable water and led to Knappa Dock. Along the marsh on the way to the dock, a young fox trotting along the nearby mudflat stopped and watched me paddle by, and then scooted into the underbrush.

The tide was no longer in my favor, but I still had a weak current. Rather than take a break at Knappa Dock, I continued along Knappa Slough to take advantage of the rapidly diminishing current. Within a few miles, I paddled through the narrow and much shallower Calendar Slough south of tiny Minaker Island. I realized that in a "slough" I'd have to be prepared to bottom out on the sandbars and mudflats, but in a "channel" there would be deeper water somewhere. Calendar Slough was short and led me back to the larger Prairie Channel, which had come around from Karlson Island. I stayed more or less in the center of the channel to avoid the wide underwater sandbars near Russian Island.

I faced another decision at the southwest end of Russian Island: take Prairie Channel south of **Lois Island** and north to Tongue Point, or the northern channel, which went north along the west side of Russian and McGregor islands? From my vantage point low in the water, there were half a dozen temporary sand islands showing in Cathlamet Bay. I took the north channel, but made the mistake of taking a shortcut between two sand islands and was soon bottomed out in the tidal flats. After poling and pulling my kayak 0.5 mile (0.8 km), I finally found deeper water and set course for Tongue Point.

The tide had turned and the closer I got to Tongue Point, the stronger it pushed against me. Tongue Point is known as a constriction point where the flow of the Columbia is squeezed into a smaller area because of the rocky point sticking so far out into the river. As I got closer to the point and the paddling got tougher, I moved off the main flow of the river coming around the point toward the inner shoreline to find an eddy or at least dead water. It worked, and I made the shore just south of the tip of Tongue Point.

I had to get around the point, so I paddled to the rocky tip and stayed close to the shoreline to catch the eddy created by the incoming tide. I could see Pier 39 2.5 miles (4 km) away, but with the incoming tide and the wind suddenly blowing 15 to 20 mph (24.1 to 32.2 kmph) on the Astoria side of Tongue Point, the paddle was going to be difficult. After an hour of wind and waves, and paddling against the strong tidal current, I reached the Astoria Marina entrance and the take-out. Joyce was there as usual, this time with cheese, crackers, and a bottle of sparkling cider to celebrate my arrival in Astoria.

Joyce and I made a great team and found new adventure in our lives and along the river.

An Astoria-based fishing trawler catches the ebb tide on its way to the mouth of the Columbia.

LEG 35: Astoria Marina to Clatsop Spit

Distance: 13.8 miles (22.2 km)
Paddle Time: 3 to 5 hours

River View

The final leg, from **Astoria Marina** to **Clatsop Spit** (taking out at Fort Stevens's **South Jetty**), is one of the classic paddles on the Columbia, combining a paddler's view of the Astoria historical pier district; an open-water paddle across **Youngs Bay;** and the challenge of strong tides and breakers as the river and ocean collide at the end of Clatsop Spit. The distance is short, but the journey is challenging given the deep channel tide near shore, large-ship traffic, and the chance of a headwind across Youngs Bay. The key to paddling the 14 miles (22.5 km) is timing—get an early start and coincide your arrival in Youngs Bay with the change of tide.

The put-in is the boat ramp at the Astoria Marina. You'll know you're at the launch by the noisy barking and grunting from the hundred or more sea lions lying on the floating docks inside the marina. Oregon's Department of Fish & Wildlife has tried trapping and shipping the animals back to their natural habitat along the coast, but the sea lions know a food trough when they swim in it, so the offenders return hundreds of miles (200 to 300 km) in just a few weeks back to the salmon buffets migrating in the Columbia River.

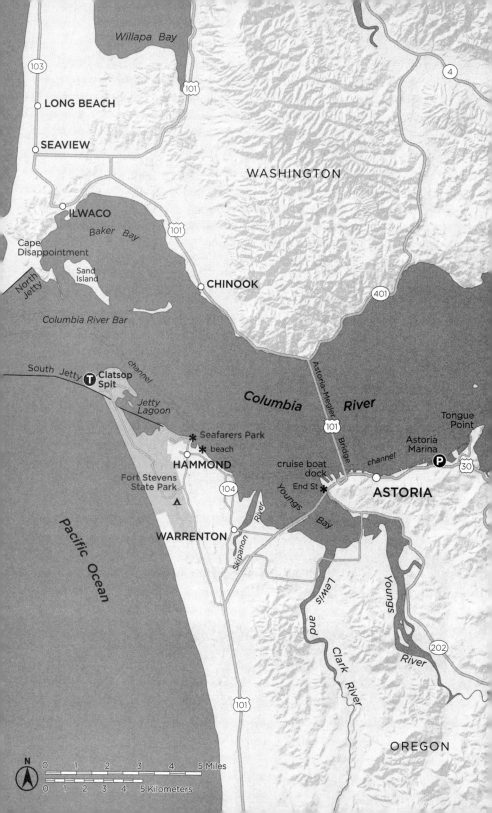

Once outside the marina, paddle close to the piers as you make your way to the **Astoria–Megler Bridge** (US Highway 101), which begins crossing the Columbia in downtown Astoria. The deep-water shipping channel is between 300 and 400 yards (274 to 366 m) offshore, so the tide near shore is like a fast-flowing river during the peak hours. Stay inside the first bridge piling and then close to the Portway Street Pier (the cruise ship dock) and Piers 2 and 3. Pier 3 is the farthest point west before entering Youngs Bay.

If the tide is neutral or incoming, the paddle route can be straight across the bay 1.8 miles (2.9 km) to the mouth of the **Skipanon River.** But if it is an outgoing tide, I strongly suggest paddling into Youngs Bay to the US 101 bridge to use the tide's power as you cross over and also to prevent being carried out into the shipping channel, which is not far from the entrance to the bay. This area is also known for its east winds, so expect waves in the open water if there's more than just a breeze. From Pier 3 to the east end of the bridge is tidal mudflats, which can be avoided by staying offshore 100 yards (91 m), especially if it's a low tide.

The bay on the west end of the US 101 bridge is protected from the wind but is mudflats as well. Angle from the bridge to the mouth of the Skipanon River and then paddle along the shoreline past the big piers to either a small park beach just south of the **Hammond Marina** or to **Seafarers Park,** adjacent to and north of the marina and 2.5 miles (4 km) from the Skipanon River. Both are excellent spots to pull out and rest. Seafarers Park has restroom facilities, while the beach access is a bit more primitive but has a nicer beach.

My face-off with the 93,500-ton cruise ship *Norwegian Jewel* as I made my way to Youngs Bay was brief, but exciting.

CHANGING THE MOUTH OF THE COLUMBIA

Since first discovered by Captain Robert Gray in 1792, the channel to the mouth of the Columbia and shorelines of the Pacific has changed dramatically due to the river's flow, tides, storms, and dams. In order to maintain the navigational channel depth without dredging, three jetties were built over a period of fifty-four years.

Construction of the first 4.5 miles (7.2 km) of the South Jetty was begun in 1885 and completed in 1895. An extension of 2 miles (3.2 km) was built from 1903 to 1913. The South Jetty is built of rocks averaging 10 tons (9.1 t), with some weighing as much as 25 tons (22.7 t). The giant boulders were carried by rail on three trestles that extended over the top of the jetty and placed by machine or dumped. The jetty's height averages 76 feet (23.2 m), with 26 feet (7.9 m) above mean low water. Its width ranges from 45 to 70 feet (13.7 to 21.3 m) across the top, with a base width of 1000 feet (305 m) near shore to 150 feet (45.7 m) at the north end.

Powerful ocean storms have damaged the outer jetty over the years, requiring major repair work from 1931 to 1936. Over 2.2 million tons (2 million metric tons) of stone was placed to strengthen the structure at that time. To stabilize the outer end, concrete was used from shoreward to within 3900 feet (1189 m) of the end of the jetty.

The 2.5-mile-long (4 km) North Jetty, a smaller structure, was built from 1913 to 1917 using only 3 million tons (2.7 million metric tons) of rock. Jetty "A" inside the mouth was built to offset changing channel conditions caused by the other two jetties, and was completed in 1938. The three jetties are believed to have had more influence on sediment transport along the Pacific coast than all the dams put together.

A mile (1.6 km) past Seafarers Park is a rock jetty built to protect **Jetty Lagoon** from filling up with sediment. There will be some tidal chop as you paddle around this obstruction, but once you are past the jetty, the paddle is easy in windless conditions to the sandy beaches on the south and east side of Clatsop Spit. There will be more tidal chop just offshore, as the tidewater fights its way out of the lagoon and around the spit. At the northeast end of the spit, there are swells coming off the **Columbia Bar** where the river and Pacific collide. The bar is several miles (3.2 km) out, but the turmoil of two great water bodies gnashing teeth in such a small area creates strong currents and conditions that result in breakers along the north shore of the spit.

There is a calm area between the beach and breaking waves farther out. Paddle just offshore west to the South Jetty and, as the surf and beach meet, turn your bow toward the sand and let the breakers push you in to end the leg.

Hazards include strong tidal current; high wind and large waves; breakers on the northeast end of Clatsop Spit; mudflats in Youngs Bay; and cruise ships and large boats docking at the piers.

FLOW AND SEASON: With an ebb tide, the flow rate on this leg can be as high as 6 to 7 mph (9.7 to 11.3 kmph) in the main channel or much slower near the shore. There is a steady current with the outgoing tide, which is reversed by a strong incoming tide. This leg can be paddled all year round, but the best time is from April through October.

PUT-IN: Astoria Marina, 37th St off US 30.

TAKE-OUTS: Tidal flat off End St, 4.1 miles (6.6 km), Youngs Bay; unmaintained beach, 8.7 miles (14 km), intersection of Iredale St and Iredale Dr, Hammond; Seafarers Park, 9.1 miles (14.6 km), end of Lake Dr, Hammond; Clatsop Spit, 11.5 miles (18.5 km), parking lot at south end of Jetty Rd; South Jetty beach, 13.8 miles (22.2 km), 0.4 mile (0.6 km) north of the South Jetty parking lot. All distances are from the Astoria Marina put-in.

SERVICES: Astoria is a full-service community with excellent motels and restaurants, coffee shops, bakeries, grocery stores, gas stations, and paddling shops.

CAMPING: Fort Stevens State Park, E Harbor St off US 101 to OR 104 to Pacific Dr; Astoria KOA, Ridge Rd off US 101 to Hammond.

Passage

Amid the barking and groaning of over a hundred sea lions lying on the docks at the Astoria Marina, I paddled west along the old piers and new buildings lining the Astoria waterfront. The outgoing tide along the waterfront was swift and strong. Just off the support tower under the Astoria–Megler Bridge (US 101), which is close to the deep shipping channel, I felt as though I could be swept out to sea in an hour.

Less than 0.5 mile (0.8 km) from the bridge, I found myself in a face-off with the 93,500-ton cruise ship *Norwegian Jewel,* 100 yards (91 m) seaward and coming in to the dock at the Portway Street Pier. High on the pier above me were two men in uniform with radios guiding the big ship in. I gauged the distance between the ship and me, and decided to paddle through rather than wait and go around the ship. The 965-foot-long (294 m) ship must have been using bow and stern thrusters, because it was coming in fast. I yelled up at the two officers (who didn't look all that concerned), "I'll be quick about it!" And then one of them replied with a grin, "Well, slow down, this is a no-wake zone!"

With the tide ripping me along the pier, I made the distance in minutes, while passengers, some still in their robes, watched the scene from their staterooms amused, I'm sure. I paddled around Pier 3 and turned into Youngs Bay. The wind had picked up around the corner and this, coupled with the outgoing tide, convinced me to take out on the west end of **End Street** near the Oregon Coast US 101 bridge over the bay and wait for the tide change the next day. The next morning a low-pressure system had descended on Astoria and the wind was 20 to 25 mph (32.2 to 40.2 kmph) with gusts in the 40s (64 kmph). I would have to return at a later time.

Two months later, after a trip to India, I returned to my take-out point in Youngs Bay near the bridge. There was a light wind and it looked like rain, but the bay seemed calm and there was a tiny hint of morning sun touching the clouds. To catch the slack tide at 6:45 AM, just before the ebb, I unloaded my boat at 6 AM and set off from the rocky beach. It was not predicted to be a fast outgoing tide, so I paddled parallel to the bridge 100 yards (91 m) to the northwest as I made the 1.5-mile (2.4 km) crossing in rough chop to **Warrenton,** and then turned downriver well offshore from the acres of tidal flats on the southwest side of the bay.

I skirted the protruding landform jetties and delta from the Skipanon River flowing out through Warrenton, and then paddled by multiple three-pole marker pilings, each one occupied by a bald eagle. The first couple of eagles flew off as I approached, but as I continued downriver, some of them held their pilings, just as curious about me as I was of them.

The tidal current lightly pulled me past a sawdust chip plant protruding into the bay that had conveyor belts dumping sawdust into a high-walled rusty barge. The operator never looked up from his book, as I caught the surge of trapped tidal water trying to get around the pier and was swept along to where Joyce was standing on a 0.5-acre (0.2 ha) sandy beach just before the Hammond Marina and a little less than 5 miles (8 km) from my put-in. This was not Seafarers Park, on the other side of the marina, but a classic Columbia beach nevertheless. I didn't know where I was going to pull out at Fort Stevens State Park because of the breakers on the northwest side of Clatsop Spit, so I told Joyce to just look for me somewhere on the beach.

Bald eagles were my constant companions. This one stood firm on the beach near the South Jetty as I ended my journey.

The tide was picking up steam as I passed the two rock jetties at the mouth of the marina and continued along the mostly rock riprap shoreline of Fort Stevens State Park toward Jetty Lagoon, named for the railroad trestle used to build the South Jetty between 1885 and 1895. At the south end to Jetty Lagoon, I rounded a small rock jetty protruding 300 yards (274 m) into the channel and paddled 1.3 miles (2.1 km) to the southeast beach on Clatsop Spit. I wanted a taste of salt water, so kept going along the east shoreline, through rough tidal chop, and then turned the corner inside the breakers just offshore.

Four bald eagles were feeding on the carcass of a 4-foot (1.2 m) white sturgeon that had drifted onto the beach, and only one of them stood its ground as I paddled by. A mile (1.6 km) farther along the north shore of the spit, I reached the pounding waves alongside the South Jetty and, with the power of a few waves pushing me from behind, beached the kayak. Joyce found me dragging it farther onto the shore, ran up, and gave me a big hug. Our multiyear journey of discovery, not only of the river but of ourselves, was finally complete.

As I towed my kayak from the South Jetty beach to the parking lot in Fort Stevens State Park, I thought about how fabulous my trip with Joyce had been and how lucky I am to live in the Pacific Northwest.

OPPOSITE: We are all *Wy-Kan-Ush-Pum*, Salmon People. Smoker Marchand's *The Chief* watches over the Columbia from Beebe Springs Natural Area south of Wells Dam.

RESOURCES

Recommended Reading

Freeman, Lewis R. *Down the Columbia.* New York: Dodd, Mead, and Company, 1921.

Harden, Blaine. *A River Lost: The Life and Death of the Columbia.* New York: W. W. Norton & Co., 1996.

Landers, Rich, Dan Hansen, Verne Huser, and Doug North. *Paddling Washington.* Seattle: Mountaineers Books, 2008.

Lichatowich, Jim. *Salmon without Rivers.* Washington, DC: Island Press, 1999.

Nisbet, Jack. *Sources of the River.* Seattle: Sasquatch Books, 1994.

Environmental Agencies and Awareness

American Rivers, 877-347-7550, www.americanrivers.org

Center for Environmental Law & Policy, 206-829-8366, www.celp.org

Columbia River Estuary Study Taskforce, www.columbiariverestuary.org

Columbia Riverkeeper, 541-387-3030, http://columbiariverkeeper.org

Friends of the Columbia Gorge, 503-241-3762, www.gorgefriends.org

Lower Columbia Estuary Partnership, 503-226-1565, www.estuarypartner ship.org

Sierra Club Washington state chapter, 206-378-0114, http://cascade .sierraclub.org

Swim for a Healthy World: Christopher Swain www.swimforcleanwater.org

Trout Unlimited, 800-834-2419, www.tu.org

Voyages of Rediscovery, 509-675-5592, www.voyagesofrediscovery.org

Wild Steelhead Coalition, http://wildsteelheadcoalition.org

Regional Paddling and Camping

Destination British Columbia, www.hellobc.com
Guide to Northwest camping, www.freeguidetonwcamping.com
Lower Columbia Water Trail, 503-226-1565, www.estuarypartnership.org
Wenatchee Outdoors, www.justgetout.net/Wenatchee

Tribal Government

Columbia River Inter-Tribal Fishing Commission, 541-296-6010, www.critfc.org
Confederated Tribes of the Colville Reservation, www.colvilletribes.com
Spokane Tribe of Indians, 509-458-6500, www.spokanetribe.com

Canadian Government Agencies

BC Hydro, www.bchydro.com
British Columbia government, http://www2.gov.bc.ca
British Columbia Parks: www.env.gov.bc.ca/bcparks, reservations:
    204-983-3500, or 800-689-9025 (outside Canada), www.env.gov.bc.ca
    /bcparks/reserve
British Columbia: Stream flow data, www.wateroffice.ec.gc.ca/index_e.html
British Columbia: Road status, www.gov.bc.ca/tran
British Columbia: Customs and border crossings, 800-461-9999, www.cbsa
    -asfc.gc.ca
Parks Canada, www.pc.gc.ca
Weather, http://weather.gc.ca

Canadian City Government

Fairmont Hot Springs, www.fairmonthotsprings.com
Invermere, 403-464-8727, www.invermere.ca
Nakusp, 250-265-3689, www.nakusp.com
Radium Hot Springs, 250-347-6455, www.radiumhotsprings.ca
Revelstoke, 250-837-2161, www.cityofrevelstoke.com
Trail, 250-364-1262, www.trail.ca

US City Government

Astoria, 503-325-5821, http://astoria.or.us
Boardman, 541-481-9252, www.cityofboardman.com
Cascade Locks, 541-374-8484, www.cascade-locks.or.us
Clatskanie, 503-728-2622, www.cityofclatskanie.com
The Dalles, 541-296-5481, www.ci.the-dalles.or.us
Hood River, 541-386-1488, http://ci.hood-river.or.us

Kennewick, 509-585-4200, www.go2kennewick.com
Pateros, 509-923-2571, www.grandcouleedam.com
Portland, 503-823-4000, www.portlandonline.com
Rainier, 503-556-7301, www.cityofrainier.com
Richland, 509-942-7390, www.ci.richland.wa.us
Wenatchee, 509-888-6200, www.wenatcheewa.gov

Ferries

BC Interior ferry schedules:
Arrow Park, Needles, and Upper Arrow Lake, www.th.gov.bc.ca/marine/ferry
    _schedules.htm
Cathlamet–Westport Ferry, 360-795-9996, www.cathlametchamber.com/ferry
    _schedule.php
Gifford–Inchelium Ferry, www.colvilletribes.com/inchelium_gifford_ferry
    _schedule.php
Keller Ferry, 888-808-7977, www.wsdot.wa.gov/regions/eastern/kellerferry

British Columbia Kayak Clubs and Outfitters

Columbia River Kayak and Canoe, Invermere, 250-342-7397,
    http://columbiariverkayakcanoe.com
Columbia Valley Canoes, Golden, 250-272-0859, www.goldencanoerentals.com
Endless Adventures Kayaking, Crescent Valley, 877-386-8181,
    http://endlessadventure.ca
Natural Escapes Kayaking, Revelstoke, 250-837-2679, www.naturalescapes.ca

US Kayak Clubs and Outfitters

Columbia River Kayaking, 360-747-1044, Skamokawa, WA,
    www.columbiariverkayaking.com
Lower Columbia Canoe Club, Portland, OR, www.l-ccc.org
Oregon Ocean Paddling Society (OOPS), Portland, OR, https://daniel-mccarty
    .squarespace.com
Spokane Canoe and Kayak Club, Spokane, WA, www.sckc.ws
Wenatchee Row and Paddle Club, Wenatchee, WA,
    www.wenatcheepaddle.org

Public Utility Districts

Chelan County PUD, 509-663-8121, www.chelanpud.org
Douglas County PUD, 509-884-7191, www.douglaspud.org
Grant County PUD, 509-754-0500, www.grantpud.org

State of Washington

Northwest Power and Conservation Council, 800-452-5161, www.nwcouncil.org
Washington State Department of Fish and Wildlife, http://wdfw.wa.gov
Washington State Parks and Recreation, 360-902-8844, www.parks.wa.gov

State of Oregon

Oregon State Parks, 800-551-6949, www.oregonstateparks.org

Federal Agencies

US Army Corps of Engineers, www.usace.army.mil/
US Army Yakima Training Center, www.lewis-mcchord.army.mil/yakima
US Coast Guard, Columbia River Sector, www.uscg.mil/d13/sectcolrvr
US Department of Commerce NOAA, www.noaa.gov
US Department of Energy, Hanford, www.hanford.gov
US Department of Interior, Bureau of Reclamation, www.usbr.gov
US Fish and Wildlife Service, www.fws.gov
US Fish and Wildlife Service National Refuge System, www.fws.gov/refuges
US Geological Survey Current Water data, www.waterdata.usgs.gov/nwis/rt

History

Canadian Pacific Railway: General information, Canada, 888-333-6370; US,
    413-319-7000; www.cpr.ca/en/about-cp
Center for Columbia River History, www.ccrh.org
The Columbia River, a photographic journey, http://columbiariverimages.com
The Corps of Discovery, Public Broadcasting System, www.pbs.org/weta
    /thewest/program/episodes/one/corpsof.htm
Hydroelectric development in southeastern British Columbia, www.musee
    virtuel-virtualmuseum.ca
Geology of Washington's Columbia Basin, www.dnr.wa.gov/researchscience
    /topics/geologyofwashington
Ice Age Floods Institute, www.iceagefloodsinstitute.org
Lewis and Clark Expedition, http://lewis-clark.org

Land Managers and Other Sources

Segment 1

BC Parks Reservation System, 800-689-9025, www.env.gov.bc.ca/bcparks
    /reserve
British Columbia iMap, http://maps.gov.bc.ca/ess/sv/imapbc

Columbia Valley Chamber of Commerce, 250-342-2844, www.cvchamber.ca
Columbia Valley Wetlands, www.wildsight.ca/columbiawetlands
Destination British Columbia, www.hellobc.com
Tourism Golden, 250-439-1111, www.tourismgolden.com
Yoho National Park, 250-343-6783, www.pc.gc.ca/eng/pn-np/bc/yoho
    /index.aspx

Segment 2

Arrow Lakes, www.bchydro.com/community/recreation_areas/arrow_lakes
    _reservoir.html
Arrow Lakes Provincial Park, www.env.gov.bc.ca/bcparks/explore/parkpgs
    /arrow_lks
BC Hydro Hugh Keenleyside Dam, www.bchydro.com/community/recreation
    _areas/hugh_keenleyside_dam.html
Blanket Creek Provincial Park, www.env.gov.bc.ca/bcparks/explore/parkpgs
    /blanket_crk
Burton Historical Park Campground, http://burtonhistoricalpark.com/home
Columbia River: Flow at Birchbank, BC: www.wateroffice.ec.gc.ca/graph
    /graph_e.html?stn=08NE049
Kinbasket Lake Resort, 250-344-1270, www.kinbasketlakeresort.com
Martha Creek Provincial Park, www.env.gov.bc.ca/bcparks/explore/parkpgs
    /martha_crk
Nakusp and Arrow Lakes tourism, 250-265-4234, http://nakusparrowlakes.com
Nakusp Municipal Campground, www.nakuspcampground.com
Revelstoke Dam, www.bchydro.com/community
Syringa Provincial Park, www.env.gov.bc.ca/bcparks/explore/parkpgs/syringa

Segment 3

Aquaculture on Rufus Woods Lake, www.epa.gov/region10/pdf/permits/npdes
    /wa/pac_aqua_site3_draft_ea_2012.pdf
Chief Joseph Dam, 206-764-3742, www.nws.usace.army.mil/Missions
    /CivilWorks/LocksandDams/ChiefJosephDam.aspx
Columbia River Dams, www.cbr.washington.edu/hydro
Colville Confederated Tribes Parks and Recreation, 509-634-3142,
    www.colvilletribes.com/tourism_parks_and_recreation.php
Grand Coulee Dam, BOR, www.usbr.gov/pn/grandcoulee
Grand Coulee Dam tourist information, 509-633-9265, www.grandcouleedam
    .com/welcome.html
Lake Roosevelt Forum, 509-535-7084, www.lrf.org
Lake Roosevelt National Recreation Area, 509-754-7800, www.nps.gov/laro
Rufus Woods Lake tourism, US Army Corps of Engineers, 509-686-5501,
    http://corpslakes.usace.army.mil/visitors/projects
Two Rivers Resort on Lake Roosevelt, www.two-rivers-resort.com

Segment 4

Beebe Bridge Park, www.chelanpud.org/beebe-bridge-park.html
Chelan County parks and recreation, 509-663-8121, www.chelanpud.org
    /parks-and-recreation.html
Columbia Plateau, 800-452-5161, www.nwcouncil.org/history/ColumbiaPlateau
Hanford Nuclear Reservation River Corridor, www.hanford.gov/page.cfm
    /RiverCorridor
Hanford Reach, www.fws.gov/refuges
Hood Park, reservations, 877-444-6777, www.nww.usace.army.mil/Missions
    /Recreation/McNaryDamandLakeWallula/HoodPark.aspx
Hoover Park and other Benton County parks, 509-783-3118, www.co.benton
    .wa.us
McNary National Wildlife Refuge, 509-546-8300, www.fws.gov/mcnary
National Weather Information System: Water flow below Priest Rapids Dam
    (monitored by USGS), www.usgs.gov/water
NOAA Northwest River Forecast: Current river flow, regional office,
    503-326-7401, www.nwrfc.noaa.gov/rfc
Northwest Discovery Water Trail, www.ndwt.org
Priest Rapids Dam, 509-754-0500, www.grantpud.org
Rock Island Dam, 509-663-8121, www.chelanpud.org
Rocky Reach Dam, 509-663-8121, www.chelanpud.org
Saddle Mountain National Wildlife Refuge, 509-546-8300, www.fws.gov
    /refuges
Wanapum Dam, 509-754-0500, www.grantpud.org
Washington Department of Fish and Wildlife Columbia Basin Wildlife Area,
    http://wdfw.wa.gov/lands/wildlife_areas/columbia_basin
Wells Dam, 509-884-7191, www.douglaspud.org

Segment 5

Boardman Marina Park, 888-481-7217, www.boardmanmarinapark.com
Bonneville Dam, 541-374-8442, www.nwp.usace.army.mil/Locations
    /ColumbiaRiver/Bonneville.aspx
Clatskanie City Park: 503-728-3094, www.freeguidetonwcamping.com
Columbia County: Tourist information, www.travelcolumbiacounty.com
Columbia River Bar: Current conditions, www.wrh.noaa.gov/pqr/marine/bars
    _mover.php
Columbia River Inter-tribal Fish Commission: Treaty access sites, 541-296-6010,
    www.critfc.org/for-tribal-fishers/in-lieutreaty-fishing-access-sites
The Dalles Dam, 541-506-7819, www.nwp.usace.army.mil/Locations
    /ColumbiaRiver/TheDalles.aspx
iWindSurf: Wind, tide, and temperature conditions for users of the lower
    Columbia; http://global.iwindsurf.com

John Day Dam, 541-506-7819, www.nwp.usace.army.mil/Locations
/ColumbiaRiver/JohnDay.aspx

Kelley Point Park, Portland, 503-823-7529, www.portlandoregon.gov
/parks/finder

Lewis & Clark National Wildlife Refuge, 360-795-3915, www.fws.gov/refuges

McNary Dam, 541-922-3211, www.nww.usace.army.mil/Locations
/DistrictLocksandDams/McNaryLockandDam.aspx

Portland boat launch facilities, www.oregonmetro.gov

SailFlow: Wind, tide, and weather data for river users; www.sailflow.com

Tidespy: Tide data from OceanFun Publishing, http://tidespy.com

Waterkeepers Swim Guide: Pollution levels at Columbia River beaches,
www.theswimguide.org

INDEX

ABOUT THE AUTHOR

Author and photographer John Roskelley is a dabbler in everything outdoors. If he's not dodging rocks on some alpine face in Canada or scratching his way up a frozen waterfall, John can be found hunting pheasants along the breaks of the Snake River or paddling the Columbia River from source to mouth. Adventuring flows in his blood. In his first half century, John fought his way up four of the highest peaks on Earth, including K2 and Everest, plus a plethora of devilishly hard, unclimbed Himalayan mountain faces and ridges.

"Paddling and climbing have many similarities." John says, "The most obvious, of course, is a front row seat to nature's unlimited marvels."

John's occupation changes as frequently as the weather. A graduate of Washington State University in geology, he's worked as a geologist, a marketing consultant, an elected Spokane County commissioner, and a governor appointee to Washington State's Growth Management Hearings Board. Through the years, he has written four books and numerous national magazine articles, and his photography has been on the cover of *National Geographic*.

John lives in Spokane with his wife, Joyce. "Paddling the Columbia was a team effort," he says. "Joyce always knew where I was on the river, even when I didn't." They have been married since 1972 and have three wonderful and productive kids, Dawn, Jess, and Jordan.

MOUNTAINEERS BOOKS is a leading publisher of mountaineering literature and guides—including our flagship title, *Mountaineering: The Freedom of the Hills*—as well as adventure narratives, natural history, and general outdoor recreation. Through our two imprints, Skipstone and Braided River, we also publish titles on sustainability and conservation. We are committed to supporting the environmental and educational goals of our organization by providing expert information on human-powered adventure, sustainable practices at home and on the trail, and preservation of wilderness.

The Mountaineers, founded in 1906, is a 501(c)(3) nonprofit outdoor activity and conservation organization whose mission is "to explore, study, preserve, and enjoy the natural beauty of the outdoors." One of the largest such organizations in the United States, it sponsors classes and year-round outdoor activities throughout the Pacific Northwest, including climbing, hiking, backcountry skiing, snowshoeing, bicycling, camping, paddling, and more. The Mountaineers also supports its mission through its publishing division, Mountaineers Books, and promotes environmental education and citizen engagement. For more information, visit The Mountaineers Program Center, 7700 Sand Point Way NE, Seattle, WA 98115-3996; phone 206-521-6001; www.mountaineers.org; or email info@mountaineers.org.

Our publications are made possible through the generosity of donors and through sales of more than 500 titles on outdoor recreation, sustainable lifestyle, and conservation. To donate, purchase books, or learn more, visit us online:

MOUNTAINEERS BOOKS
1001 SW Klickitat Way, Suite 201 • Seattle, WA 98134
800-553-4453 • mbooks@mountaineersbooks.org • www.mountaineersbooks.org

Mountaineers Books is proud to be a corporate sponsor of The Leave No Trace Center for Outdoor Ethics, whose mission is to promote and inspire responsible outdoor recreation through education, research, and partnerships • The Leave No Trace program is focused specifically on human-powered (nonmotorized) recreation • Leave No Trace strives to educate visitors about the nature of their recreational impacts and offers techniques to prevent and minimize such impacts • Leave No Trace is best understood as an educational and ethical program, not as a set of rules and regulations • For more information, visit www.lnt.org, or call 800-332-4100.

OTHER TITLES YOU MIGHT ENJOY FROM MOUNTAINEERS BOOKS

Paddling Washington
Rich Landers, Dan Hansen, Verne Huser,
and Douglass A. North
The only all-in-one guide to the best Northwest
flatwater and whitewater paddling routes.

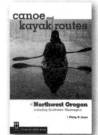

Canoe and Kayak Routes of Northwest Oregon and Southwest Washington
Philip N. Jones
The only complete guide to flatwater
canoe and kayak routes in northwest
Oregon and southwest Washington.

The Don't Drown Out There Deck
Learn water safety tips from this compact,
water-resistant deck of playing cards.

Sea Kayaking
Mountaineers Outdoor Expert series
Dan Henderson
The only guide that applies the efficient tech-
niques of science to recreational paddling.

The Northern Forest Canoe Trail
Northern Forest Canoe Trail, Inc.
The official guide to one of the
country's most alluring water treasures.

Washington's Channeled Scablands Guide
John Soennichsen
Explore Washington's canyons of ice age
wonders—great trails, stunning scenery,
and amazing history.